T0137047

Lecture Notes in Information Systems and Organisation

Volume 63

Series Editors

Paolo Spagnoletti, Rome, Italy

Marco De Marco, Rome, Italy

Nancy Pouloudi, Athens, Greece

Dov Te'eni, Tel Aviv, Israel

Jan vom Brocke, Vaduz, Liechtenstein

Robert Winter, St. Gallen, Switzerland

Richard Baskerville, Atlanta, USA

Lecture Notes in Information Systems and Organization—LNISO—is a series of scientific books that explore the current scenario of information systems, in particular IS and organization. The focus on the relationship between IT, IS and organization is the common thread of this collection, which aspires to provide scholars across the world with a point of reference and comparison in the study and research of information systems and organization. LNISO is the publication forum for the community of scholars investigating behavioral and design aspects of IS and organization. The series offers an integrated publication platform for high-quality conferences, symposia and workshops in this field. Materials are published upon a strictly controlled double blind peer review evaluation made by selected reviewers.

LNISO is abstracted/indexed in Scopus

Gheorghe Cosmin Silaghi ·
Robert Andrei Buchmann · Virginia Niculescu ·
Gabriela Czibula · Chris Barry · Michael Lang ·
Henry Linger · Christoph Schneider
Editors

Advances in Information Systems Development

AI for IS Development and Operations

 Springer

Editors
Gheorghe Cosmin Silaghi ⓘ
Business Informatics Research Center
Babes-Bolyai University
Cluj-Napoca, Romania

Robert Andrei Buchmann ⓘ
Business Informatics Research Center
Babes-Bolyai University
Cluj-Napoca, Romania

Virginia Niculescu ⓘ
Department of Computer Science
Babes-Bolyai University
Cluj-Napoca, Romania

Gabriela Czibula ⓘ
Department of Computer Science
Babes-Bolyai University
Cluj-Napoca, Romania

Chris Barry ⓘ
Business Information Systems Discipline
University of Galway
Galway, Ireland

Michael Lang ⓘ
Business Information Systems Discipline
University of Galway
Galway, Ireland

Henry Linger ⓘ
Department of Human-Centred Computing
Faculty of Information Technology
Monash University
Clayton, VIC, Australia

Christoph Schneider ⓘ
IESE Business School
University of Navarra
Barcelona, Spain

ISSN 2195-4968   ISSN 2195-4976 (electronic)
Lecture Notes in Information Systems and Organisation
ISBN 978-3-031-32417-8   ISBN 978-3-031-32418-5 (eBook)
https://doi.org/10.1007/978-3-031-32418-5

© The Editor(s) (if applicable) and The Author(s), under exclusive license to Springer Nature Switzerland AG 2023
This work is subject to copyright. All rights are solely and exclusively licensed by the Publisher, whether the whole or part of the material is concerned, specifically the rights of translation, reprinting, reuse of illustrations, recitation, broadcasting, reproduction on microfilms or in any other physical way, and transmission or information storage and retrieval, electronic adaptation, computer software, or by similar or dissimilar methodology now known or hereafter developed.
The use of general descriptive names, registered names, trademarks, service marks, etc. in this publication does not imply, even in the absence of a specific statement, that such names are exempt from the relevant protective laws and regulations and therefore free for general use.
The publisher, the authors, and the editors are safe to assume that the advice and information in this book are believed to be true and accurate at the date of publication. Neither the publisher nor the authors or the editors give a warranty, expressed or implied, with respect to the material contained herein or for any errors or omissions that may have been made. The publisher remains neutral with regard to jurisdictional claims in published maps and institutional affiliations.

This Springer imprint is published by the registered company Springer Nature Switzerland AG
The registered company address is: Gewerbestrasse 11, 6330 Cham, Switzerland

Conference Organization

Conference Chairs

Gheorghe Cosmin Silaghi, Babeș-Bolyai University, Romania
Gabriela Czibula, Babeș-Bolyai University, Romania

Program Chairs

Robert Buchmann, Babeș-Bolyai University, Romania
Virginia Niculescu, Babeș-Bolyai University, Romania

Proceedings Chair

Darius Bufnea, Babeș-Bolyai University, Romania

Publicity and Social Media Chair

Ana-Maria Ghiran, Babeș-Bolyai University, Romania

Conference Office

Cristina Osman, Babeș-Bolyai University, Romania

Virtualization and Web Chairs

Adrian Sterca, Babeș-Bolyai University, Romania
Daniel Mican, Babeș-Bolyai University, Romania

International Steering Committee

Chris Barry, National University of Ireland Galway, Ireland
Michael Lang, National University of Ireland Galway, Ireland
Henry Linger, Monash University, Australia
Christoph Schneider, IESE Business School, Spain

Track Chairs

Managing IS Development and Operations

Emilio Insfran, Universitat Politècnica de València, Spain
Alberto Rodrigues da Silva, University of Lisbon, Portugal

IS Methodologies and Education

Björn Johansson, Linköping University, Sweden
Tomas Gustavsson, Karlstad University, Sweden

Knowledge Science, Knowledge Management and Knowledge Representation in IS

Knut Hinkelmann, FHNW University of Applied Sciences and Arts Northwestern Switzerland
Aurona Gerber, University of Pretoria, South Africa

AI-Empowered IS

Adrian Iftene, Alexandru Ioan Cuza University of Iași, Romania
Ioan Petri, Cardiff University, UK

Usability, Trust and Sustainability in IS

Dorina Rajanen, University of Oulu, Finland
Alvaro Arenas, IE Business School Madrid, Spain

Current Topics in IS Development

Alfred Zimmermann, Reutlingen University, Germany
Rainer Schmidt, Munich University of Applied Sciences, Germany
Rainer Alt, University of Leipzig, Germany

Program Committee Members

Track: Managing IS Dev and Ops

Abel Gómez, Universitat Oberta de Catalunya, Spain
Ana C. R. Paiva, University of Porto, Portugal
António Rito Silva, Universidade de Lisboa, Portugal
Carmine Gravino, University of Salerno, Italy
Christopher Vendome, Miami University, USA
Dominique Blouin, Telecom Paris, France/Hasso-Plattner-Institut, Germany
Dušan Savić, University of Belgrade, Serbia
Fernando González-Ladrón-de-Guevara, Universitat Politècnica de València, Spain
Giuseppe Scanniello, University of Basilicata, Italy
Ilias Gerostathopoulos, Vrije Universiteit Amsterdam, The Netherlands
Jabier Martinez, Tecnalia, Spain
João Faria, Universidade do Porto/Institute for Systems and Computer Engineering, Technology and Science, Portugal
Juan Manuel Vara, University Rey Juan Carlos, Spain
Julio Sandobalin, Escuela Politécnica Nacional, Ecuador
Luca Cernuzzi, Universidad Católica "Nuestra Señora de la Asunción", Paraguay
Mariana Peixoto, Universidade Federal de Pernambuco, Brazil
Marta Fernández-Diego, Universitat Politècnica de València, Spain
Maya Daneva, University of Twente, The Netherlands
Miguel Mira Da Silva, Universidade de Lisboa, Portugal
Olga Korableva, Saint Petersburg State University, Russia
Paulo Rupino Da Cunha, University of Coimbra, Portugal
Priscila Cedillo, Universidad de Cuenca, Ecuador
Silvia Abrahao, Universitat Politècnica de València, Spain

Track: IS Methodologies and Education

Alexandra Cristea, Durham University, UK
Amin Jalali, Stockholm University, Sweden
Andreas Hedrén, Uppsala University, Sweden
Ann Svensson, University West, Sweden
Asif Akram, Chalmers University of Technology, Sweden
Bo Andersson, Linnaeus University, Sweden

Claes Thorén, Uppsala University, Sweden
Jacob Nørbjerg, Copenhagen Business School, Denmark
Jānis Grabis, Riga Technical University, Latvia
Janis Stirna, Stockholm University, Sweden
Kai Wistrand, Örebro University, Sweden
Kurt Sandkuhl, The University of Rostock, Germany
Mairéad Hogan, National University of Ireland Galway, Ireland
Michael Lang, National University of Ireland Galway, Ireland
Odd Steen, Lund University, Sweden
Peter Bellström, Karlstad University, Sweden
Torben Tambo, Aarhus University, Denmark
Victoria Paulsson, Linköping University, Sweden

Track: Knowledge Science, Knowledge Management and Knowledge Representation in IS

Ana-Maria Ghiran, Babeş-Bolyai University, Romania
Andreas Martin, FHNW University of Applied Sciences Northwestern Switzerland, Switzerland
Ansgar Bernardi, German Research Center for Artificial Intelligence (DFKI), Germany
Dimitris Apostolou, University of Piraeus, Greece
Emanuele Laurenzi, FHNW University of Applied Sciences and Arts Northwestern Switzerland, Switzerland
Hanlie Smuts, University of Pretoria, South Africa
Hans Friedrich Witschel, FHNW University of Applied Sciences and Arts North-western Switzerland, Switzerland
Heiko Maus, German Research Center for Artificial Intelligence (DFKI), Germany
Jan Vanthienen, Katholieke Universiteit Leuven, Belgium
Ludger Van Elst, German Research Center for Artificial Intelligence (DFKI), Germany
Marie Hattingh, University of Pretoria, South Africa
Rainer Telesko, FHNW University of Applied Sciences and Arts Northwestern Switzerland, Switzerland
Robert Buchmann, Babeş-Bolyai University, Romania
Sunet Eybers, University of South Africa, South Africa
Ulrich Reimer, Eastern Switzerland University of Applied Sciences, Switzerland

Track: AI-Empowered IS

Adrian Popescu, CEA LIST, France
Alexandru Burlacu, University of Medicine and Pharmacy "Gr. T. Popa", Iasi, Romania

Allan Hanbury, TU Wien, Austria
Christian Haas, Vienna University of Economics and Business, Austria
Daniela Zaharie, West University of Timisoara, Romania
Diana Trandabat, "Alexandru Ioan Cuza" University of Iasi, Romania
Florin Leon, "Gheorghe Asachi" Technical University of Iasi, Romania
Gabriela Czibula, Babeș-Bolyai University of Cluj Napoca, Romania
Heitor Murilo Gomes, University of Waikato, New Zealand
Lenuța Alboaie, "Alexandru Ioan Cuza" University of Iasi, Romania
Luiz Fernando Bittencourt, University of Campinas, Brazil
Magdalena Punceva, University of Applied Sciences Western Switzerland, Switzerland
Mihaela Breaban, "Alexandru Ioan Cuza" University of Iasi, Romania
Mihai Dascălu, University Politehnica of Bucharest, Romania
Pinar Duygulu Sahin, Hacettepe University, Turkey
Radu Ionescu, University of Bucharest/SecurifAI, Romania
Rafael Tolosana-Calasanz, Universidad de Zaragoza, Spain

Track: Usability, Trust and Sustainability in IS

Achim D. Brucker, University of Exeter, UK
Aggeliki Tsohou, Ionian University, Greece
Ahmed Seffah, Zayed University, United Arab Emirates
Benjamin Aziz, University of Portsmouth, UK
Chris Barry, National University of Ireland Galway, Ireland
Coral Calero, Universidad de Castilla-La Mancha, Spain
Costin Pribeanu, National Institute for Research & Development in Informatics, Romania
Daniela S. Cruzes, Norwegian University of Science and Technology, Norway
David Langley, TNO/University of Groningen, The Netherlands
Efpraxia Zamani, The University of Sheffield, UK
Irene Lizeth Manotas Gutiérrez, IBM, USA
Jose Angel Bañares, University of Zaragoza, Spain
Ma Ángeles Moraga, Universidad de Castilla-La Mancha, Spain
Marco Winckler, Université Côte d'Azur, France
Marianne Kinnula, University of Oulu, Finland
Mikko Rajanen, University of Oulu, Finland
Netta Iivari, University of Oulu, Finland
Norbert Pataki, Eötvös Loránd University, Hungary
Patricia Lago, Vrije Universiteit Amsterdam, The Netherlands
Ruzanna Chitchyan, University of Bristol, UK

Track: Current Topics in ISD

Abdellah Chehri, University of Quebec in Chicoutimi, Canada
Colin Atkinson, University of Mannheim, Germany
Dimitris Karagiannis, University of Vienna, Austria
François Charoy, Université de Lorraine—LORIA—Inria, France
Giancarlo Guizzardi, Free University of Bozen-Bolzano, Italy/University of Twente,
The Netherlands
Giuseppe Scanniello, University of Basilicata, Italy
Henderik A. Proper, Luxembourg Institute of Science and Technology, Luxembourg
Jānis Grabis, Riga Technical University, Latvia
Janis Stirna, Stockholm University, Sweden
Juan Velasquez, University of Chile, Chile
Kathrin Kirchner, Technical University of Denmark, Denmark
Kurt Sandkuhl, The University of Rostock, Germany
Marco Aiello, University of Stuttgart, Germany
Matthias Wißotzki, Wismar University of Applied Sciences: Technology, Business
and Design, Germany
Oleg Svatoš, University of Economics in Prague, Czech Republic
Ovidiu Noran, Centre for Enterprise Architecture Research and Management/Griffith
University, Australia
Selmin Nurcan, Université Paris 1 Panthéon—Sorbonne, France
Stefanie Rinderle-Ma, Technical University of Munich, Germany
Ulrike Steffens, HAW Hamburg, Germany
Václav Řepa, Prague University of Economics and Business, Czech Republic
Xiaohui Tao, University of Southern Queensland, Australia

Additional Reviewers

Alidéou Prosper Ayégnon, University of Stuttgart, Germany
Daniel Gaspar Figueiredo, Universitat Politècnica de València, Spain
Evrim Güner, Stockholm University, Sweden
Harald Kühn, BOC Group, Austria
Kawsar Haghshenas, University of Stuttgart, Germany
Vlad-Sebastian Ionescu, Babeș-Bolyai University, Romania
Rakshit Mittal, Télécom Paris, France
Robin Pesl, University of Stuttgart, Germany
Ana Carolina Moises de Souza, Norwegian University of Science and Technology,
Norway
Alexandru Ioan Stan, Babeș-Bolyai University, Romania
Wilfrid Utz, OMiLAB NPO, Germany

Preface

The **International Conference on Information Systems Development** (ISD) is an academic conference where researchers and practitioners share their knowledge and expertise in the field of information systems (IS) development. As an Affiliated Conference of the Association for Information Systems, the ISD conference complements the international network of general IS conferences (ICIS, ECIS, AMCIS, PACIS, HICSS). ISD continues a tradition started with the first Polish-Scandinavian Seminar on Current Trends in Information Systems Development Methodologies, held in Gdansk, Poland, in 1988, which evolved into the International Conference on Information Systems Development. In this volume we mark the death of Prof. Stanisław Wryzca this year. Prof. Wryzca was instrumental in initiating the workshop on ISD in 1988—the beginning of the ISD conference—and was associated with the conference for a number of years.

Throughout its history, the conference has focused on different aspects, ranging from methodological, infrastructural, and educational challenges in the ISD field to bridging gaps between industry, academia, and society.

The 30th Information Systems Development Conference was hosted by the Faculty of Economics and Business Administration (FSEGA) at Babeș-Bolyai University in Cluj-Napoca, Romania, during August 31–September 2, 2022. All accepted papers have been published in the AIS eLibrary, which is accessible at https://aisel.aisnet.org/isd2014/proceedings2022/.

This volume contains extended and revised versions of some of the best papers, as selected by the ISD2022 Proceedings Editors. The theme of the conference was *AI for IS development and operations* and included two specific AI-oriented tracks (*AI-empowered IS* and *Knowledge Science, Knowledge Management and Knowledge Representation in IS*) in addition to traditional tracks of the conference. Therefore, the conference focused on how Artificial Intelligence can empower Information Systems and how it can facilitate digital transformation in various aspects—organizational structures, enterprise architectures, decision-making, business processes, etc.

The ISD2022 conference attracted contributions in the general area of information systems development, as well as in specialized areas represented by each track: *Managing IS Development and Operations; IS Methodologies and Education;*

Knowledge Science, Knowledge Management and Knowledge Representation in IS;
AI-Empowered IS; Usability, Trust and Sustainability in IS. The conference was held
in a hybrid format and received submissions by authors from 27 countries. The selection presented in this volume balances empirical and design-oriented approaches as
two key research streams to inform further advancements in the field of Information
Systems.

Cluj-Napoca, Romania   Gheorghe Cosmin Silaghi
Cluj-Napoca, Romania   Robert Andrei Buchmann
Cluj-Napoca, Romania   Virginia Niculescu
Cluj-Napoca, Romania   Gabriela Czibula
Melbourne, Australia   Henry Linger
Galway, Ireland   Chris Barry
Galway, Ireland   Michael Lang
Barcelona, Spain   Christoph Schneider

Contents

A DSR Study on Iterative Tool Development to Measure IT Process Maturity in an Agile Context

Björn Johansson, Henn Jaadla, and Tomas Gustavsson

Abstract This paper presents the design of a tool for recurring quantitative self-assessment of IT Service Management (ITSM) process maturity in a financial institution implementing agile software development as a new way of working. This change brought on an increased need to monitor ITSM process performance, and a Design Science Research (DSR) project was launched to create an ITSM maturity assessment tool. Continual improvement of ITSM processes can be measured by performing a process maturity assessment, comparing the organization's process performance against a best-practice reference set of processes. This paper reports a development project for a quantitative measuring survey-based tool. Due to the increasing use of agile methods, there is an increase in research attention to the coexistence of agile and ITSM maturity assessment tools. The results show that a company-wide ITSM process maturity assessment can be established as a survey-based self-assessment in an agile software development context. The aggregate scores from this self-assessment present a good indicator of the organization's process performance, especially when complemented by a reference score. A key learning is that the iterative DSR methodology made it possible to create a tool that in good way measure ITSM process maturity in an agile context.

Keywords ITSM · IT service management · IT maturity · Process maturity · Quantitative self-assessment

B. Johansson (✉)
Department of Management and Engineering, Division of Information Systems and
Digitalization, Linköping University, Linköping, Sweden
e-mail: bjorn.se.johansson@liu.se

H. Jaadla
Swedbank AS, Tallinn, Estonia
e-mail: henn.jaadla@swedbank.ee

T. Gustavsson
Karlstad Business School, Karlstad University, Karlstad, Sweden
e-mail: tomas.gustavsson@kau.se

© The Author(s), under exclusive license to Springer Nature Switzerland AG 2023

G. C. Silaghi et al. (eds.), *Advances in Information Systems Development*,
Lecture Notes in Information Systems and Organisation 63,
https://doi.org/10.1007/978-3-031-32418-5_1

1

1 Introduction

IT services are under constant pressure to become better, faster and cheaper [1] and IT Service Management (ITSM) processes are constantly evolving. The continual improvement of IT service management processes can be measured by performing a process maturity assessment, comparing the organization's process performance against a best-practice reference set of processes [2, 3]. There are several assessment frameworks available, but most existing assessments are very resource demanding, which makes them expensive to apply—especially when repeated regularly. As an alternative organizations has started to seek after lighter assessments methods to perform self-assessments [4].

However, at the same time as business demand drives improvement of ITSM processes, many IT Service Management organizations are adopting agile software development methods [5, 6]. They do so in order to improve time-to-market [7] as well as improve customer satisfaction [8]. The essence of agile ways of working is the ability to embrace change, rather than believe too much in detailed planning [7]. By working in short iterations, both the software and the processes are continuously developed in short cycles. Also, it is aimed at putting more focus on people and communication rather than plans and formal contracts [7].

Despite the fact that the agile way of working improves the speed of development and alignment with customer needs, the more informal way of working may create gaps in process compliance as well as in process maturity [9]. This is especially likely during the transition to the new way of working, while process participants are still adjusting to new roles and responsibilities [7]. Organizational change may impact control and feedback cycles of IT processes due to low process awareness, incomplete role adoption and other transitional effects. In addition, differences between waterfall models and agile ways of working may exacerbate negative effects, if not mitigated properly [7, 10].

Therefore, when IT departments are undergoing organizational changes to agile ways of working, it would be prudent to evaluate process maturity throughout the change, to ensure that lapses in process compliance and maturity can be handled swiftly [7, 8, 10]. In this paper we describe development of a survey-based tool for self-assessment of IT process maturity at a large financial institution, aiming at indicating process maturity level at the financial institution.

The research question addressed in this paper is: How can we implement a tool for measuring IT process maturity in an agile software development context? This question was studied in a DSR project implementing a quantitative self-assessment survey-based tool where development was transformed into using agile ways of working.

The rest of the paper is organized in the following way: Sect. 2 presents previous research on process maturity assessments and Sect. 3 the context of the project. This is followed by an overview of the development approach (Sect. 4) and research methodology (DSR) in Sect. 5. Section 6 presents findings of three iterations of development and testing of the maturity assessment tool. Section 7 discusses the results and the development approach, and the final section presents concluding thoughts.

2 Process Maturity Assessments

Process maturity level is an indication of how well a process achieves its objectives, and whether the process is capable of continuous improvement [11]. The assessment of process maturity is commonly used as the starting point for ITIL implementations [12] to pinpoint improvements that would be the most beneficial to perform. However, assessments are equally valuable for understanding as-is state for planning continuous improvements and evaluating overall performance of IT organizations [12]. So, whenever an organization is undertaking a process improvement initiative, or going through organizational change, there is a need for assessing process maturity [13]. Furthermore, to gauge the progress of improvements, or the impact organizational changes cause to processes over time, the measurement should be applied at regular intervals and cover the key roles and organizational departments. The most common approaches to measure maturity are qualitative assessments, conducted through interviews or extensive questionnaires, which are complex, time consuming, and expensive to apply [14].

The most commonly used maturity model is Capability Maturity Model Integrated (CMMI) [15]. The CMMI framework describes performance of individual process areas in terms of capability, and the overall performance of the IT processes in terms of maturity. The capability levels indicate the extent of implementation and performance of the processes corresponding to a given process area. The four capability levels are numbered 0 through 3. Capability levels serve as an indicator for improving individual processes.

Maturity levels apply to an organization's process improvement achievement across multiple process areas. These levels are a means of improving processes corresponding to a given set of process areas (i.e., maturity level). The five maturity levels are numbered 1 through 5. Table 1 presents the alignment of the four capability levels and the five maturity levels.

Table 1 Capability and maturity levels as per CMMI [16]	Level	Continuous representation capability levels	Staged representation maturity levels
	Level 0	Incomplete	
	Level 1	Performed	Initial
	Level 2	Managed	Managed
	Level 3	Defined	Defined
	Level 4		Quantitatively managed
	Level 5		Optimizing

CMMI-SVC draws on concepts and practices from CMMI and other service focused standards and models, including ITIL, ISO/IEC 20,000: Information Technology—Service Management, Control Objectives for Information and related Technology (COBIT) and Information Technology Services Capability Maturity Model (ITSCMM) [16].

Although high levels of CMMI maturity have been shown to improve project success in waterfall environments [17], these higher maturity levels have been found to be incompatible with agile ways of working without sacrificing the benefits of agility being sought [18]. These two approaches have even been informally characterized as having the same relationship as oil and water [19]. This incompatibility might depend on the different focus areas between agile methods and CMMI. Agile software development methodology is an iterative software development methodology where the main objectives are lower cost, high productivity and a satisfied customer [19]. In other words, agile methods are focusing on software delivery in the single teams while CMMI is focusing more on the organizational level [19]. The CMMI tends not to focus on the software process but on an organization's business objectives in their software process improvement program [19]. According to several researchers, the highly collaborative and self-organizing team approach of agile methods means an agile principle-based maturity model would be better suited for use in agile environments [20].

At the same time, studies have found successful implementations of agile methods are most likely in mature CMMI environments [21]. Given the significant investment in advancing in CMMI maturity and the continued increase in agile adoption [22], the increase in research attention in the coexistence of agile and CMMI is unsurprising.

3 The Case Organization

The context of this project is a large multinational financial institution with around 16,000 employees. A majority of the company's systems are created in-house due to the nature of the business, and the existence of a lot of legacy systems. The internal IT development process has been heavily influenced by hardware-oriented development approaches and has historically been built around a waterfall approach. The development process has been well-integrated with IT governance, resource management, and financial process. However, from a user perspective the waterfall approach has the downside of long lead times and slow feedback cycles.

To mitigate downsides (long lead time and slow feedback) of the waterfall approach, the company introduced an agile approach in some teams over a period of 3 years, and since 2018, the agile approach is fully implemented throughout all business areas.

The department-based way of working with clear distinction between IT development and maintenance roles was replaced with cross-functional teams handling both development and operations while working with a common product backlog.

The change to an agile software development process affected the ITSM processes by changing roles and responsibilities, organization structure and the speed of introducing new services into the production environment. The changed dynamics of the way services were developed and operated impacted the IT process maturity in various ways, and therefore it was important to evaluate process maturity changes across different affected teams throughout and after this organizational change. This resulted in the situation that there was a need for having a recurring and effective way of measuring IT process maturity.

Several risks arising from the organizational transition from centralized, waterfall-based way of working to decentralized, agile way of working have been identified, which can impact IT process maturity and compliance [8, 9]. According to respondents in this case organization, negative transitional effects are incomplete role adoption, low process awareness and team motivation issues during formation of new cross-functional teams. The decentralization led to uneven performance between different business units due to different adoption speed of new ways of working. Additionally, the decentralization resulted in inefficiencies and duplication of control and management activities.

Also, issues may arise from conflicting priorities between development and maintenance tasks, as work is handled by the same cross-functional team and prioritized in the same product backlog [9].

All this made it necessary to get a better understanding of IT maturity in the financial institution and this reason was the starting point of the project that aimed at developing a tool for measuring IT maturity. In this paper, the specific focus is on development of a self-assessment tool for measuring IT maturity.

4 Development of the Self-Assessment Tool

The choice of Design Science Research (DSR) [23] was based on the premise that DSR methodology can support an adaptive and responsive design process which aligns with the agile IT management practices introduced in the organization in question. In DSR, creation of an artefact is central [23, 24]. In this case it is a survey-based tool that contains questions as well as storage of results and possibilities to evaluate and present the results in different ways.

To be able to gauge the impact of organizational changes to the process maturity level, maturity assessment needs to be performed regularly [23], so it can identify trends and provide feedback while the new way of working becomes the norm. A full CMMI assessment is unsuitable for establishing trends in a short timeframe due to the cost, disruption and long feedback cycle [23]. Therefore, the IT Process Maturity Assessment project aimed to implement a survey-based self-assessment, which can be applied repeatedly across a broad spectrum of roles and business areas within an IT organization.

The framework selected as basis for the process maturity assessment initiative was CMMI-SVC [16]. CMMI® (Capability Maturity Model® Integration) models

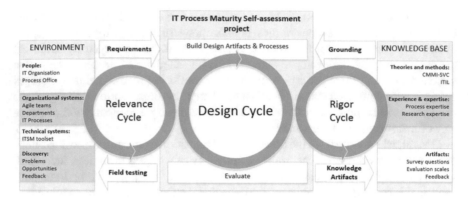

Fig. 1 The DSR framework adopted in the project

are collections of best practices that help organizations to improve their processes [16].

The research used the three-cycle view of the DSR methodology [23, 24] and in Fig. 1 we show our adoption of the framework to the specific context of the project.

5 Method

The research method used in this design science research project, Hevner's 3 cycle model [23], bridges contextual environment with design science activities, and design science activities with the knowledge base. The research was conducted mainly by two researchers working on the project. One of the researchers worked at the financial institution and was dedicated to work with the development of the tool. This setting could be related and described to what Goldkuhl [25] define as practice research. The researcher conducted research as a master student before the project started, and his master thesis was one of the starting points for the project. When presenting the master thesis to the financial institution, the organization decided to continue with developing a tool for measuring IT maturity in the financial institution.

The other researcher first acted as supervisor of the master thesis. Based on the case organizations decision to continue the development of the tool, a design science research method approach was decided for this study. This also meant that it had a pragmatic stance as presented by Goldkuhl and Lind [26] when they present a multi-grounded design process. The combination of the practice researcher and the university researcher made it possible to execute the project as a design science research project in which the two researchers had a good combination of insights. The project was conducted in three iterations. Before and in between each iteration workshops were conducted. In these workshops the tool was presented and discussed by different experts and engaged stakeholders both from the IT department and from different business departments. This made two of the cycles, relevance cycle and rigor cycle [23, 24], to be considered extensively in the project. The relevance cycle provided input from the contextual environment of the research project to the design science activities. The rigor cycle was used to bridge the design science activities with the knowledge base of scientific foundations, domain experience, and expertise that provided guidance to the research project. The central design cycle iterated between the core activities of building and evaluating the design artefacts and processes of the research.

6   Results

In this paper we describe development of the tool for measuring IT process maturity at the financial institution through its first three iterations. The project was performed during the agile transformation of the IT organization. The tool selection for establishing the IT process assessment program was based on the main considerations that the surveys would need to be digitally accessible within the financial institution IT environment. Therefore, the artefacts and data were stored using the existing collaboration tools. The chosen survey platform was Netigate digital survey tool,[1] since that tool was already in use within the financial institution. The data were processed in MS Access and MS Excel.

The assessment focused on the IT service providers feedback and the key characteristics of their perception of process outcomes. The targeted process roles as users of the tool in the financial institution IT service management organization were service portfolio managers, service owners, service managers and team managers.

6.1   Iteration 1—Pilot Survey

The pilot survey was initially planned to cover only three process areas, and initially selected process areas were Service Design, Incident Resolution and Prevention, and Service Continuity. The idea of this restriction was to verify the survey method and test the assumptions in a reasonably short timeframe with manageable effort. However, it was decided to extend the limited scope, since it was assumed that a such a limited scope would not have provided enough insight to demonstrate the value of the model. The scope was extended to cover CMMI process areas from several maturity levels to allow the results to be mapped to a process capability score and a relative process maturity score. The project team therefore selected several well-established IT-processes and mapped these to CMMI process areas.

This meant that the pilot survey investigated 11 processes as shown in Table 2, which presents the survey scope as applied to selected IT-processes, and the respective counts of questions asked in the tool. The number of questions for each process was

---

[1] Netigate AB, Sweden.

Table 2 Financial institution
IT processes in scope of the
test of the assessment tool

Financial institution IT process	Number of questions
Availability management	2
Capacity management	2
Change management	4
Incident management	5
IT service continuity management	3
Problem management	4
Service asset and configuration management	2
Service level management	5
Service portfolio and catalog management	2
Continual service improvement	4
Service transition	1

decided by the researchers after discussions with process experts at the financial institution. The specific number of questions was seen as enough for stating the maturity level on each process. Regarding the specific number of questions, this was a trade-off between having a questionnaire that takes too long to answer and having trusted answers. The final decision on the number of questions was based on input from process experts in the case organization. Fewer, rather than too many questions, was decided on since the goal was not to draw any statistical inference.

When mapped to CMMI process areas, the survey scope refers to maturity levels one to four (see Table 1). This limitation, excluding level five, was deliberate, as the likely maturity score at the time of the initiation of the project was seen as be around level two, and there would be less benefit in designing questions that cover level five features.

The CMMI process area specific goals and respective specific practices form the basis for designing the questionnaire as well as the questions, which addressed key outcomes of the processes, as described by CMMI-SVC [16]. The survey was designed with closed questions, with only a fixed range of answer options on an ordinal scale.

In the first iteration, response options were a mix of binary "yes-or-no" choices and some ranges of Likert-type items. The logical order of the questions was defined using the ITIL Service Lifecycle steps [27] of Service Strategy, Service Design, Service Transition, Service Operation and Continual Service Improvement. The questionnaire was developed in close cooperation with process experts at the financial institution to ensure that the use of terminology and wording would be familiar to survey participants.

The pilot survey was launched at a time when the agile transformation change had just taken effect and the recruitment process had not finished, so the new Service

Provider roles were not fully established in the organization. The respondents for the pilot survey were selected from the people who were in a Service Provider role in the previous organization and had retained the equivalent role in the new organizational setup. This decision regarding population selection would ensure that respondents were familiar with the process framework and would be knowledgeable for providing feedback to the survey content and format.

The final agreed population for the survey contained 229 respondents. This list comprised all people marked as a Service Owner for active services in the IT service portfolio. The selected population formed an estimated 20% of the total direct participants of IT service management processes at the time. The survey was open for 11 days, 72 people responded and 53 people completed the survey.

In an ordinal scale, responses can be rated or ranked, but the distance between responses is not measurable. Thus, the differences between "most," "some," and "few" on a frequency response Likert scale used in the survey are not necessarily equal.

Descriptive statistics, such as means and standard deviations, have unclear meanings when applied to Likert scale responses. For example, what would the average of "most" and "some" really mean? Furthermore, if responses are clustered at the high and low extremes, the mean may appear to be the neutral or middle response, but this may not fairly characterize the data.

In this case, means are of limited value for describing the results, as the data does not follow a classic normal distribution, so instead a frequency distribution of responses was used. The results were summarized to divide process areas into two: those receiving on average higher scores, and those with a majority of low scores. "Don't know" was counted towards low score. Table 3 presents the processes with indicative good and bad performance.

The survey participants were also asked to provide feedback to the survey content and process. 16 respondents left a comment in the survey, and a few more participants provided direct feedback to the project team either by email or verbally. The main feedback was related to the issue of comprehension. This feedback was then used as input for improvements of the tool before testing it in iteration 2.

The adjusted response rate after excluding invalid responses was 32% and the aggregated results of the survey can be considered statistically significant. As the total population of Service Owners at the time of the pilot survey was 229, the total of 72 responses indicates a 9.5% margin of error at a 95% confidence level. The results should be considered nonparametric, as the sample was chosen based on their specific role in IT service management.

6.2   Iteration 2—Q4 2018 Survey

The second iteration of the self-assessment tool for IT process maturity was developed in Q4 of 2018 and targeted an increased range of service management roles in the IT organization. The population of interest for the second iteration covered the

Table 3 Pilot survey results

	Low score	High score
Service design	Service commitments	Service definitions
	Service reporting	
	Recovery plan testing	
Service transition	Configuration management	Change management
	Service handover	
Service operation	Outage registration	Incident management
		Problem management
Continual service improvement	Using operational metrics	Root cause analysis
	Using KPI for improvements	

roles of Service Owner, Team manager and Service manager for all active services in the IT Service Portfolio. These roles are the key actors in the ITSM processes, so responses from this population would reflect the state of the whole IT organization.

The assessment added a more detailed perspective of process capability level. The specific goals and the respective specific practices for the CMMI Process Areas forming the basis for designing the questionnaire are stated in a hierarchical order. This means the questions could be mapped to respective process capability level. Each question was mapped to the specific practices it referred to, so the response could be translated to a capability score, as well as a maturity level.

The final agreed distribution list for the survey contained 504 names, and this population formed an estimated 40% of the total IT service management process participants at the time of the survey. The invitations to participate in the Q4 process maturity survey were sent out and the survey was open for 10 days. Out of 504 invitees, 195 people responded, and 167 people completed the survey.

To report outcomes in terms of process maturity and capability, the frequency table was matched to the questions table. This allowed for the results to be compared to the maximum possible score for each process area.

The results in iteration 2 were presented in a more detailed way, expressing both the maximum possible process capability score as covered by the assessment, and the resulting capability score. The processes were presented in the overall process maturity steps by matching CMMI specific goals and specific practices to the organization's IT processes. The resulting graph is presented in Fig. 2.

In this graph, the financial institution's IT process areas are mapped to CMMI maturity levels on the horizontal axis, and the specific process capability results (green) are presented against a possible maximum score (red) on the vertical axis.

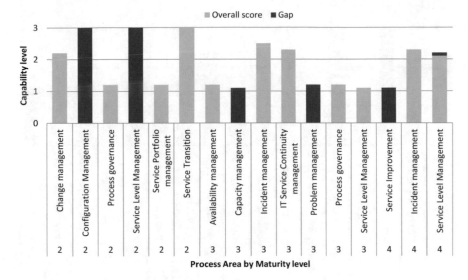

Fig. 2 Iteration 2 results by process area

The red areas highlight the process capability gaps, where the specific goals of the process are not achieved by the organization. As the respondents' results are subjective and depend on the process, each participant's knowledge, experience and attitude towards IT processes, the negative results may indicate both a problem with process capability and a lack of knowledge among process participants.

To distinguish between areas where the gaps are related to process participant's awareness, as opposed to process capability, the score achieved by the process participants was compared to a reference score compiled by process experts (Fig. 3). This score is based on expert opinion and operational statistics from the organization.

The comparison of results in Figs. 2 and 3 indicates, that the low results in Service Level management, Problem management and Service Improvement area may be due to a low awareness, or misunderstood questions. However, the relatively low scores for Configuration management and Capacity management are likely due to low process capability.

The larger sample in iteration 2 allowed for responses to be summarized by business area and role, so gaps could be identified, and specific mitigation actions suggested for IT management in general, and for business area management teams specifically.

The adjusted response rate for the Q4 survey was 39%. The aggregated results of the survey can be considered statistically significant. As the total population of Service Owners at the time of the pilot survey was 504, the total of 195 responses indicates a 5,5% margin of error at a 95% confidence level. The results can be considered parametric, with non-normal distribution for role.

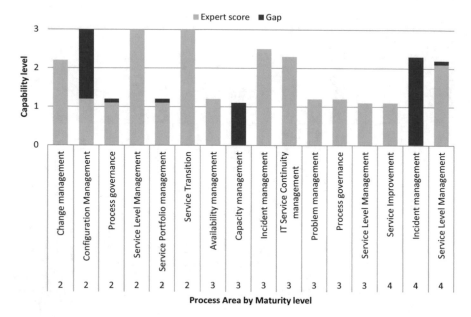

Fig. 3 Iteration 2 expert score by process area

6.3   Iteration 3—Q2 2019 Survey

The third iteration of the self-assessment tool for IT process maturity was developed in Q2 of 2019. In the third iteration, target population remained the same as in the second iteration, but the scope of process outcomes was increased. The capability ranges covered by the assessment were harmonized, so process scores would be comparable, allowing better visualization of process capability results using a spider-web graph.

The distribution list for the survey contained 558 names, and this population formed an estimated 40% of the total IT service management process participants at the time of the survey. The invitations to participate in the Q2 process maturity survey were sent out and the survey was open for 16 days. Out of 558 invitees, 199 people responded, and 153 people completed the survey.

The results in iteration 3 were presented as a spiderweb graph, with processes divided into the process maturity steps as prescribed by CMMI-SVC [16]. This view expresses both the maximum possible process capability scores as covered by the assessment, and the resulting capability scores, and highlights process capability gaps for each ITSM process maturity level. The resulting graph is presented in Fig. 4.

The results were also cascaded by role and organization structure, which meant that the gaps could be identified, and specific mitigation actions suggested for specific roles and for business area management teams.

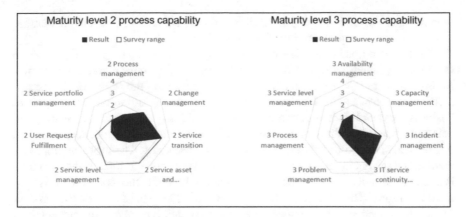

Fig. 4 Iteration 3 results by process area

The main improvement idea from project stakeholders for the third iteration was related to the process capability ranges covered by the survey. The idea for next iterations was to harmonize the ranges, so that all individual process results could be matched to a capability score of 0–3. This will improve the ability to pinpoint improvement activities and enable the calculation of a CMMI-SVC maturity score above level 3. This presents a challenge in terms of survey scope, as the number of survey questions and the average time to complete the assessment would increase.

7 Discussion

The research question investigated in this paper is: How can we implement a tool for measuring IT process maturity in an agile software development context? To answer this question, a design science research method approach was performed, based on Hevner's three cycle model [23, 24]. The method bridges contextual environment with design science activities, and design science activities with the knowledge base. By iterating through these cycles, the developed artefact (the survey-based tool) is expected to contribute with new knowledge to the scientific evidence, and to the real-world applications [28]. In this study, the contextual environment is the case organization with its people, processes and tools. By bringing the developed artefact into the case environment, the research gained feedback about its applicability and usefulness to the participants and stakeholders. This iterative nature of the method supports an adaptive and responsive design process, which enables the improvement of the requirements, the knowledge base and the developed artefact throughout the development process. This process is similar to the central idea of agile software development, in which design practices are reviewed, acted upon and adjusted to changing user requirements [29]. This study reflects the view of Conboy, Gleasure and Cullina [30], which points out that the problem space in DSR projects could be seen as emerging and evolving in tandem with the solution space, and encourages an agile approach to problem identification.

This first iteration of the relevance cycle [23], was intended to provide input from the contextual environment of the research project to the design science activities. In this first iteration, management stakeholders receiving the report of the assessment results provided feedback on the lack of granularity of the results in terms of business areas and roles. According to Hevner [23], the results of field testing will determine whether additional iterations of the relevance cycle are needed. Based on this feedback, an additional iteration was deemed necessary. Therefore, an improvement in the second iteration was to extend the survey scope to more roles across all business areas and presenting the results accordingly. While the report on the assessment results in the first iteration was simple and provided a brief overview of process areas which needed improvements, the second iteration results were presented in the dimensions of capability and maturity. The added perspective was appreciated by the stakeholders, but the presentation was considered too complex. In the third iteration, the capability ranges covered by the assessment were harmonized, so the process scores were comparable. This allowed for better visualization of the process capability results using a spider-web graph. The third iteration can be seen as a rigor cycle as it provides past knowledge to the research project to ensure its innovation [23].

Previous research [31] has indicated that self-assessments tend to have an upward bias on the capability scores when compared to an in-depth analysis of IT process performance. Johansson, Eckerstein and Malmros [31] associated this bias with the participants' low specialist knowledge in process areas in question and surmised that the results would be more reflective of the true state if all survey participants were ITIL-educated.

In our research at the financial institution, existence of the bias problem was tested by comparing survey results to an expert score established by process managers using operational data and in-depth knowledge of the individual processes. This bias was not observed, and the difference with previous research may be attributable to two factors: the wording of the questions and the interpretation of the responses.

First, in this survey tool wording of questions was tailored to fit the organization by using terminology which is used in the organization's ITSM tool, work instructions and training materials. The wording and presentation of questions was also reviewed and improved in several iterations to make it as intuitive and clear as possible.

The maturity assessment is currently focused on level 2 and 3 process areas, as the target organization is operating at this level. However, as the organization is also on an agile journey, there may arise potential conflicts between the goals of CMMI-SVC maturity and agile methods [32]. The reason for the mismatch is the different objectives: while agile is aimed at lowering cost, improving productivity and customer focus [19], CMMI is more broadly aimed at governance on the organizational level [19]. A literature review performed by Henriques and Tanner [32] also indicates that agile and CMMI are not a natural fit at higher maturity levels, and further points to a lack of research into the use of agile methods to achieving CMMI maturity levels beyond level three.

Boehm and Turner [33] have pointed out, that while in principle agile methods are in line with level 5 maturity concept of constant adaptation of operations to improve performance, most agile methods do not support the degree of documentation and infrastructure required for achieving lower-level maturity. This is another area where the DSR approach may benefit the project, as the knowledge base and the maturity evaluation criteria will need to evolve along with the assessment tool itself.

The design science research presented in this paper is subject to several possible limitations. The participatory approach of the study can have several biases, including becoming too much of a supporter of the tool under study and not spending enough time for observations [34]. These biases were mitigated by keeping knowledge of the potential problems explicit. There was also dedicated time to be spent on observation and reflection during the project. Another limitation is the difficulty in generalizing a single study to other similar studies. In design science research, the aim of the rigor cycle is to demonstrate the feasibility of the design artefact. The results after the third iteration have arguably demonstrated such feasibility, but as identified by other researchers, design science research outcomes in one project may not generalize to other projects [35]. It is essential that further cases or action research studies be undertaken, possibly using a replication logic.

8 Concluding Remarks

The creation of an IT process maturity self-assessment tool has a pragmatic focus due to its emphasis on relevance—the outcome needs to be useful for the organization; the application environment. In this way, a DSR approach for developing assessment is quite appropriate as it focuses on applicability of the developed artefact. However, practical utility alone is not enough. It is the synergy between relevance and rigor and the contributions along both relevance cycle and rigor cycle that define good design science research [24], and this is achieved in this case by using Hevner's three cycle model [23].

This research is centered on designing a self-assessment survey-based tool for measuring IT process maturity where the trigger for organizational change was an agile transformation of IT development and operations in the organization. As the transformation continues, the maturity assessment activity should also continue, as process performance can be considered an emergent property, which is a function of organization culture, tools and technology, and the process framework. Thus, it is constantly changing in response to changes in the organization, the tools in use and the processes themselves. Therefore, any initiative to measure process maturity should be continuous, and constantly evolving. The same need for process maturity assessment may arise from any other major reorganization of the business, e.g. mergers and acquisitions, major changes to business model etc. To measure process maturity, as in this case, can provide opportunity to identify trends and to assess impact of improvement activities. The simplified nature of the tool means that it can be applied regularly, and the iterative nature of the way the tool is managed means it can be adaptive and responsive to enable its use for monitoring process maturity trends in a changing organization.

We believe that despite the differences of approach, CMMI is an appropriate framework for improving ITSM processes in organizations in their path to implement agile ways of working. Future development of the tool will hopefully contribute to the understanding of what level 4 and 5 maturity means in an agile environment.

In the future, one avenue of research to explore could be to compare the process maturity assessment results with Employee Net Promoter Score (eNPS) results and other internal performance metrics to see whether there is any correlation, e.g. between process performance and employee satisfaction. This would provide an interesting perspective to both process improvements and HR initiatives.

References

1. Leopoldi, R. (2015). *Employing ITSM in value added service provisioning* (p. 5). RL Information Consulting LLC.
2. Marquis, H. (2006). ITIL: What it is and what it isn't. *Business Communications Review, 36*(12), 49.
3. Obwegeser, N., Nielsen, D. T., & Spandet, N. M. (2019). Continual process improvement for ITIL service operations: A lean perspective. *Information Systems Management, 36*(2), 141–167.
4. Lacerda, T. C., von Wangenheim, C. G., & Hauck, J. C. (2018). *A mapping study on software process self-assessment methods.* arXiv:1812.09112.
5. Lee, J.-C., & Chen, C.-Y. (2019). Investigating the environmental antecedents of organizations' intention to adopt agile software development. *Journal of Enterprise Information Management.*
6. Gerster, D., Dremel, C., & Kelker, P. (2019). How enterprises adopt agile structures: A multiple-case study. In *Proceedings of the 52nd Hawaii International Conference on System Sciences.*
7. Ince, C. S. (2015). Approaches and benefits for adopting agile methods. *Insight, 18*(3), 18–20.
8. Lindvall, M., et al. (2004). Agile software development in large organizations. *Computer, 37*(12), 26–34.
9. Dikert, K., Paasivaara, M., & Lassenius, C. (2016). Challenges and success factors for large-scale agile transformations: A systematic literature review. *Journal of Systems and Software, 119*, 87–108.
10. Jaadla, H., & Johansson, B. (2018). *Developing a tool for self-assessment of IT process maturity: A design science research initiative.* In *2018 Joint of the 17th Business Informatics Research Short Papers, Workshops and Doctoral Consortium, BIR-WS 2018.* CEUR.
11. Srinivasan, S., & Murthy, M. (2018). *Process maturity model can help give a business an edge.* Retrieved April 01, 2018, from https://www.isixsigma.com/methodology/business-process-management-bpm/process-maturity-model-can-help-give-business-edge/.
12. McNaughton, B., Ray, P., & Lewis, L. (2010). Designing an evaluation framework for IT service management. *Information & Management, 47*(4), 219–225.
13. Sahid, A., Maleh, Y., & Belaissaoui, M. (2018). A practical agile framework for IT service and asset management ITSM/ITAM through a case study. *Journal of Cases on Information Technology (JCIT), 20*(4), 71–92.
14. Göbel, H., Cronholm, S., & Seigerroth, U. (2013). Towards an agile method for ITSM self-assessment: A design science research approach. In *Proceedings of the International Conference on Management, Leadership and Governance (ICMLG2013).*
15. Leppänen, M. (2013). A comparative analysis of agile maturity models. In J. C. Rob Pooley (Ed.), *Information systems development, reflections, challenges and new directions* (pp. 329–343). New York: Springer.

16. CMMI Institute. (2019). *Build capability, improve maturity*. Retrieved April 11, 2019, from https://cmmiinstitute.com/.
17. Humble, J., & Russel, R. (2009). *The agile maturity model applied to building and releasing software*. Thoughtworks Web Publishing.
18. Frietzsche, M., & Keil, P. (2007). Agile methods and CMMI: Compatibility or conflict? *e-Informatica Software Engineering Journal*, 9–26.
19. Patel, C., & Ramachandran, M. (2009). Agile maturity model (AMM): A software process improvement framework for agile software development practices. *International Journal of Software Engineering*, 3–28.
20. Gren, L., Torkar, R., & Feldt, R. (2015). The prospects of a quantitative measurement of agility: A validation study on an agile maturity model. *The Journal of Systems and Software, 107*, 38–49.
21. Sutherland, J., Jakobsen, C. R., & Johnson, K. (2008). Scrum and CMMI level 5: The magic potion for code warriors. In *Proceedings of the 41st Hawaii International Conference on System Sciences* (pp. 1–9). IEEE.
22. Digital.ai. (2022). The 15th state of agile report. Retrieved May 05, 2022, from https://digital.ai.
23. Hevner, A. R. (2007). A three cycle view of design science research. *Scandinavian Journal of Information Systems, 19*(2), 4.
24. Hevner, A., et al. (2004). Design science in information systems research. *MIS Quarterly, 28*(1), 75–105.
25. Goldkuhl, G. (2012). From action research to practice research. *Australasian Journal of Information Systems, 17*(2).
26. Goldkuhl, G., & Lind, M. (2010). A multi-grounded design research process. In *International Conference on Design Science Research in Information Systems*. Springer.
27. Agutter, C. (2015). *ITIL foundation handbook*. TSO (The Stationery Office).
28. Costa, E., Soares, A. L., & de Sousa, J. P. (2016). Situating case studies within the design science research paradigm: An instantiation for collaborative networks. In *Working Conference on Virtual Enterprises*. Springer.
29. Conboy, K. (2009). Agility from first principles: Reconstructing the concept of agility in information systems development. *Information systems research, 20*(3), 329–354.
30. Conboy, K., Gleasure, R., & Cullina, E. (2015). Agile design science research. In *International Conference on Design Science Research in Information Systems*. Springer.
31. Johansson, B., Eckerstein, J., & Malmros, J. (2016). Evaluating a quantitative IT maturity self-assessment approach: Does it give a good way of the as-is state? In *ICMLG2016–4th International Conference on Management, Leadership and Governance: ICMLG2016*. Academic Conferences and publishing limited.
32. Henriques, V., & Tanner, M. (2017). A systematic literature review of agile and maturity model research. *Interdisciplinary Journal of Information, Knowledge and Management*, 53–73.
33. Boehm, B., & Turner, R. (2005). *Management challenges to implementing agile processes in traditional organisations*. IEEE Software (pp. 30–39).
34. Yin, R. K. (2017). *Case study research and applications: Design and methods* (6th ed.). SAGE Publications.
35. Markus, M. L., Majchrzak, A., & Gasser, L. (2002). A design theory for systems that support emergent knowledge processes. *MIS Quarterly, 26*, 179–212.

A Living Lab Perspective on Information Systems Development Process

Abdolrasoul Habibipour and Anna Ståhlbröst

Abstract This article explores the information systems development (ISD) process when ISD follows a living lab approach. A living lab is an innovation development approach in which stakeholders are involved in cocreating, implementing, testing and adopting innovations in a real-life setting. Several aspects of living lab settings, such as the voluntary nature of user engagement, the real-life context of innovation development and the resulting difficulty of observation, and the immaturity of innovation in living lab activities, influence the ISD process in living lab settings. Accordingly, the aim of this paper is to understand how the ISD process is shaped when ISD follows a living lab approach. The aim will be achieved by conducting four participatory knowledge generation workshops as the primary sources of empirical data in the context of three European projects (namely, AdaptUrbanRail, UNaLab, and LiLaCC) as well as an international conference (DLLD20). A SWOT (Strengths, Weaknesses, Opportunities, and Threats) analysis of the ISD process following the living lab approach will also be presented.

Keywords Information systems development · Living lab · Workshop · Innovation development · SWOT

1 Introduction

Information systems development (ISD) has always been one of the fundamental research themes within information systems research [23] from the first introduction of information systems as an independent research discipline [4]. Despite this, ISD has widely been interpreted as developing information systems within the realm of

A. Habibipour (✉) · A. Ståhlbröst
Information Systems, Luleå University of Technology, Luleå, Sweden
e-mail: Abdolrasoul.Habibipour@ltu.se

A. Ståhlbröst
e-mail: Anna.Stahlbrost@ltu.se

© The Author(s), under exclusive license to Springer Nature Switzerland AG 2023
G. C. Silaghi et al. (eds.), *Advances in Information Systems Development*,
Lecture Notes in Information Systems and Organisation 63,
https://doi.org/10.1007/978-3-031-32418-5_2

19

an organisation [3], and less attention has been given to ISD when ISD boundaries are beyond the organisational context; this topic deserves further research [24].

Currently, information systems in many ways are innovations that, unlike traditional information systems, are developed in interaction with society by engaging volunteer citizens and users [47]. Consequently, these innovations will affect people's daily lives in various ways, and therefore, humans morally and ethically have the right to be engaged in the development of innovations by which they might later be affected [8]. This is in line with the participatory design approach adopted in information systems research [7, 27] with the difference that it is mainly moving out from the realms of an organisation.

Living labs are one of the most well-known participatory design approaches that facilitate multistakeholder engagement throughout ISD processes, in which innovations are cocreated, implemented, tested and evaluated by various stakeholders and voluntary contributors (e.g., potential end-users) in a real-life context [5, 28, 36]. However, there is a dearth of research on what should be taken into consideration under each ISD phase and what actions and activities can be taken when ISD follows a living lab approach. Several aspects, such as the voluntary nature of user engagement [40], a real-life context of innovation development and the resulting difficulty of observation [29, 38], as well as the immaturity of many innovations in living lab activities [36], will influence the ISD process in a living lab setting. Accordingly, the aim of this paper is to understand how an ISD process can be shaped when ISD follows a living lab approach.

To achieve this goal, this article uses four participatory knowledge generation workshops as the primary sources of empirical data. The workshops were conducted within the context of three European projects, namely, UNaLab, AdaptUrbanRail, and LiLaCC, as well as an international conference (DLLD20). The workshops aimed to understand the innovation development process in a living lab setting. In addition, a SWOT (Strengths, Weaknesses, Opportunities, and Threats) analysis [18] of the ISD process following the living lab approach will be presented.

The remainder of this article is structured as follows. The next section presents the theoretical background of this study and reviews some related work. The third section outlines the methodology and research process for this article. The ISD process in a living lab setting is presented in the fourth section, and the paper ends with a SWOT analysis, together with the limitations of this study and suggestions for future research.

2 Background

2.1 Information Systems and Participatory Design

The information systems research field has a history of more than 60 years, origi-nating and evolving from the management information systems discipline [23]. Since then, the ongoing growth of the information systems field has made it an independent discipline that has its own right [4], instead of being a subdivision of management information systems research. Consequently, the information systems field has been recognised as a unique research discipline, and numerous research streams have emerged within the field. Its research themes include, but are not limited to, infor-mation systems development (ISD), information systems adoption and diffusion, decision support systems, information systems evaluation and so forth [23].

Currently, information systems are more heterogeneous, more complicated to develop and less defined compared to earlier systems, making it difficult to convey the sociotechnical perspective [22] from an organisation to real-life situations [1]. This complexity and the uncertainty of various ISD approaches in turn call for more inno-vative information systems that integrate both social and technical aspects of devel-oped systems or innovations [31]. Therefore, in many ways, information systems are innovations that are developed outside of organisational boundaries, have users who are not necessarily organisational employees and aim to integrate both social and technical aspects of innovations in real-life settings [32, 47]. Accordingly, innova-tions and the innovation development process together form the core focus of this study regarding both information systems and the ISD process.

One central aspect of ISD is associated with the engagement of individual users in the innovation and development process. Involving users in the development process is of vital importance [21], and it has been acknowledged since the early 1960s, when the participatory design tradition was pioneered in Scandinavia [7, 27]. In this regard, all the technical structures of the system, the social interactions supported by the system, and the other sociotechnical aspects are influential through the way that users recognise and interpret their experiences, and consequently, user behaviours are affected by these aspects [15]. The core idea of participatory design is that people in societies expect to have a voice in the final systems or innovations that will influence many different aspects of their lives [1].

Even though participatory design as an approach has been acknowledged in a wide range of disciplines (with different levels of technological engagement), the technological aspects of innovations in participatory design activities have always been of fundamental importance, whether as supporting infrastructure for partici-patory design activities or as the final outcome of participatory design actions [1]. Although the term "democratising innovation" [45] is a relatively new concept within the information systems literature, the main rationale for the participatory design approach was to democratise workplaces in Scandinavia in the late 1970s. This was accomplished by engaging the organisational workers in the ISD process [8].

Despite the fact that the user engagement movement in the information systems development process within organisations has existed for a long time, the central approach has still revolved around designing systems "for" users, as promised in the user-centred design approach [17]. However, what distinguishes participatory design from other traditional development approaches (such as user-centred design), is that it relies on the active engagement of users throughout innovation processes [33], as well as designing systems not only for users but "with" and "by" users [17]. Hence, in the participatory design approach, users are not used as the subject only to gain commercial benefits or as information repositories; they are also engaged with the goal of distributing decision-making power in society among different actors, including public and private sectors and citizens [6, 13]. In a study on participatory design, Pilemalm et al. [32] highlighted the significance of active user engagement all the way through the ISD process and argued that this topic deserves further research.

Over the past two decades, the information systems literature has emphasised the importance of innovativeness and creativity throughout the development process by involving individual users in the entire ISD process [42]. This is in line with the concept of open innovation, a term first coined by Chesbrough [11] Following the open innovation approach, external sources of knowledge and ideas become key contributors, and individual users in these innovation processes have proven to be valuable external resources [25]. Consequently, engaging users in innovation processes is one of the key aspects of open innovation activities, contributing to different aspects of developed innovations, including success, acceptance and user satisfaction [2, 46]. Both information systems and open innovation fields are focused on individual users as active participants and sources of knowledge and experience with the power of decision-making [25, 44].

2.2   Living Labs

Considering information systems as sociotechnical systems, the incorporation of societal structures and heterogeneous perspectives with technical functions has been a fundamental problem of sociotechnical systems [22]. One of the most well-known approaches to designing and developing innovations is the "living lab", which aims to integrate technical and social structures in a highly complex sociotechnical setting related to various stakeholders and their perspectives [29]. Accordingly, living labs can be seen as an approach for facilitating innovation processes, as they allow one to simultaneously focus on individuals, technologies, tasks and structures and the interactions between different stakeholders [35].

One of the fundamental premises of living lab activities is that users are voluntarily engaged to explore, cocreate, implement, test and evaluate innovations in open, collaborative, multicontextual real-world settings [5, 28, 39]. In contrast with traditional research and development projects, in which prototyped products, services or systems are in focus [9], living labs present an outstanding approach that focuses on cocreative innovations [30]. Therefore, in the living lab context, the aim is to actively engage users throughout the entire innovation processes, from exploring the innovation to its test and adoption in a real-life context [36, 39]. Consequently, living lab research has been heavily inspired by both participatory design and open innovation [8, 14].

There is no clear consensus on the ISD phases when the innovation process follows a living lab approach. For example, Schuurman et al. [37] highlight three main innovation development phases in living lab settings, namely, exploration, experimentation and evaluation. Despite this, the experimentation phase may contain various activities from the early design phase until the final implementation phase. That might be very difficult to explore as a single phase of the ISD process.

FormIT, as one of the most well-known living lab methodologies, employs four key phases: exploration, cocreation, implementation and evaluation [39]. However, Shin [38] highlights adoption, which can be considered the post evaluation phase, as one of the key phases of innovation development in a living lab setting. In another study, Bergvall-Kareborn et al. [5] also highlight the importance of the planning phase in living lab activities, even before starting the exploration phase in innovation development. Accordingly, by synthesizing these studies, this article uses six main phases throughout the ISD process to explore different actions and activities under each ISD phase. These six phases are planning, exploration, cocreation, implementation, evaluation, and finally, adoption. The overall framework has been built based on the FormIT living lab approach [39] and the inclusion of planning and adoption phases.

In a study that aims to identify the key constructs of urban living labs, Chroneer et al. [12] identified seven key components that have been used as the basis for all living lab actions. These seven key components are governance models, including management structure, politics, and policies; financing and business models; physical representation that takes place in a real-life setting in the city context; an innovation to experiment with; partners and end-users; approaches for engaging different stakeholders and collecting data; and finally, ICT and infrastructure, such as Internet of Things (IoT) devices. The combination of these seven key components on the one hand (as one dimension) and the six ISD phases in living labs (as the second dimension) has been used to investigate the ISD process in living lab settings.

Table 1 outlines the overall framework that was employed as the primary data gathering tool to collect empirical data, as described in the next section.

3   Research Methodology

This study adopts a qualitative research methodology [16] using four participatory knowledge generation workshops by involving a number of experts in the area of innovation management, open innovation, participatory design, living labs, etc., from both academia and industry. The aim of the workshops was to identify the main actions and activities that should be taken into consideration in regard to the ISD

Table 1 Overall framework for the collection of empirical data

	Planning	Exploration	Cocreation	Implementation	Evaluation	Adoption
Governance and management						
Financing and business models						
A real-life context						
Innovation						
Key stakeholders						
Methods of engagement and data collection						
ICT infrastructure						

process, following a living lab approach. To achieve this goal, the developed framework in the previous section (Table 1) was used as the basis for the data collection through these four workshops. Before each workshop, one training session on the concept of living labs was organised so that the participants could translate the information systems and living lab concepts into their own setting.

The workshops were conducted within the context of three European projects as well as an international conference from 2020 to 2022. The projects were called UNaLab, LiLaCC and AdaptUrbanRail, and the conference was the main annual conference of the European network of living labs, namely, Open Living Lab Days 2020. The workshop participants were mainly project partners with some degree of knowledge about innovation development but in different contexts. Table 2 shows an overview of the workshops, timeline, participants, etc.

Table 2 Summary of workshops

Workshop number	Context	Time	Participants	Number of participants
Workshop #1	DLLD conference	September 2020	Living lab and innovation experts, conference participants	56 participants in 11 groups
Workshop #2	UNaLab	November 2020	UNaLab Project partners, city representatives, innovation experts outside of the project	39 participants in 9 groups
Workshop #3	LiLaCC	March 2021	LiLaCC Project partners	13 participants in 2 groups
Workshop #4	AdaptUrbanRail	January 2022	AdaptUrbanRail Project partners	11 participants in 2 groups

The UNaLab (Urban Nature Labs) project incorporated ten European cities, aiming at developing nature-based solutions to problems in these cities by engaging citizens throughout the innovation development process following a living lab approach. The project started in 2017 and will be finished in 2022.

The aim of the LiLaCC (Living Laboratory in Climate Change) project is to improve and adjust the educational systems of partner universities via knowledge and technology transfer in the field of disruptive information technologies to study and mitigate climate change. The aim will be achieved with the help of developing massive open online courses (MOOCs), with a particular emphasis on developing MOOCs on the usage of disruptive information technologies (DITs) as tools to work on climate change mitigation. The LiLaCC project follows living lab methodology as the main innovation development approach. The project started in 2020 and will be finished in 2023.

The aim of the AdaptUrbanRail (Adapting Urban Rail Infrastructure to Climate Change) project is to improve the resilience of urban railway infrastructure to adverse future climate conditions by implementing a climate adaptation strategy in design, construction, operation, and maintenance. The aim will be achieved by developing a decision support system (DSS) that integrates urban railway infrastructure features with climate change models and satellite images and climate data. The development of DSS in this project follows the living lab approach. The project started in 2021 and will be finished in 2024.

The Open Living Lab Days (OLLD) conference is the annual event organised by the European Network of Living Labs. The event offers a space or a platform for public officials, companies, entrepreneurs, academics, living lab representatives, and innovators to connect and work together, to create new products and services, to set the basis for the debate and exploration of theories and to discuss and process policy recommendations within the practical elements of open and user-driven innovation. The 2020 edition (DLLD20) of the conference was held in digital format due to the COVID-19 pandemic and was called Digital Living Lab Days. Table 2 shows a summary of the conducted workshops.

The qualitative data from the workshops were synthesised, interpreted and analysed following an explanatory approach through content analysis [43] as well as qualitative coding as one of the most flexible methods of qualitative content analysis [26]. Since the most important element within coding analysis is being grounded in the data, researchers do not restrict themselves to a preestablished theory or categories of data. This approach facilitated insights and comparisons of the different theoretical concepts [26] and enables this study to better understand the main actions and activities that should be taken into account throughout the ISD process in living labs. As seen, in this study, the ISD process may refer to the development of various innovations, from large-scale sociotechnical innovations such as nature-based solutions (in the context of the UNaLab project) to MOOC courses (in the context of the LiLaCC project). This research employed Microsoft Excel for data synthesis and data analysis.

4   ISD in Living Labs

The results of this study demonstrate that different researchers and innovation experts have highlighted various actions in ISD phases, depending on the nature of the project (context), as well as their expertise area. To give the readers a general picture of the workshops, Fig. 1 shows an overview of the results from one group in one of the workshops. In the following, the results of the workshop based on the six phases of ISD in living labs (as presented in the background chapter) are presented.

4.1   Planning

In regard to the planning phase, it is of vital importance to obtain as much information as possible regarding the background, aim and scope of the innovation, different perspectives on the innovation, relevant skills that are needed within the ISD team, the context of the ISD (urban or rural context, organisations, home environment, etc.) in which the project is located and finally the constraints and boundaries that need to be clearly defined and agreed upon.

In this phase, it is necessary to achieve a shared perspective on the objectives of the ISD. A mixture of various competences stimulates knowledge sharing and enhances understanding of the various stakeholders' visions (i.e., public sector, private sector, research institutions and citizens).

In the planning process, it is important to take the five living lab key principles (namely, value, sustainability, influence, realism and openness) into consideration [5]. For example, the ISD team should think about how value can be cocreated for all stakeholders, how users can influence the ISD process, how sustainability takes form,

	Planning	Exploration	Co-creation	Implementation	Test & evaluation	Adoption
Governance and management	Develop a vision and prospective; Definition of a timeline	defining managing body/organisation	ensure good moderation of process and that all stakeholders are heard			e.g., scalling up the NBS, refine the process and activities undertaken in ULL, ensure maintenance
Financing and business models	Rough Value proposition of the solutions that will be developed	Setting up boundaries and limits for the business case (what budget do we have available	Setting up an worst case and best case business scenario	Use all available data to setup a healthy business model and get the finance done by agreements		e.g., ownership cost for regular use of NBS
Real-life context	PESTEL analysis	status quo assessment / benchmark analysis	analyze viable options in the city centre that can be used and set up an SWOT analyses to determine	Execute all field research and perform a risk analyses to tackle all events at the project site.	e.g., field test in real life	
NBS	Prioritize the different components and then perform a SWOT analysis	field research e.g., map existing NBS solutions	Simulation of some of the solutions and their potential impacts/benefits	preparing the project site		
Key stakeholders	e.g., stakeholder identification, lobbying	precising key stakeholders and adressing them / first contact / needs assessment	Involving key stakeholders in thedevelopment of suitable NBS solutions; deal with conflicting interests and trade-offs	e.g., barriers of stakeholder engagement in implementation phase	User testing and feedback	
Methods of engagement and data collection		Communication / (Marketing)	Brainstorming / Design Thinking	Data collection by different means during the project		
ICT infrastructure	e.g., discover opportunities for collaboration platform	Deep dive in existing databases (e.g. GIS) to see what is already there	Online / remote option of handing in ideas (to make sure many citizens can be reached)			ICT tools and data to help in performance monitoring and support maintenance processes

Fig. 1 An example (excel sheet) of the collected data from the workshops

how openness should be considered [11], and so on. In addition, the planning phase highlights how the innovation process should be designed to capture a situation that is as realistic as possible, i.e., innovation implementation, evaluation and adoption should be carried out in a real-life context. One important aspect in the planning phase is to be aware of the challenges of living lab activities. The challenges include but are not limited to the voluntary nature of participation, difficulties with the observation of living lab activities due to the nature of real-life activities, and finally issues associated with the immaturity level of innovation, which in turn may create frustration for the users and other involved stakeholders (the so-called quadruple-helix actors, namely, public sectors, private sectors, research institutions and individual users [19]). In this phase, questions such as those presented below are relevant.

- What is the goal of the intervention?
- What is the specified aim of the ISD within the living lab team?
- What competencies and resources need to be involved in the process?
- What are the important frames for the project (e.g., ethics, economics, resources)?

4.2 Exploration

In the exploration phase, it is important to gain as much information as possible about the underlying circumstances for the ISD process. The key difference between planning and exploration is that in exploration, innovation is in focus, while in the planning phase, the whole ISD process is at the centre of attention. One important aspect of the exploration phase is to gain insights into the needs of citizens with respect to innovation. Here are some examples of the questions and points that need to be considered in this phase.

- In which social, physical, technical, and organisational context is the ISD planned to be implemented? How might that affect the process?
- What ICT infrastructures for the ISD process are needed? For example, hardware, software, data (public, private), and networks (4G, fibre, etc.).
- Does ISD stimulate creativity and support the generation of new thoughts?
- Are the relevant delegates from the ISD team involved in the exploration phase?
- Who are the target users for the innovation? Who benefits from the innovation?
- What is the aim of user (real or potential) engagement? How should citizens be recruited? What are the recruited citizens expected to do?
- Which questions will stimulate rich storytelling and explanations so that needs can be constructed?

4.3 Cocreation

The aim of the cocreation phase is to develop concepts or rough prototypes of inno-vation based on the identified needs from the two previous phases, i.e., the planning and exploration phases. The concepts need to be detailed enough for the users to understand the basic objective with the functions of the innovation. Examples of the questions that project partners need to think about before starting the cocreation of innovation in the living lab context are presented below. When all these questions have been addressed and discussed, the ISD in the living lab context can proceed forwards into the next phase (implementation).

- How should users be engaged in the ISD process? Interviews? Workshops? Focus groups? Mock-ups? Observations? Scenarios, visual? Narratives? Other?
- Which user requirements are most relevant in relation to the purpose of the innovation?
- What value is cocreated in the process for all stakeholders?
- What information needs to be classified, categorised, and organised from the exploration phase?
- How can we capture insights from the data produced and collected from the cocreation activities? Camera, notes, video, audio, etc.
- What supportive tools are required for cocreation?

4.4 Implementation

Within the implementation phase, it is important to discuss the users' requirements (needs, goals, values, etc.) that have been identified and presented in the exploration and cocreation phases. Examples of questions in this phase are as follows:

- How should the risks associated with innovation development in the living lab context be managed?
- Who can experiment with the innovation? How can they experiment with it, and which activities will they do?
- At what maturity level should innovation be implemented?
- Where is the ISD setting?
- Who owns the innovation setting? For example, who can stop the ISD process?
- Who has access to the developed innovation? Is it open or restricted?
- Which activities does the physical context of ISD currently support and for whom?
- Is the context in which the innovation is planned to be implemented a real-life context?

4.5 Evaluation

The aim of this phase is to test and evaluate developed innovation in the living lab context in a real-life setting (the so-called living lab field test). Within the test and evaluation phase, it is important to encourage users to express their thoughts and attitudes towards the cocreation and implementation activities from the previous phases. Examples of the questions that need to be considered in this phase are as follows:

- To what extent can the test and evaluation process in a real-life setting be observed and controlled? How should the activities be documented to overcome this issue?
- How should user drop-out from field tests in living labs be handled?
- How should the test participants be motivated to test the innovation? For example, winning the prize, monetary incentives, learning, etc.
- What is the aim of the test and evaluation of the innovation? What do the ISD teams want to achieve?
- What ethical considerations (in relation to voluntary engagement) need to be handled during the test and evaluation process of the innovation?
- Which data collection methods should be used in the innovation test and evaluation? Observations? Interviews? Focus Groups? Diaries? Questionnaires?
- For how long should the living lab field test continue?
- What technical equipment does the innovation test and evaluation require?
- How many users should be recruited for the innovation testing and evaluation?

4.6 Adoption

As Rogers [34] states, a successful test of innovations will lead to a higher level of innovation adoption because testing the innovation by (real or potential) users is one of the fundamental aspects of all living lab activities [36, 38]. In this phase, the developed innovation in the context of living labs is adopted by the final users, including citizens, in the users' everyday use setting. Various actions should be considered in the adoption phase in living labs. Examples of the questions that need to be handled in this phase are as follows:

- How should the knowledge gained from the ISD process be shared among various stakeholders and citizens?
- Who are the main adopters of the innovation in the living lab context?
- What are the future plans for the context of innovation development?
- In which social, physical, technical, and organisational context is the ISD planned to be adopted?
- How should the innovation results be disseminated?
- What technical equipment does the innovation adoption require?
- What barriers are associated with the adoption of the innovation in living lab settings?
- How should the identified innovation adoption barriers be approached?

As the final remarks, the next chapter outlines the SWOT analysis [18] of the results based on the outcomes from the workshops.

5   Final Remarks

The abovementioned actions and activities that were identified from the workshops clearly show the prominent role of individual users and citizens in the ISD process in the living lab context. This is in line with most of the previous research, for example [12, 14, 15, 19, 38], which highlights user engagement as the core focus of living lab activities. In addition, the voluntary nature of user engagement throughout the ISD process in living labs [40] is of vital importance and is highlighted in various ISD phases. Furthermore, the level of innovation maturity, particularly when it is in its fuzzy front-end stage, should be taken into account in various ISD phases [41], mainly in the last three phases, namely, implementation, evaluation and adoption. Lack of control over the ISD process in living lab settings and difficulty in observing the activities in a real-life context [14, 20, 30] were also highlighted as key differences between traditional ISD and living lab settings.

The results also showed that ISD in living labs is a combination of an iterative process in the middle and a single entry and exit point. That is, the process should always be started from planning and be ended by adoption. However, the four middle stages, i.e., exploration, cocreation, implementation and evaluation, are iterative in nature, and each phase can be met several times throughout the ISD process in living labs. This is in line with what is recommended by the FormIT living lab methodology, as explained earlier [39]. Figure 2 shows the ISD process in living labs, as explained.

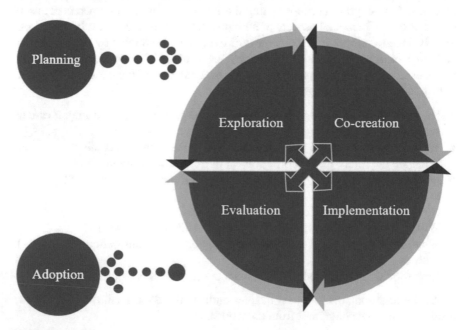

Fig. 2 ISD process in living labs

This article contributes to the body of information systems and living lab literature by discussing the ISD process, when information systems are developed outside the realm of an organisation (i.e., in a real life setting), following a living lab approach. The findings from this study can also be put into practical use by information systems and, more particularly, living lab researchers and practitioners to understand what activities should be done under each ISD phase and what aspects should be taken into consideration by them when the innovation process follows the living lab approach.

5.1 SWOT Analysis

SWOT analysis is known as an appropriate way to analyse the strengths, weaknesses, opportunities, and threats in relation to an organisation [10]. However, several other applications for SWOT analysis have been identified, including the evaluation of an approach, a solution, barrier analysis, and so on [18]. The SWOT framework includes both internal and external factors that need to be considered in regard to identifying strengths, weaknesses, opportunities, and threats. Strengths and weaknesses mainly refer to internal factors, while opportunities and threats are associated with external factors. The SWOT analysis was performed after all the workshops were conducted and when all the results were synthesized from the four conducted workshops. Table 3 shows an overview of the SWOT analysis for living labs as an ISD approach based on the results from the workshop.

The SWOT analysis highlights different aspects in relation to all seven key components of living labs [12], including the governance and management of living labs, the

Table 3 SWOT analysis of the living lab approach for ISD

Strengths	Weaknesses
• Value cocreation • Flexibility and dynamic nature of living labs • Inclusive • Participatory leading ISD • Early stakeholder engagement	• Difficulty in observing activities • Immaturity of innovation • Lack of control over innovation activities • Sometimes not a separate institution with a physical location
Opportunities	*Threats*
• Openness • Multistakeholder engagement • Knowledge sharing and dissemination • Research-oriented	• Voluntariness of participation (drop-out concerns) • A real-life setting related issues • Scaling-up challenges • Ownership of shared tools and resources • Funding issues

financing and business model, the ICT infrastructure, the stakeholder engagement, the context of ISD, the innovation approach and the innovation itself. Many of these aspects, such as the voluntary nature of participation in living lab activities, real-life experimentation, and immaturity of developed innovation emphasise the differences between ISD in an organisational setting and the ISD process in living labs.

5.2 Limitations and Future Research

This study has its own limitations. One limitation was that some workshop participants were project partners who were not familiar with the concept of living labs. However, before each workshop, one training session on the concept of living lab was organised so that the participants could translate the information systems and living lab concepts into their own setting. However, the results could still be triangulated by the same group of participants (i.e., data triangulation [16]) in the later stages of the project. This would be an interesting direction to expand this research. In addition, in regard to SWOT analysis, using quantitative data may strengthen the analysis [10], and this can also be considered an avenue for future research in information systems and living lab research.

Acknowledgements This work was funded by Vinnova in the context of AdaptUrbanRail (Grant Agreement No. 2021-02456), the European Commission in the context of the Horizon 2020 project UNaLab (Grant Agreement No. 730052), and Erasmus+ LiLaCC—Living Laboratory in Climate Change project (Grant Agreement No. 618209), which is gratefully acknowledged.

References

1. Bannon, L., Bardzell, J., & Bødker, S. (2018). Introduction: Reimagining participatory design—Emerging voices. *ACM Transactions on Computer-Human Interaction, 25*(1), 1–8. https://doi.org/10.1145/3177794
2. Bano, M., & Zowghi, D. (2015). A systematic review on the relationship between user involvement and system success. *Information and Software Technology, 58*, 148–169. https://doi.org/10.1016/j.infsof.2014.06.011
3. Bansler, J. (1989). Systems development research in Scandinavia: Three theoretical schools. *Scandinavian Journal of Information Systems, 1*(1), 3–20.
4. Baskerville, R. L., & Myers, M. D. (2002). Information systems as a reference discipline. *MIS Quarterly, 26*(1), 1–14. https://doi.org/10.2307/4132338
5. Bergvall-Kareborn, B., Hoist, M., & Stahlbrost, A. (2009). Concept design with a living lab approach. In *2009 42nd Hawaii International conference on system sciences* (pp. 1–10). IEEE.
6. Bergvall-Kåreborn, B., & Ståhlbrost, A. (2008). Participatory design: One step back or two steps forward? In *Proceedings of the tenth anniversary conference on participatory design* (pp. 102–111). Luleå University of Technology.
7. Bjerknes, G., & Bratteteig, T. (1995). User participation and democracy: A discussion of Scandinavian research on system development. *Scandinavian Journal of Information Systems, 7*(1), 1.

8. Björgvinsson, E., Ehn, P., & Hillgren, P.-A. (2010). Participatory design and "democratizing innovation". In *Proceedings of the 11th Biennial participatory design conference* (pp. 41–50). ACM.

9. Brønnum, L., & Møller, L. (2013). The dynamics and facilitation of a living lab construct. In *ISPIM conference proceedings* (p. 1). ISPIM.

10. Chang, H.-H., & Huang, W.-C. (2006). Application of a quantification SWOT analytical method. *Mathematical and Computer Modelling, 43*(1), 158–169. https://doi.org/10.1016/j.mcm.2005.08.016

11. Chesbrough, H. (2003). *Open innovation: The new imperative for creating and profiting, from technology*. Harvard Business School Press.

12. Chronéer, D., Ståhlbröst, A., & Habibipour, A. (2019). Urban living labs: Towards an integrated understanding of their key components. *Technology Innovation Management Review, 9*, 50–62. https://doi.org/10.22215/timreview/1224.

13. Clemmensen, T., Rajanen, D., Rajanen, M., & Abdelnour-Nocera, J. (2019). Introduction to the special issue on HCI in a sharing society. *AIS Transactions on Human-Computer Interaction, 11*(3), 107–116. https://doi.org/10.17705/1thci.00115.

14. Dell'Era, C., & Landoni, P. (2014). Living lab: A methodology between user-centred design and participatory design. *Creativity and Innovation Management, 23*(2), 137–154. https://doi.org/10.1111/caim.12061

15. Di Gangi, P. M., & Wasko, M. (2009). The co-creation of value: Exploring user engagement in user-generated content websites. In *Proceedings of JAIS theory development workshop. Sprouts: Working papers on information systems* (pp. 9–50).

16. Flick, U. (2014). *An introduction to qualitative research*. Sage.

17. Gulliksen, J., Göransson, B., Boivie, I., Blomkvist, S., Persson, J., & Cajander, Å. (2003). Key principles for user-centred systems design. *Behaviour & Information Technology, 22*(6), 397–409. https://doi.org/10.1080/01449290310001624329

18. Gurl, E., & Tat, M. (2017). SWOT analysis: A theoretical review. *The Journal of International Social Research, 10*, 994–1006. https://doi.org/10.17719/jisr.2017.1832.

19. Habibipour, A. (2020). *User engagement in living labs: Issues and concerns*. Doctoral dissertation, Luleå University of Technology.

20. Habibipour, A., Lindberg, J., Runardotter, M., Elmistikawy, Y., Ståhlbröst, A., & Chronéer, D. (2022). Rural living labs: Inclusive digital transformation in the countryside. *Technology Innovation Management Review, 11*(9/10), 59–72. https://doi.org/10.22215/timreview/1465.

21. He, J., & King, W. R. (2008). The role of user participation in information systems development: Implications from a meta-analysis. *Journal of Management Information Systems, 25*(1), 301–331. https://doi.org/10.2753/MIS0742-1222250111

22. Herrmann, T. (2009). Systems design with the socio-technical walkthrough. In B. Whitworth & A. de Moor (Eds.), *Handbook of research on socio-technical design and social networking systems* (pp. 336–351). IGI Global.

23. Hirschheim, R., & Klein, H. K. (2012). A glorious and not-so-short history of the information systems field. *Journal of the Association for Information Systems, 13*(4), 188–235. https://doi.org/10.17705/1jais.00294.

24. Ismagilova, E., Hughes, L., Dwivedi, Y. K., & Raman, K. R. (2019). Smart cities: Advances in research—An information systems perspective. *International Journal of Information Management, 47*, 88–100. https://doi.org/10.1016/j.ijinfomgt.2019.01.004

25. Jespersen, K. (2010). User-involvement and open innovation: The case of decision-maker openness. *International Journal of Innovation Management, 14*(3), 471–489. https://doi.org/10.1142/S136391961000274X

26. Kaplan, B., & Maxwell, J. A. (2005). Qualitative research methods for evaluating computer information systems. In J. G. Anderson & C. E. Aydin (Eds.), *Evaluating the organizational impact of healthcare information systems* (pp. 30–55). Springer.

27. Kensing, F., & Blomberg, J. (1998). Participatory design: Issues and concerns. *Computer Supported Cooperative Work, 7*(3), 167–185. https://doi.org/10.1023/A:1008689307411

28. Leminen, S., Westerlund, M., & Nyström, A.-G. (2012). Living labs as open-innovation networks. *Technology Innovation Management Review, 2*(9), 6–11. https://doi.org/10.22215/timreview/602.
29. McNeese, M. D., Perusich, K., & Rentsch, J. R. (2000). Advancing socio-technical systems design via the living laboratory. In *Proceedings of the human factors and ergonomics society annual meeting* (pp. 2–610). SAGE Publications Inc.
30. Mulder, I. (2012). Living labbing the Rotterdam way: Co-creation as an enabler for urban innovation. *Technology Innovation Management Review, 2*(9), 39–43. https://doi.org/10.22215/timreview/607.
31. Mumford, E. (2000). A socio-technical approach to systems design. *Requirements Engineering, 5*(2), 125–133. https://doi.org/10.1007/PL00010345
32. Pilemalm, S., Lindell, P.-O., Hallberg, N., & Eriksson, H. (2007). Integrating the rational unified process and participatory design for development of socio-technical systems: A user participative approach. *Design Studies, 28*(3), 263–288. https://doi.org/10.1016/j.destud.2007.02.009
33. Robertson, T., & Simonsen, J. (2012). Challenges and opportunities in contemporary participatory design. *Design Issues, 28*(3), 3–9. https://doi.org/10.1162/DESI_a_00157
34. Rogers, E. M. (2010). *Diffusion of innovations.* Simon and Schuster.
35. Schaffers, H., Merz, C., & Guzman, J. G. (2009). Living labs as instruments for business and social innovation in rural areas. In *2009 IEEE International technology management conference (ICE)* (pp. 1–8). IEEE.
36. Schuurman, D. (2015). *Bridging the gap between open and user innovation? : Exploring the value of Living Labs as a means to structure user contribution and manage distributed innovation.* Ghent University
37. Schuurman, D., Marez, L., & Ballon, P. (2013). Open innovation processes in living lab innovation systems: Insights from the LeYLab. *Technology Innovation Management Review, 3*(11), 28–36. https://doi.org/10.22215/timreview/743.
38. Shin, D. (2019). A living lab as socio-technical ecosystem: Evaluating the Korean living lab of internet of things. *Government Information Quarterly, 36*(2), 264–275. https://doi.org/10.1016/j.giq.2018.08.001
39. Ståhlbröst, A. (2008). *Forming future IT—The living lab way of user involvement.* Doctoral dissertation, Luleå Tekniska Universitet.
40. Ståhlbröst, A., & Bergvall-Kåreborn, B. (2013). Voluntary contributors in open innovation processes. In J. S. Z. Eriksson Lundström, M. Wiberg, S. Hrastinski, M. Edenius, & P. J. Ågerfalk (Eds.), *Managing open innovation technologies* (pp. 133–149). Springer.
41. Takey, S. M., & Carvalho, M. M. (2016). Fuzzy front end of systemic innovations: A conceptual framework based on a systematic literature review. *Technological Forecasting and Social Change, 111*, 97–109. https://doi.org/10.1016/j.techfore.2016.06.011
42. Tiwana, A., & McLean, E. R. (2005). Expertise integration and creativity in information systems development. *Journal of Management Information Systems, 22*(1), 13–43. https://doi.org/10.1080/07421222.2003.11045836
43. Vaismoradi, M., Turunen, H., & Bondas, T. (2013). Content analysis and thematic analysis: Implications for conducting a qualitative descriptive study. *Nursing & Health Sciences, 15*(3), 398–405. https://doi.org/10.1111/nhs.12048
44. Vines, J., Clarke, R., Wright, P., McCarthy, J., & Olivier, P. (2013). Configuring participation: on how we involve people in design. In *Proceedings of the SIGCHI conference on human factors in computing systems* (pp. 429–438). ACM.
45. von Hippel, E. (2005). Democratizing innovation: The evolving phenomenon of user innovation. *Journal für Betriebswirtschaft, 55*(1), 63–78. https://doi.org/10.1007/s11301-004-0002-8
46. West, J., Salter, A., Vanhaverbeke, W., & Chesbrough, H. (2014). Open innovation: The next decade. *Research Policy, 43*(5), 805–811. https://doi.org/10.1016/j.respol.2014.03.001
47. Yoo, Y., Henfridsson, O., & Lyytinen, K. (2010). Research commentary—the new organizing logic of digital innovation: An agenda for information systems research. *Information Systems Research, 21*(4), 724–735. https://doi.org/10.1287/isre.1100.0322

Cloud-Based Business Intelligence Solutions in the Management of Polish Companies

Damian Dziembek and Leszek Ziora

Abstract The paper aims to indicate the role, scale, and benefits resulting from the application of Business Intelligence systems in the cloud computing model in the management of Polish companies. The paper characterizes cloud-based BI systems and its role in the support of a contemporary company's management. It focuses on the cloud as a factor positively affecting business organization development where the research was conducted on a sample of 400 medium and large Polish companies in the 2021 year. The research part indicates benefits resulting from the application of Cloud BI systems by medium and large companies in Poland, the popularity of Cloud BI systems, threats and barriers resulting from the application of Cloud BI systems, assessment of Cloud BI systems application in the scope of the decision and business processes support and evaluation of the application of Cloud BI systems in supporting key company's areas and activities.

Keywords Business intelligence systems · Cloud computing · Cloud-based BI · Business analytics · Decision making support

1 Introduction

Business Intelligence systems are currently one of the most important IT tools supporting the process of contemporary company management, especially playing a crucial role in the support of decision making at all levels of management. "Dynamic development in the area of IT, growing needs of recipients, and the increasing competition among suppliers of IT solutions, contributed to the rising of new forms of purchase and utilization of Business Intelligence systems. An alternative for the

D. Dziembek · L. Ziora (✉)
Czestochowa University of Technology, Czestochowa, Poland
e-mail: leszek.ziora@pcz.pl

D. Dziembek
e-mail: damian.dziembek@pcz.p

© The Author(s), under exclusive license to Springer Nature Switzerland AG 2023
G. C. Silaghi et al. (eds.), *Advances in Information Systems Development*,
Lecture Notes in Information Systems and Organisation 63,
https://doi.org/10.1007/978-3-031-32418-5_3

traditional model (on-premise) which bases itself on own IT resources of the recipient, is the possibility of purchase and utilization of Business Intelligence systems in the cloud" [5]. In the paper the authors posed the following research questions:

(1) Which Cloud BI solutions are used in medium and large companies?
(2) What were the motives for using Cloud BI in medium and large companies?
(3) What benefits and threats resulting from using Cloud BI systems are indicated by medium and large enterprises?
(4) What is the assessment of Cloud BI systems in terms of supporting decision-making processes, business processes, and projects as well as key areas in the business activity of the company.

According to Gartner "leading organizations are now creating resilient business foundations using cloud computing" [12]. J. Idemudia states that "Business Intelligence involves making data-driven decisions allowing users to get real-time business data to: identify marketing trends, structure unstructured data, analyze supply chain data, generate real-time automated reports, set business goals, identify and eliminate inefficient processes, provide affordable business communications, help businesses reduce costs and this author names two significant reasons businesses should consider cloud BI such as multi-device accessibility and simple user-friendly interface" [12].

2   Characteristics of Cloud-Based Business Intelligence Systems

The literature of subject presents multiple definitions of Business Intelligence systems e.g. IGI Global conducts a review of 62 definitions [3]. The worth mentioning is the one by Forrester Research where BI is defined as "a set of methodologies, processes, architectures, and technologies that transform raw data into meaningful and useful information used to enable more effective strategic, tactical, and operational insights and decision-making" [3]. The second definition on which this paper is based on is the one by Gartner Group where "Business intelligence (BI) is an umbrella term that includes the applications, infrastructure and tools, and best practices that enable access to and analysis of information to improve and optimize decisions and performance" [3].

S. Ouf and M. Nasr state that BI enables "making better decisions through the use of people, processes, data, and related tools and methodologies" [19]. "Cloud BI (Business Intelligence) and analytics refer to the applications hosted on the cloud, used to provide an organization with access to BI-related data—dashboards, KPIs, and other business analytics. It synergizes BI with business and predictive analytics, delivering information and insights in real-time on multiple devices and web browsers" [27]. Another crucial components of such systems include portals, predictive analytics tools, data and text mining solutions, alerts and notifications, workflow, querying and reporting, etc. [26].

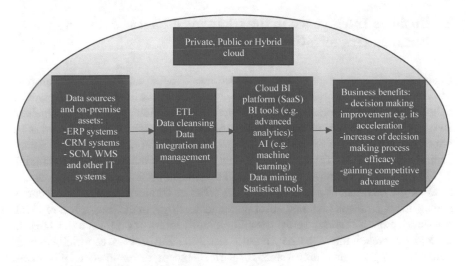

Fig. 1 Cloud BI environment. *Source* Authors' contribution

The cloud BI environment proposed in Fig. 1 utilizes data sources and on-premise assets including IT systems implemented in contemporary companies such as ERP systems, CRM systems, SCM, and WMS systems applied in the logistics domain as well as other ones applicable in a specific area. The data from those systems undergo the extraction, transformation, and load process (data cleansing) and with the application of the Cloud BI platform e.g. SaaS deployment, different BI analyses are conducted such as clustering, regression analyses, and so on. In order to carry out such analyses the artificial intelligence solutions (machine learning with deep and reinforcement learning), advanced statistics, data mining methods, techniques, and tools are applied. The application of the Cloud BI platform brings multiple benefits to the companies such as the improvement of the decision-making process with its acceleration, increasing efficiency and efficacy of the decision-making process, and many others which were presented in the research part of this paper.

A. Duggal states that "cloud Business Intelligence refers to the deployment of Business Intelligence tools over cloud infrastructure which can then be accessed using virtual networks including the Internet and enumerates such key advantages of Cloud BI as: cost-effectiveness, scalability of deployment, easier setup and operation, reduced overhead expenditures, advanced data sharing and improved reliability" [4]. C. Olszak states that "cloud BI has been developed in order to enhance the efficiency and productivity of business intelligence and increase the performance of BI software. It helps in shortening BI implementations, and reduction of BI application costs" [18]. W. Thompson and J. S. Walt underline the advantages of BI SaaS solution as cost reduction and "having access to the latest software which will give the business an edge on their competition" [23]. The challenges related to the utilization of Cloud BI may be connected with security concerns and data latency and also availability, performance, integration, regulatory issues, and constraints on network bandwidth [21].

3   Business Intelligence in the Cloud as a Factor Affecting Business Organization Development

Business Intelligence deployed in the cloud model as an innovative solution may contribute to business organization development. Business intelligence (BI) can be defined "as a decision-making process supported by the integration and analysis of an organization's data resources" [25]. Al Aqrabi et al. claim that the "cloud is an important part of future BI and offers several advantages in terms of cost efficiency, flexibility, and scalability of implementation, reliability, and enhanced data sharing capabilities" [1]. According to the research conducted by E. Indriasari et al. on the basis of the financial sector, the functional areas of Cloud BI embrace: executive management, strategic planning, information technology, marketing, sales, research and development, finance, human resources, and centers of competencies [13]. In the logistics area, it improves the whole decision-making process, especially in relation to the supply chain, improvement of performance in different areas of business activity, cost reduction and optimization in reverse logistics, improve the efficacy of transportation, and allows for better inventory management [9]. The deployment of Cloud BI brings multiple benefits to the company which utilizes such a solution. M. Kasem and E. Hassanein enumerate such advantages as: lower costs, scalability, flexibility, and disaster recovery [15]. Other advantages of BI on-premise, as well as cloud BI, embrace: "getting in one place reliable and coherent data and information from all areas of an organization's activity,facilitated access to data coming from different sources,shortening the time of analysis, decision making and increasing efficiency of management,efficient planning, simulation, and prognosis in different angles,quick reaction to appearing market trends, detection of threats and chances in the area of leading activity,current analysis of the financial situation; lowering the number of persons involved in decision-making processes; increase of efficiency and efficacy of undertaking decisions" [7].

Business Intelligence systems enable the processing of data coming from various sources and generate valuable information for decision-makers regarding the current and future state of various areas of company business activity. Knowledge derived from the information obtained from BI systems, allows making decisions important for the functioning and development of both large, small and medium-sized companies. Significant potential in the use of BI systems in the group of small and medium-sized is constituted by the SaaS model, which is a component of Cloud Computing. The use of BI systems by companies in the SMB sector can generate a number of strategic, organizational, economic, technological and social benefits" [6].

BI enables "turning data into valuable information in support of the management's decision making and the cloud addresses the problem of scalability, agility and cost" [16]. It has significant and positive impact on many industries such as sales, marketing or inventory management e.g. in the area of sales and marketing "BI systems provide information on customer needs across many segments to help managers better match products to market demands,in the inventory management area BI can provide historical information on stock-outs permitting better forecasting and generally BI application speeds up information processing" [22]. J. Ereth and D. Dahl enumerate factors that bring benefits to companies such as "the reduction of costs or the increasing focus on key competencies, but also criteria which are more complicated to identify, for instance, the enabling of competitive advantages and new business models [8]. "Compared to traditional on-premise BI software, cloud BI solutions are more affordable to implement and give a business greater agility in how they operate. These tools also scale with a company and improve collaboration within the workplace" [24]. F. Hamidinava et al. claim that "BI tools enable the effective management of companies of all sizes by providing analytic data and critical performance indicators" [11]. Y. S. Gurjar and V. S. Rathore state that "BI on the Cloud offers huge possibilities for removing barriers to decision making by integrating high volume and mission-critical business processes. Therefore, a Cloud BI solution may be a feasible answer to the challenges of the economic crisis" [10]. L. Menon et al. present Return on Investment (ROI) for a cloud BI implementation with "financial metrics including e.g. cost reduction or revenue increase, non-financial benefits including improved customer satisfaction (i.e. Customer Satisfaction Index CSI), better information, shorter cycle-time" [17]. I Aslan et al. claim that "most organizations realize the necessity of using data as efficient as possible in order to gain competitive advantage by making both strategic and tactical decisions" [2]. Jalil et al. underline the fact that "Business Intelligence has a critical role in terms of organizational development as Business Intelligence (BI) is able to provide a competitive advantage in the context of achieving positive information asymmetry, that is, unifying and making useful heterogeneous data" [14].

4 The Scale of Cloud BI Application Among Medium and Large Companies in Poland

In order to identify the scope of management support of medium and large companies by Cloud BI solutions, the authors conducted a survey in the first half of 2021, among 400 medium and large companies doing business in Poland, and which declared the use of BI systems in cloud computing. The distribution of companies in terms of their size was proportional: 50% of medium-sized and 50% of large companies operating in different industries participated in the survey. The questionnaire included questions with single and multiple answer choices and used a 5-point Likert scale. The research was conducted using the CAWI (Computer Assisted Web Interview) method, in which the respondent filled out a questionnaire posted on a website. MS Excel was used for data processing and analysis.

The analysis of the collected data shows that the largest percentage of the surveyed companies belonged to the industry sector (50%) and trade (20%). Other industries (i.e. construction, transport and inventory management, accommodation, and catering) had a much smaller share (about 10%). Among the respondents, the largest groups were IT department specialists (76%) and management representatives (19%). Managers of other departments and specialists constituted a small number of people participating in the survey (3%). Thus, the research involved personnel who understand the role and importance of IT solutions and decide/co-decide on the purchase and implementation of IT systems in the cloud, and have knowledge on the effects of using Cloud BI systems in the enterprise. On average, the surveyed enterprises in Poland have been using Cloud BI for over 5 years, which indicates that this is the period to gather sufficient knowledge and experience on the effects of using this type of solution in the business activities of medium and large companies.

The most popular Cloud BI system used in medium and large companies in Poland is Power BI (71%). A much smaller share is held by Tableau (27%) and Qlick Sense (2%). The popularity of Cloud BI systems among the surveyed enterprises is shown in Fig. 2. ERP systems are the main source of power for Cloud BI systems. The dominant ERP system in medium and large companies is SAP (85%). Much less popular in this group of enterprises are ERP systems from the Polish company Comarch (about 15%) and other ERP systems (about 1%).

Among the surveyed group which belonged to medium and large companies, Cloud BI systems were most often hosted in a private cloud (70%), although this type of cloud is characterized by significant implementation costs and limited flexibility. The high popularity of BI systems hosted in a private cloud may result from the need for its direct control by the company's IT staff and the lack of the need to transfer data to an external provider. Cloud BI systems in the surveyed group of Polish companies are much less often deployed in the public cloud (30%), although this type of cloud has many advantages (e.g. no investment in infrastructure, provider responsibility for IT resources, a wide selection of services, scalability of services, low cost of BI system purchase). None of the enterprises indicated that they use other types of clouds e.g. hybrid, partner, or dedicated cloud. Respondents using Cloud BI equally utilize both SaaS and PaaS services (50% each). In the IaaS model, in addition to the necessary hardware and software infrastructure, an internal or external supplier also provides a software environment for operating BI systems, while in the SaaS model

Fig. 2 Popularity of Cloud BI systems among medium and large companies in Poland. *Source* Authors' study based on the conducted research

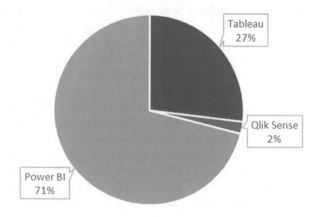

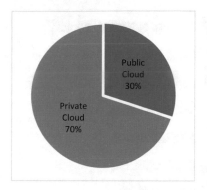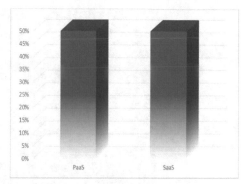

Fig. 3 Popularity of particular types of clouds and services for Cloud BI systems among medium and large companies in Poland. *Source* Authors' study based on the conducted research

the supplier takes full responsibility for the operation of Cloud BI systems. Cloud BI systems in the IaaS model were not mentioned by any surveyed Polish company classified as a large or medium-sized business entity. The popularity of a particular type of cloud and services for Cloud BI systems is presented in (Fig. 3).

Decisions to apply Cloud BI systems were made by respondents under the influence of various (i.e., external and internal) factors. A list of the most important factors is presented in Fig. 4. The most important sources for the making of the decision were factors in the business environment (expert opinions—40%, recommendations from another business entity—30%, and standards and regulations—30%). Decisions to use Cloud BI were also inspired by internal factors, i.e. recommendations from the company's own IT staff (30%). According to respondents, slightly less influence on the decision to apply Cloud BI came from industry articles and publications, IT system offerings exclusively in a cloud environment, and their own analysis of documented projects (20%). Interestingly, Cloud BI vendor offerings had limited influence on the decision to apply Cloud BI (only 10% of indications) and the pandemic and its effects had no relevance to the application of business intelligence systems in the cloud.

The main motives for applying BI systems in the cloud computing were: ensuring adequate security of the analyzed data (40%), greater availability of analysis (31%), optimization and predictability of costs (19%), improving the quality and pace of analysis (13%) and increasing the development opportunities of the company and the need for digital transformation (13%). It may be somewhat surprising that such a factor as the ability to quickly adapt analytics to changing needs in such a dynamic and unpredictable business environment was not indicated as important by respondents. The main motives for using Cloud BI systems among medium and large enterprises in Poland are presented in Fig. 5.

Thus, it can be observed that the main factors for applying Cloud BI in medium and large companies in Poland were not only the increased accessibility and acceleration of performing business analyses on positive or negative phenomena occurring in particular areas of the company and the business processes realized in the era

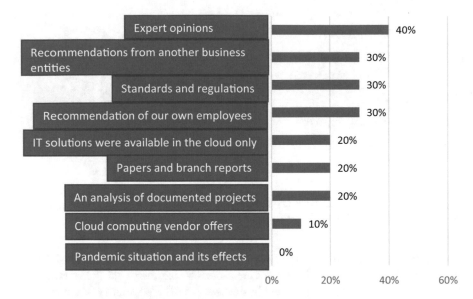

Fig. 4 Factors influencing the decision to apply Cloud BI systems among medium and large enterprises in Poland. *Source* Authors' study based on conducted surveys

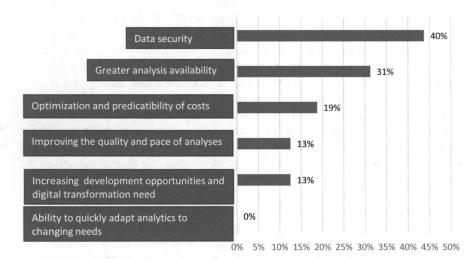

Fig. 5 Main motives for applying Cloud BI systems among medium and large enterprises in Poland. *Source* Authors' study based on conducted surveys

of Digital Economy, but primarily the increased security of processed data while optimizing IT investment costs. Cloud BI systems do not play an important role, according to respondents, due to the need to dynamically adapt analytics to the changing needs of the enterprise, as well as the development opportunities and the realization of the enterprise's digital transformation. In contrast, such factors are indicated in the literature as accompanying the use of Cloud BI systems.

The above-mentioned motives seem to be accurate, considering the fact that as many as 70% of respondents have previously used traditional BI systems (on-premise model) and gained a lot of experience using this type of system, and only 30% of respondents had no previous local BI system installations and immediately used Cloud BI.

Medium and large companies decide to use Cloud BI systems due to the numerous benefits they gain from their acquisition and operation. The benefits of using Cloud BI systems indicated by the respondents are presented in Table 1. For each benefit of Cloud BI systems, the corresponding mean values are presented, the percentage of respondents' answers defining the given benefit on a five-point Likert scale as important (4) and very important (5), the value of the dominant, and the standard deviation. A dominant value of 3 indicates that most respondents ranked the presented Cloud BI benefits as fairly important. A low standard deviation value indicates that the individual Cloud BI benefits are centered around the mean.

Many publications identify potential benefits and barriers of Cloud BI e.g. [[1, 18, 20], but typically they are not identified on the basis of company research but a literature review. The research shows that the most important benefits that have been identified in this group of companies are of a qualitative, economic, environmental, and organizational nature. Qualitative benefits play an important role for the respondents (continuous access to the latest versions of Cloud BI, optimization of organizational processes and data processing, reliable access to the Cloud BI system, high flexibility, scalability and efficiency of Cloud BI, faster and easier implementation of Cloud BI, high level of security, substantive and technological advancement of Cloud BI). Economic benefits are also important (relatively lower costs of acquisition, maintenance, and development of Cloud BI, no need to purchase and development of IT infrastructure, reduction of investment risk in the Cloud BI). An important benefit associated with the use of Cloud BI solutions was also environmental protection associated with the use of BI systems in the cloud and lower CO_2 emissions (indicated as important or very important by 20% of respondents). Among the benefits of organizational nature, respondents indicated: the simplicity of sharing information and knowledge from Cloud BI systems, support for mobile business, and transferring responsibility for the operation and development of Cloud BI to the provider.

There is also a group of risks associated with the application of Cloud BI. Threats and challenges concerning the application of Cloud BI systems indicated by the respondents are presented in Table 2, where also presented are the average values for each benefit, the percentage of responses identifying the problem as important and critical, the value of the dominant, and the standard deviation.

Table 1 Benefits resulting from the application of Cloud BI systems by medium and large companies in Poland

Advantage	Average	Percent (4 and 5) (%)	Dominant	Standard deviation
Constant access to current versions of cloud BI system	3.51	40	3	0.69
No need to purchase and develop IT infrastructure	3.30	30	3	0.46
Low cost of acquisition, maintenance, and development of a cloud BI system	3.30	30	3	0.46
Faster and easier implementation of cloud BI	3.20	30	3	0.60
Support for mobile business operations of a company	3.10	30	3	0.70
High level of system security	3.17	30	3	0.83
Optimization of organization processes and data processing	3.30	30	3	0.46
Better predictability of IT costs	3.00	20	3	0.63
Reducing investment risk in cloud BI	3.16	20	3	0.67
High flexibility, scalability and performance of cloud BI	3.26	20	3	0.55
Transfer of liability to the supplier	3.06	20	3	0.76
Reliable enterprise access to cloud BI	3.26	20	3	0.56
The advanced nature and technology of the cloud system	3.16	20	3	0.67
Simplicity of sharing information and knowledge	3.10	20	3	0.34
Environmental protection (reduction of CO_2 emissions)	3.20	20	3	0.40
Less demand for IT specialists	2.90	10	3	0.54

(continued)

Table 1 (continued)

Advantage	Average	Percent (4 and 5) (%)	Dominant	Standard deviation
Professional and flexible technical support	3.12	10	3	0.38
User-friendliness of the cloud BI system	3.00	10	3	0.45
Cloud BI independence from hardware and software platform	2.90	10	3	0.54

Source Authors' study based on the conducted research

The most important disadvantages and limitations of Cloud BI (with the highest number of indications as very important and critical), respondents from large and medium companies included problems of the following nature:

– technical and organizational, i.e.: Internet network failures preventing access to and use of Cloud BI system, risk of IT knowledge loss, partial dependence on the provider (resulting in, among others, weakening the ability to manage own IT area), concerns related to data security (e.g. provider's bankruptcy, protection of data sent to Cloud BI systems, lack of physical security of data sent to Cloud BI systems, lack of physical security of data sent to Cloud BI systems), incomplete possibilities to adjust the Cloud BI system to the needs of the recipient, the possibility of difficulties in data migration, lack of local technical support, lack of qualified staff and necessary competencies to implement and develop Cloud BI
– economic, i.e.: the need to incur additional expenditures on data integration (e.g. from different IT systems), the risk of hidden costs of using Cloud BI systems, high cost of required broadband Internet connections, the possibility of incurring higher than expected costs (e.g. due to unsatisfactory level of services).

Some barriers (e.g. the risk of losing IT knowledge, the need to incur expenditures on data integration, Internet network failures, the high cost of Internet connections) had a higher value of standard deviation—which means that the indicated problems both deviated from the average and at the same time were evaluated differently by the respondents (a lot of answers that the given problem is perceived by some respondents as not very important and by the rest as very important). Other barriers and problems of using Cloud BI in large and medium companies were more centered around the average.

Most of the risks mentioned above relate to Cloud BI providers in the public cloud. The application of Cloud BI in the form of a private cloud can significantly change and reduce the number of highlighted threats and drawbacks. Minimizing the risks of Cloud BI in a public cloud can be supported by, among other things, a long time of testing Cloud BI in order to fully understand the technical conditions of the service (e.g. data portability, cooperation with local IT systems, optimization possibilities) and establishing the principles of service operation (along with controlling the level of provider support). It is also important to precisely determine the business objectives of

Table 2 Threats and barriers resulting from the application of Cloud BI systems in medium and large companies in Poland

Threats and barriers	Average	Percent (4 and 5) (%)	Dominant	Standard deviation
Internet network failures	3.32	40	3	0.67
Risk of losing IT knowledge	3.30	30	3	1.04
Partial dependence on the cloud BI provider	3.11	20	3	0.55
Data security concerns and issues	3.21	20	3	0.42
The need to spend money on data integration	3.09	20	3	0.88
Risk of hidden costs of using cloud BI systems	3.12	20	3	0.58
Incomplete possibilities of cloud BI system adaptation to customer's needs	3.00	10	3	0.48
The high cost of Internet connections	2.89	10	3	0.60
The possibility of incurring higher than expected costs	3.00	10	3	0.50
The potential for difficulties in data migration	3.01	10	3	0.49
Lack of local technical support	2.89	10	3	0.57
Lack of qualified staff and competence in cloud BI	3.00	10	3	0.46
Temporary degradation of cloud BI performance	2.90	0	3	0.30
Risk of creating additional functionality necessary for the client	2.80	0	3	0.40
Risk of unsatisfactory technical parameters occurrence of cloud BI	2.79	0	3	0.45
Legal issues	2.68	0	3	0.51
No or limited control over the vendor's activities	2.90	0	3	0.32
Uncertainty and reluctance to implement cloud BI	3.00	0	3	0.00

Source Authors' study based on the conducted research

enterprises and adjust the Cloud BI system to the reported needs and expectations. The dynamic technological progress, the development of the Cloud Computing market, and new regulations on the provision of services in cloud computing will probably influence the reduction of threats and problems associated with the use of Cloud BI systems.

Table 3 summarizes the respondents' answers regarding the assessment of the application of Cloud BI systems for decision support in medium and large companies in Poland. The measurement was made on an ordinal scale where a value of 1 means "strongly disagree" and a value of 5 means "strongly agree".

The analysis of the effects of Cloud BI application in supporting decision-making processes in the surveyed group of companies allows us to state that:

– All respondents confirmed that the application of Cloud BI increased the effectiveness of the decision-making process (defining its role as quite important or important). None of the respondents (0%) considered that Cloud BI does not improve the efficiency of the decision-making process. However, enterprises did not indicate (0%) that Cloud BI systems definitely increase the effectiveness of decision-making processes—which ultimately allows us to conclude that the application of Cloud BI systems has significantly increased the effectiveness of decision-making processes.
– In the opinion of 90% of respondents, the application of Cloud BI systems increased the effectiveness of decision-making processes. 11% of respondents claimed that the role of Cloud BI systems in the scope of the effectiveness of decision-making processes is small or very small. However, the surveyed companies did not indicate (0%) that Cloud BI systems definitely increase the effectiveness of decision-making processes—which ultimately allows us to conclude that the use of Cloud Bi systems to a large extent increases the effectiveness of decision-making processes.

Table 3 Assessment of cloud BI systems application in the scope of decision processes support, according to medium and large enterprises in Poland

Assessment	Assessment of cloud BI systems application in the scope of decision making processes support			
	Cloud BI increased the efficiency of decision-making processes	Cloud BI increased the efficacy of decision-making processes (%)	Cloud BI increased the speed of decision making (at all levels of business management) (%)	Cloud BI enabled real-time decision making (%)
1	0	1	0	1
2	0	10	0	19
3	50	20	60	40
4	50	70	40	30
5	0	0	0	10

Source Authors' study based on the conducted research

- 100% of the respondents confirmed that the application of Cloud BI systems increased the speed of decision-making (at all levels of enterprise management) defining its role in this area as somewhat important or important. Also, in this case, the surveyed companies did not indicate (0%) that Cloud BI systems significantly increase the speed of decision-making—which ultimately allows us to conclude that the application of Cloud BI systems significantly increased the speed of decision-making the effectiveness of decision-making processes at all levels of company management.
- 80% of respondents said that Cloud BI systems enabled decision-making in real-time, compared to 20% who said that the role of Cloud BI systems in this area is not significant. 10% of the surveyed enterprises indicated that Cloud BI systems significantly facilitated real-time decision-making—which allows us to conclude that the application of Cloud BI systems to a large extent enabled real-time decision-making in a group of medium-sized companies in Poland.

Table 4 presents the respondents' answers regarding the evaluation of the application of Cloud BI systems in terms of supporting business processes and projects. The value 1 means "strongly disagree" and the value 5 means "strongly agree".

All respondents indicated that the application of Cloud BI systems significantly influenced the improvement and optimization of business processes (of which 48% described this impact as important and 12% as very important.

The role of Cloud BI systems in providing information on existing and new business processes was positively assessed by 70% of respondents, while 29% of the surveyed companies described this impact as important and 1% as very important.

Similarly, they evaluated the role of Cloud BI systems in terms of efficacy of monitoring the effects of ongoing projects. 50% of respondents indicated a positive

Table 4 Assessment of cloud BI systems application in the support of business processes and projects

Assessment	Assessment of cloud BI systems application in the support of business processes and projects			
	Cloud BI has allowed to improve and optimize business processes (%)	Cloud BI provides information on current and new business processes (%)	Cloud BI enabled more effective monitoring of the effects of realized projects (%)	Cloud BI increased efficiency in the utilization of the company's resources (%)
1	0	0	0	0
2	0	0	0	10
3	40	70	50	40
4	48	29	48	50
5	12	1	2	0

Source Authors' study based on the conducted research

impact of BI systems in this area, while the remaining respondents considered this role to be important or very important (48 and 2% respectively).

Only 10% of respondents disagree with the statement that Cloud BI systems have increased efficiency in the use of company resources. The rest of the respondents (40%) agreed that BI systems have increased the efficiency of using enterprise resources and 50% of them agreed that this impact is important.

Table 5 shows the respondents' responses regarding the evaluation of the application of Cloud BI systems in supporting key enterprise areas and activities. As with the previous tables, the measurement was carried out on an ordinal scale in which a value of 1 means "strongly disagree" and a value of 5 means "strongly agree".

The analysis of the assessment of Cloud BI systems application in supporting key areas and activities of the company allows to formulate the following conclusions:

- 11% of respondents believe that Cloud BI systems do not affect the ability to create and monitor the enterprise's business strategy. The opposite opinion is held by 89% of respondents—which allows us to conclude that Cloud BI significantly affects the ability to create and monitor business strategy.
- All respondents confirmed that Cloud BI allows for better control of production costs or provision of services (with 40% of respondents confirming that this impact is important or very important).
- Better implementation of promotional and sales campaigns with the support of Cloud BI systems—also confirmed by all respondents. Some of them indicated that in this area Cloud BI systems play an important (37%) or very important role (3%).

Table 5 Evaluating the application of cloud BI systems in supporting key company areas and activities

Assessment	Evaluating the application of cloud BI systems in supporting key company's areas and activities					
	Cloud BI affected the ability to create and monitor a business strategy (%)	Cloud BI allowed for better control of costs of production or provision of services (%)	Cloud BI allowed for better analysis of promotional and sales campaigns (%)	Cloud BI enabled a more effective value chain analysis (%)	Cloud BI enabled more effective customer profiling (%)	Cloud BI impacted better inventory and distribution analytics (%)
1	1	0	0	0	0	0
2	10	0	0	0	10	0
3	60	60	60	60	80	90
4	29	38	37	38	9	10
5	0	2	3	2	1	0

Source Authors' study based on the conducted research

– All companies agreed that Cloud BI systems allow for more effective value chain
analysis, many respondents confirmed that the role of Cloud BI systems in this
area is important (38%) or very important (2%).
– Cloud BI systems also influence better inventory analysis and distribution analysis—which was confirmed by 90% of the companies surveyed, and 10% of them
considered this influence to be important. None of the enterprises indicated that
the role of Cloud BI systems in this area is very important.

It is worth mentioning that a particularly useful aspect of adopting Cloud BI
solution is fast access to professional analyses (some entities declared readiness to
use detailed business analyses after only 7 days from the start of implementation)
and full integration with existing ERP systems used both in "on premise" and cloud
computing model.

A significant challenge but also a potential value for the adaptation of Cloud BI
systems are hybrid solutions. Hybrid solutions make it possible to combine local
BI systems with the computing power of the cloud and services offered by Cloud
Computing service providers. As a result, hybrid solutions can facilitate the transition
of medium and large enterprises from traditional to cloud-based Business Intelligence
systems, and the positive effects from the use of these solutions can increase interest
in using only Cloud Computing systems in the future. An interesting challenge in the
adaptation of Cloud BI systems might be e.g. the implementation of the multi cloud
strategy, which means the creation of a heterogeneous BI system architecture that
will use the resources of more than one cloud, each managed by a different service
provider.

5   Conclusion

In conclusion it is worth mentioning the most significant findings that Cloud BI solutions are applied in many medium and large-sized Polish companies. The prevalent
solution in Poland is Power BI (71%) and Tableau (27%) and much less common
is QlickSense (2%), and as far as the type of applied solution is concerned the
surveyed companies deploy private cloud in most cases (70%). On the basis of the
conducted research, it can be stated that the scope of decision-making processes
supporting Cloud BI solutions increased the efficiency and efficacy of decision-
making processes, increased the speed of decision making at the strategic, tactical,
and operational level of the company's management, and enabled real-time decision
making. The Cloud BI model was assessed by the respondents as providing crucial
advantages such as improvement and optimization of business processes, provision
of information on current and new business processes, ensuring more effective monitoring of the effects of realized projects, and a significant increase in the utilization of
company's resources. In the domain of supporting key company's business activities,
it positively affected the ability to create and monitor business strategy, allowed for
better control of production and services provision costs, allowed for better analysis

of promotional and sales campaigns, enabled a more effective value chain analysis, enabled more effective customer profiling and has a positive influence on inventory and distribution analytics. It brings multiple additional benefits such as no need to purchase and develop IT infrastructure, better predictability of IT costs, low cost of its acquisition, maintenance, and development, constant access to current versions of Cloud BI, and simplicity of sharing information and knowledge. There also exist some challenges and threats which were indicated by respondents such as: the risk of the Internet network failure, data security concerns, cost of the Internet connection, or legal issues.

References

1. Al-Aqrabi, H. L., Hill, R., & Antonopoulos, N. (2015, February). Cloud BI: future of business intelligence in the cloud. *Journal of Computer and System Sciences, 81*(1), 85–96.
2. İ. Aslan, Demirag, A., Akkartal, E. (2021). Collaboration of business intelligence and cloud computing and selecting the best cloud business intelligence solution. *AJIT-e Online Academic Journal of Information Technology.* https://doi.org/10.5824/ajite.2021.03.002.x.
3. Business Intelligence definitions. In *ISD2022 Conference* (2022). Retrieved March 21, 2022, from https://www.igi-global.com/dictionary/business-intelligence/3043IGI, https://isd 2022.conference.ubbcluj.ro/.
4. Duggal, A. What is cloud business intelligence? 5 Critical Points. Retrieved November 29, 2021, from https://hevodata.com/learn/cloud-business-intelligence/.
5. Dziembek, D. (2015). Analiza SWOT systemów Business Intelligence udostępnianych przedsiębiorstwom w publicznej chmurze obliczeniowej. Studia Ekonomiczne (in Polish) The SWOT Analysis of Business Intelligence Systems Made Available to Enterprises in the Public Cloud 2015/243, 50–66
6. Dziembek, D. (2015). Systemy business intelligence w modelu SaaS w działalności małych i średnich przedsiębiorstw [w:]. In: R. Knosala (red.), Innowacje w zarządzaniu i inżynierii produkcji, t. 2, Oficyna Wydawnicza Polskiego Towarzystwa Zarządzania Produkcją, Opole.
7. Dziembek D., & Ziora, L. (2014). Business intelligence systems in the SaaS model as a tool supporting knowledge acquisition in the virtual organization. *Online Journal of Applied Knowledge Management, 2.*
8. Ereth, J., & Dahl, D. (2013). Fundamentals for a service-based evaluation concept for business intelligence in the cloud. WSBI.
9. Grabińska, A., & Ziora, L. (2019). The application of business intelligence systems in logistics. Review of selected practical examples. *System Safety: Human—Technical Facility—Environment, 1*(1), 1028–1035. https://doi.org/10.2478/czoto-2019-0130.
10. Gurjar Y. S., Rathore V. S. (2013, January) Cloud business intelligence—Is what business need today. *International Journal of Recent Technology and Engineering (IJRTE), 1*(6). ISSN: 2277-3878.
11. Hamidinava, F., Ebrahimy, A., Samiee, R., & Didehkhani, H. (2021). A model of business intelligence on cloud for managing SMEs in COVID-19 pandemic (Case: Iranian SMEs). *Kybernetes, ahead-of-print No. ahead-of-print.* https://doi.org/10.1108/K-05-2021-0375.
12. Idemudia, J. (2022) *How cloud computing is influencing business intelligence.* https://www.for bes.com/sites/forbestechcouncil/2022/11/08/how-cloud-computing-is-influencing-business-intelligence-part-1/?sh=5e01d111c726.
13. Indriasari, E., Wayan, S., Gaol, F. L., Trisetyarso, A., Abbas, B. S., Kang, Ch. H. (2019). *Adoption of Cloud Business Intelligence in Indonesia's Financial Services Sector.* Springer Nature Switzerland AG. http://eprints.binus.ac.id/36305/1/Adoption%20of%20Cloud%20Business%20Intelligence.pdf.

14. Jalil, N. A., Prapinit, P., Melan, M. B., & Mustaffa, A. (2019). Adoption of business intelligence—Technological, individual and supply chain efficiency. In *2019 International Conference on Machine Learning, Big Data and Business Intelligence (MLBDBI)* (pp. 67–73).
15. Kasem, M., & Hassanein, E. (2014, February) Cloud business intelligence survey. *International Journal of Computer Applications, 90*(1). https://doi.org/10.5120/15540-4266.
16. Kazeli, H. (2014). Cloud business intelligence. *BIS. Computer Science.* https://doi.org/10.1007/978-3-319-11460-6_26.
17. Menon, L., Rehani, B., & Gund, S. Business intelligence on the cloud overview, uses cases and ROI. In *National Conference on Communication Technologies & its impact on Next Generation Computing CTNGC 2012. Proceedings published by the International Journal of Computer Applications® (IJCA).*
18. Olszak, C. M. (2014). Business intelligence in cloud. *Polish Journal of Management Studies, 10*(2).
19. Ouf, S., & Nasr, M. (2011). Business Intelligence in the cloud. IEEE. Retrieved April 15, 2022, from http://www.dl.edi-info.ir/Business%20intelligence%20in%20the%20cloud.pdf.
20. Patil, S., & Chavan, R. (2020). Cloud business intelligence: An empirical study. *Journal of Xi'an University of Architecture & Technology, XII*(II).
21. Reyes, E. P. (2010). A systems thinking approach to business intelligence solutions based on cloud computing. *Computer Science.*
22. Richards, G., Yeoh, W. G., Chong, A. Y., & Popovič, A. (2019). Business intelligence effectiveness and corporate performance management: An empirical analysis. *Journal of Computer Information Systems, 59*, 188–196.
23. Thompson, W. J. J., & van der Walt, J. S. (2010). Business intelligence in the cloud. *SA Journal of Information Management, 12*, 5.
24. ThoughtSpot. *Why cloud BI is essential to business growth.* Retrieved April 5, 2022, from https://www.thoughtspot.com/why-cloud-bi-essential-business-growth.
25. Tavera Romero, C. A., Ortiz, J. H., Khalaf, O. I., & Ríos Prado, A. (2021). Business intelligence: Business evolution after industry 4.0. *Sustainability.*
26. Turban, E., Sharda, R., Delen, D., & King, D. (2010). *Business Intelligence.* Prentice Hall.
27. Understanding Cloud BI and Analytics, IVY site. Retrieved April 15, 2022, from https://ivyproschool.com/blog/understanding-cloud-bi-and-analytics/.

Conceptualizing Node.js Projects: A Graph-Oriented Technology-Specific Modeling Method

Bianca Lixandru, Robert Andrei Buchmann, and Ana-Maria Ghiran

Abstract This paper advances our prior work in developing a modeling method for managing Node.js projects dependencies by adding a semantic analysis layer to the created models, benefitting from prior artifact-building research that makes it possible for diagrams of arbitrary semantics to be processed as RDF graphs. The purpose of models thus extends towards a knowledge-driven project management approach that handles a graph-based conceptualization of project management processes, development tasks and Node.js development resources (packages, APIs and their dependencies). With the continuous growth of the Node.js environment, managing complex projects that use this technology can be chaotic, especially when it comes to planning dependencies and module integration. The deprecation of a module can lead to serious crisis regarding various projects where that module was used; consequently, traceability of deprecation propagation becomes a key requirements in Node.js project management. The modeling method introduced in this paper provides a diagrammatic solution to managing module and API dependencies in a Node.js project. It is deployed as a modeling tool that can also generate REST API documentation and Node.js project configuration files that can be executed to install the graphically designed dependencies.

Keywords Domain-specific modeling method engineering · ADOxx · RDF · NPM ecosystem · REST API ecosystem · Dependency management

A prior version of this paper has been published in the ISD2022 Proceedings (https://aisel.aisnet.org/isd2014/proceedings2022/managingdevops/8/).

B. Lixandru · R. A. Buchmann (✉) · A.-M. Ghiran (✉)
Babeș-Bolyai University, Cluj-Napoca, Romania
e-mail: robert.buchmann@econ.ubbcluj.ro

A.-M. Ghiran
e-mail: anamaria.ghiran@econ.ubbcluj.ro

B. Lixandru
e-mail: biancastefanialixandru@yahoo.com

© The Author(s), under exclusive license to Springer Nature Switzerland AG 2023
G. C. Silaghi et al. (eds.), *Advances in Information Systems Development*,
Lecture Notes in Information Systems and Organisation 63,
https://doi.org/10.1007/978-3-031-32418-5_4

1 Introduction

This paper presents a domain-specific modeling language for describing Node.js projects extended with a semantic analysis layer by treating the domain-specific (and technology-specific) diagrams as RDF graphs that can be subjected to semantic queries for further analysis outside the modeling environment.

The initial version of the modeling method addressed challenges faced by human users dealing with Node.js projects and complex dependencies in their development ecosystem (NPM, REST APIs). We proposed a visual representation in the form of conceptual models that allowed an easy grasp and dependency overview for any stakeholder, while also making it possible to generate certain NPM project configuration files. Given that the core benefit of modeling methods is the capturing of semantics in addition to their visual aspect, we made additional steps to capture the knowledge expressed in the models in a machine-readable graph-based approach that can be an enabler for both analytics or model-driven engineering.

In our local IT outsourcing industry, Node.js has gained significant popularity—while working or collaborating in such projects we have observed a challenge in managing Node.js dependencies, considering the complexity of the NPM or REST API ecosystems and the volatility of respective dependencies. NPM modules as well as REST APIs continuously evolve, or become deprecated—see the recent case of the deprecation for the HTTP requests module that was used by countless dependent modules in the NPM ecosystem [1]. Auditing NPM dependencies across a rich portfolio of projects becomes a significant challenge—this also being one of the reasons for the recent self-criticism of Node.js's creators, which led to the introduction of Deno [2] as an alternative ecosystem offering built-in dependency auditing tools.

Node.js projects are confronted with design-related issues, which result in a high rate of improvements, updates and patches after the initial implementation of a functionality. In some cases, it even leads to problems at the projects' configuration level. Furthermore, even if the project structure and all configuration files are written by software developers, sometimes input from project owners, clients, managers, and other non-technical personnel is needed. In these situations, the project team needs a quick overview that enables everyone to visualize and discuss the project structure, its development processes and dependencies.

The main goal of this artifact-building research initiative was to propose a technology-specific modeling method that can help manage the complexity of the NPM and REST ecosystems for Node projects. The resulting functional artifact consists of a modeling language, which was built using Design Science [3] and Agile Modeling Method Engineering (AMME) [4] principles. The method's conceptualization enables a diagrammatic representation of concepts and processes surrounding Node.js projects' development; it helps developers, and non-technical stakeholders, to understand project structures and audit their dependencies, while also being able to generate project configuration files ready to install those dependencies. Following an iterative Design Science development effort, we further advanced the initial proposal towards using the conceptual models as knowledge structures, benefitting from our prior converging work on processing diagrammatic models as RDF graphs.

The remainder of the paper is structured as follows: first, in Sect. 2 we detail the motivation for the proposed method and provide context for it; in Sect. 3 we provide a high level overview of the proposed solution and the requirements it addresses; Sect. 4 details design decisions and describes running examples; Sect. 5 discusses application in real cases; Sect. 6 expands application towards the possibility to process models as graphs via semantic queries; before concluding, the paper comments on related works in Sect. 7.

2 Motivation and Background

This section describes the motivation for the adoption of the model-driven engineering paradigm in support of managing the complexity of Node.js projects.

2.1 Node.js and Its Ecosystems

Node.js is an asynchronous JavaScript runtime environment that can be used as a back-end environment for Web applications instead of more traditional approaches like PHP. Node.js encourages the use of a single programming language, JavaScript, to unify development for Web applications, both in server-side and client-side source code [5]. Comparisons between the efficiency of Node.js and PHP or Python show that Node.js can be "the best choice for I/O intensive web-sites [...], being significantly more lightweight and efficient" compared to more traditional approaches [6].

Projects using Node.js contain modules and packages, to allow easier integration with available components and libraries. All packages are managed and organized by the Node Package Manager (NPM), which oversees the downloading and installing of Node.js packages from an NPM registry, handling all the third-party Node.js modules available publicly and privately. Usually, the packages are installed within the Node.js "project" using the NPM command line, directly by the developers. After the installation is done, the package becomes a dependency in the project and is added to a dedicated configuration file named *package.json*. All the modules are stored and categorized within the specific folder *node_modules* [7].

Every package comes with its own set of dependencies, forming a dependency tree of modules. Because packages can depend on multiple other packages, the NPM can work with a range of versions required for each of them and can even compute the specific version needed to satisfy all requirements. This can lead to complex dependency paths that must keep up with updates and make organizing projects difficult, especially for the larger ones. Many times, unnecessary packages are left in the configuration of the projects and forgotten about, or outdated modules are difficult to detect and update. All these make the NPM ecosystem hard to work with, unless other processes are set in place to manage its complexity. This is also one reason for which the Node.js creator introduced Deno [2], after rethinking several features pertaining to the management of Node.js projects, including how their dependencies are audited and managed—however numerous legacy projects are still running on Node.js and are not willing to migrate in the near future to Deno, which requires a major overhaul. Node.js itself keeps evolving further encouraging adoption, rather than stepping back and promoting migration to alternatives.

Another technology-independent ingredient also raises a similar challenge of dependency traceability—REST APIs have been in vogue for some time and nowadays tend to be key ingredients in the back-ends of Web applications, including those developed in Node.js, with the help of dedicated frameworks such as Express.js [8]. In complex Web applications that are architected according to a certain (micro)service granularity, REST APIs may also be part of chains of dependencies just like NPM packages—they can actually be seen as remote modules and providers of data and functionality, whose access is based on HTTP instead of JavaScript importing and packaging mechanisms.

2.2   Domain-Specific Model-Driven Node.js Complexity Management

Model-driven engineering (MDE) [9] offered a promising approach to software development, raising the abstraction level and alleviating complexity for those involved in software projects. Node.js projects and the NPM ecosystem can get quite complex therefore they provide an appropriate testbed for model-driven engineering—not necessarily in the traditional sense of code generation, but in a complexity management sense as emphasized in our work.

An efficient management process for Node.js projects can be achieved by applying the MDE principles. A team can work on designing the modules integration by using diagrammatic means and a limited set of abstract constructs, which are captured in the conceptualization proposed in this paper. Project members or architects are empowered to create the map of the application and to analyze dependency issues before the actual implementation; ultimately they can use models as active documentation for stakeholders, even clients. The MDE approach can also be used for generating the documentation for the APIs used in the project and for generating NPM configuration files specific for Node.js projects. However, traditional MDE did not address the Node.js platform, nor the NPM ecosystem—so we needed to adopt domain-specific metamodeling to tailor a novel modeling language, tool and "code" generation for it (with "code" being limited here to configuration files and machine-readable documentation of dependencies).

In domain-specific modeling, real-world or planned objects and properties are described in diagrammatic models for representation or mediation purposes. Models are, therefore, abstractions encapsulating only the most relevant properties and characteristics [10]. As stated in [11], conceptual models "are mediators between the application world and the implementation or system world" and are designed with a specific purpose. According to [12], models are used for varied reasons, from perception support, explanation or demonstration to simulation or construction. Multiple models of the same system can be different, governed by different layers of specificity dictated either by purpose, application domain or technological environment [13]. Even though only the most relevant properties of objects and systems are captured within a conceptual model, such models have some common properties [11]—e.g. the mapping property (every model is a mapping of a real-world concept), the truncation property (some irrelevant properties of the origin are omitted in the model), the pragmatic property (models are used only by a target audience and for a specific period of time), the amplification property (the model can contain properties that are missing in the origin and are envisioned as an improvement), the distortion property (being built to improve the origin, the model is a transformed version of it), the idealization property (models have idealized properties of their respective origins), the purpose property (each model has a purpose), the carrier property (all models use languages, and because of this, every model is considered as expressive as the language it uses) and the added value property (models are created to bring an added value or utility to the modeler).

In the domain-specific paradigm, specificity is needed in order to achieve a level of detail and specialization determined by purpose. A simple definition for it is given in [14]: "a Domain-Specific Language is simply a language that is optimized for a given class of problems, called a domain". DSLs sacrifice reusability and generality for the sake of productivity and expressivity relative to the targeted problem class or environment; they also evolve faster, in response to evolving requirements [13].

Because of the complex nature of Node projects and their dependency-driven ecosystems, to achieve the best results in properly modeling Node projects, we have developed a modeling DSL whose first-class citizens are NPM modules, REST APIs, dependencies, explicit development tasks and appropriate relations between them. Mechanisms benefitting from this conceptualization beyond structuring and visualization have been built on top, as enablers for further integration or documentation.

3 The Proposed Modeling Tool

3.1 Requirements

Like in most software development projects, Node.js developers must work together with project owners, managers, analysts, and other non-technical stakeholders to assure that the implementation of the project is within the scope of the requirements. This can meet impediments when a technical subject is not properly explained or understood by all parts involved. General modeling approaches can be used to outline the architecture's outlines and the development processes, but when it comes to the particularities of Node.js or (micro)service architectures, project dependencies create an intricate system of sub-dependent modules and libraries, with open-source components being somewhat volatile as they can evolve independently of the projects using them.

The NPM network does not provide an accurate overview of all the connections between the modules of a project, so it is difficult for development teams to trace and catalogue all the dependencies that cascade with a simple installation of a module. Furthermore, developers need to manually install and update all projects' dependencies, and they need to check and replace by hand deprecated packages.

We have gained awareness of the problem by direct contact with Node.js projects in the local outsourcing industry focusing on legacy applications maintenance, therefore a Design Science approach was hereby taken to introduce a diagrammatic modeling method that keeps track of dependencies (both for NPM and REST services) in a portfolio of Node.js projects. The main purpose of the proposed method and language is to enable a diagrammatic view on the development and management of Node.js projects. Specifically, it enables the description of the management and development processes, project composition, API and NPM module integration; it repurposes the code generation algorithm towards a management perspective, by automatically generating the detailed API documentation and specific configuration files executed by the NPM environment in order to deploy a project. Further on, in the new iteration reported in this paper, it enables analysis based on semantic queries executed on an RDF representation of the inter-linked abstractions captured with the diagrammatic tool.

3.2   Methodological Aspects

According to [3], the object of Design Science is to provide an artifact that brings an improvement for the targeted situation, and then to assess the performance of the specific artifact in a determined context. In the presented case, the artifact proposed is a modeling method for managing Node.js projects. Even if, theoretically, it can be applied in any development process of any company that works with Node.js, it was inspired by the work procedures of the Company Y where the main author works as a developer, the company being specialized in outsourcing software development. During the first stage of the project, the main problem identified was the chaotic organization of Node.js projects, especially of the NPM and REST service dependencies. As an outsourcing company, Company Y adopts Node.js in most of its projects but the above-mentioned issues raise technical management obstacles. Therefore, a modeling method was proposed to integrate a dependency view on Node.js projects and a process view of their development.

Due to the nature of the proposed artifact, and the aim of developing a DSL for a particular flavor of Model-Driven Engineering, the AMME framework [4] was

adopted—Agile Modeling Method Engineering (AMME) applies agile principles
to the practice of modeling method engineering [15] resulting in the evolution of
modeling tools for various problem classes. One key ingredient of AMME is the
ADOxx metamodeling platform [16] and its native scripting language for processing
model contents—in the case of this project, for generating machine-readable Node.js
project configuration files and REST service documentations. Further resources from
our prior work have been combined to achieve the next step—the analysis of resulting
models with the help of semantic queries.

3.3 Solution Overview

The proposed modeling language consists of three types of models: Development
Workflow Model, Project Model and API Model.

- The Workflow Model (type) provides a process view, similar to BPMN but
  tailored for the taxonomy of tasks involved in Node.js project management and
  development;
- The Projects Model (type) provides a structural view and a map of project NPM
  dependencies, possibly in multiple NPM projects grouped by visual containers;
- The API Model (type) keeps track of the REST endpoints involved by a project,
  possibly also inter-dependent.

With the help of ADOScript [17], technology-specific functionality was implemented to generate REST documentation and NPM configuration files for Node.js
projects. Firstly, based on the API Model, modelers can generate detailed documentation for each end-point used within a microservice-based project. Moreover,
and most importantly, modelers can generate the entire configuration file, formatted
exactly as used by the NPM environment to install and integrate dependencies. A
bird's view architecture of the tool is provided in Fig. 1, to be detailed further in
terms of both conceptualization and scripting.

4 Design Decisions

The modeling language is the main component of the Node project management
modeling method, enabling the other components—the modeling procedure and
functionality. Its three types of models are governed by the metamodel shown in
Fig. 3, with the custom notation depicted as a legend of symbols in Fig. 2. Relationships are depicted in Fig. 3 as boxes (ADOxx classes) with "from" and "to" attributes
representing their domains and ranges, respectively. Relationships crossing between
the three types of models are implemented as hyperlinks between diagrams of the
different types. The concepts prefixed by __D__ are built-in constructs of the ADOxx

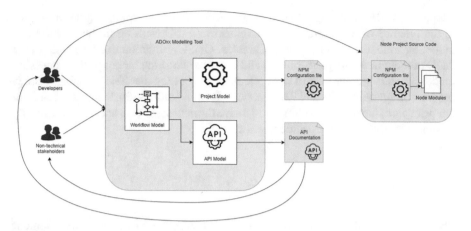

Fig. 1 Architectural view of the proposed artifact

metamodeling platform that allow the reuse some built-in properties (e.g. the "container" behavior, that generates a machine-readable relation between a container and contained elements, the management of the vector notation and machine-readable metadata attached to symbols).

The Workflow Model Type is used to diagrammatically represent the flow of tasks and decisions of development processes, in a simplified flowchart approach inspired by BPMN process diagrams but adopting a taxonomy of task types that are specific to the targeted field of activity. Additionally, domain-specific attributes can annotate and later serve to report generation based on model queries:

- *Estimation*, represents the predicted effort needed to fulfil the task;
- *Type*, with predefined values that categorize the types of tasks: *Communication, Administrative, Development, Testing, Bug fixing*. This attribute dictates the graphical variation among task types and also determines some personalized attributes for specific task types;

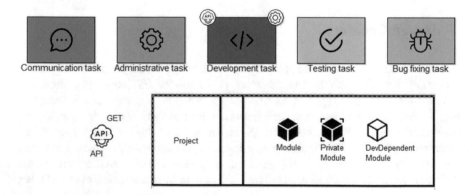

Fig. 2 Concept notations tailored for the modeling language

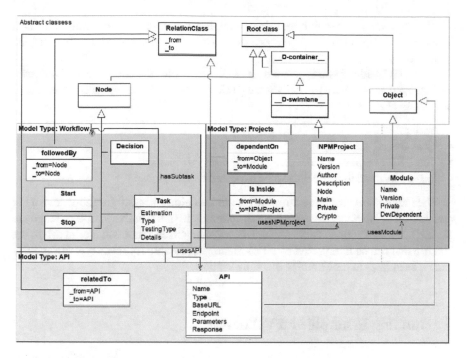

Fig. 3 The metamodel

- *TestingType*, as its name suggests, is an enumeration that allows the selection of a more precise type for the Testing Tasks. The modeler can further specialize the Testing Tasks into *Manual, Unit, Automation testing*;
- *Details*, to attach more information for a particular task;
- *usesNPMProject* and *usesModule* are hyperlinks that connect tasks from the Workflow Model to NPM project containers or directly to modules within them;
- *usesAPI*, also a hyperlink, but references an API concept from the API Model; it is only active for Development Tasks.

The Projects Model Type uses two main concepts: the *Module* class and the *Project* class. The *Project* refers to the NPM notion of "project" (and not to a software project as a whole, which is decomposed in tasks on the workflow model level). An NPM project acts as a visual container for a map of module dependencies, which will generate a machine-readable containment that allows to distinguish between different projects described on the same model canvas. Relevant attributes for a Project are:

- Basic metadata: *Name, Version, Author* and *Description*;
- *Node*, stores the Node.js version;
- *Main*, the project's main access file;
- *Private*, to set the privacy of the project if desired;
- *Crypto*, a field to gather encryption preferences.

The *Module* has similar metadata, and the possibility to indicate if it is a development dependency, i.e. ignored at runtime (this dynamically influences the notation).

The API Model Type is just a map of API endpoint dependencies, which must be managed in a (micro)service-based project. The API concept has all essential properties of APIs:

- *Name*;
- *Type*, the HTTP method;
- The URL components: *BaseURL, Endpoint, Parameters*;
- *Response*, describes the data to be expected as a response.

The functionality for generating API documentation and configuration files for the installation of NPM dependencies was implemented in the native scripting language of ADOxx, ADOScript, see a sample in Fig. 4 that parses annotated modules into the text file that can be interpreted by NPM. Examples created for these types of models can be seen later in the Running example section.

5   Running Example and Validation

The context where problem awareness was raised is an outsourcing company specialized in developing and maintaining Node.js projects. The first approach to validating the proposed artifact was to apply its ADOxx-based proof of concept in real-world project development scenarios within the company. Its applicability was internally discussed, concluding that in future iterations the configuration generation functionality should also be extended to other package management systems, e.g. Python's pip or PHP's composer.

The first project case was an extension to the Web version of Microsoft's email platform, Outlook. The requirements consisted of adding a new warning screen for displaying a user's phone number. On project management level this implied preparing the requirements, refining them, retrieving the data from the back-end application, developing the front-end part, and testing the functionality. Figures 5 and 6 depict model examples from this real-world project.

The development process for the above functionality started with the creation of the Workflow Model—a process view analogous to BPMN; however, the team lacked BPMN experience and the new model is better tailored to the task taxonomy involved in software development projects. With the help of built-in effort estimation features inherited from the underlying ADOxx metamodeling platform, the project effort was better estimated and requirements changes were easier to track.

The process described in Fig. 5 presents a sequence of tasks that are performed during the software project. The visual representation of a task is dynamically changing based on the task types selected in the *Type* attribute.

The backlog-level development tasks are detailed in a similar workflow model but describing a different level of detail, which can be semantically linked to elements

```
31  CC "Core" GET_ALL_OBJS_OF_CLASSNAME modelid:(modelid) classname:"Module"
32  CC "Core" GET_CLASS_ID classname:"Module"
33  CC "Core" GET_ALL_NB_ATTRS classid:(classid)
34  SET dependencies:("  \"dependencies\": {\n")
35  SET devDependencies:("  \"devDependencies\": {\n")
36  SET first:"true"
37  SET firstd:"true"
38  SET version:""
39
40  FOR i in:(objids)
41  {
42      CC "Core" GET_OBJ_NAME objid:(VAL i)
43      FOR j in:(attrids)
44      {
45          CC "Core" GET_ATTR_NAME attrid:(VAL j)
46          CC "Core" GET_ATTR_VAL objid:(VAL i) attrid:(VAL j)
47          IF (attrname="Version")
48          { SET version:((val)) }
49          IF (attrname="DevDependent")
50          {
51              IF ((val)="true")
52              {
53                  IF (firstd="false")
54                  { SET devDependencies:(devDependencies+",\n") }
55                  ELSE
56                  { SET firstd:"false" }
57                  SET devDependencies:(devDependencies+"    \""+objname+"\": \""+version+"\"")
58              }
59              ELSE
60              {
61                  IF (first="false")
62                  { SET dependencies:(dependencies+",\n") }
63                  ELSE
64                  { SET first:"false" }
65                  SET dependencies:(dependencies+"    \""+objname+"\": \""+version+"\"")
66              }
67          }
68      }
69  }
70  SET dependencies:(dependencies+"\n  },\n")
71  SET devDependencies:(devDependencies+"\n  }\n")
72
73  SET message:(message+dependencies+devDependencies+"}\n")
74
75  CC "AdoScript" FWRITE file:"C:\\scripts\\package.json" text:(message) append:no
76  CC "AdoScript" INFOBOX "Project config file created in C:\\scripts\\package.json"
```

Fig. 4 Scripting sample for parsing NPM module map into the dependency file package.json

from the other two model types (e.g. NPM project containers, modules, API models). For instance, the development task "Implement story" is decomposed into a sequence of 3 backlog tasks (*Get phone number*, *Create phone screen* and *Add translations*) (Fig. 6), each one will show visual cues/hyperlinks in the top corners—the "Get phone number" task is linked to the API "Get phone number" from the API model and to the web extension from the "Outlook add-in Project" (see Fig. 7 with the attributes of the task concept).

The team also represented the network of APIs used in this project (Fig. 8), with the help of the API model, and the generated documentation became part of the project's official documentation (the right side of the picture).

The most well received model type was the one for projects (Fig. 9) and their system of NPM modules—it makes it easy for beginners to understand what a module is, where is it necessary and how it impacts other modules. It is also not limited to a design-time visualization, since it also generates the package.json configuration files (the right side of the picture).

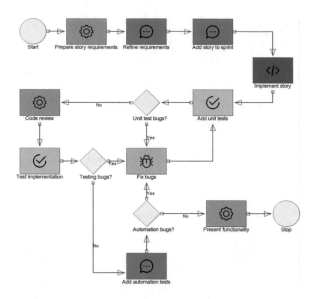

Fig. 5 Workflow of domain-specific tasks

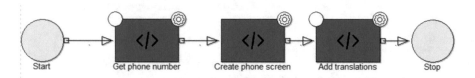

Fig. 6 "Implement story" process

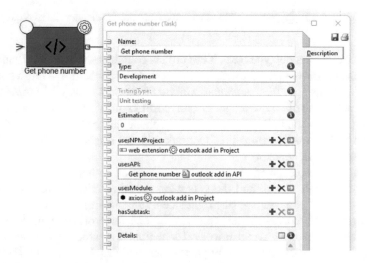

Fig. 7 Attributes for "Get phone number" task

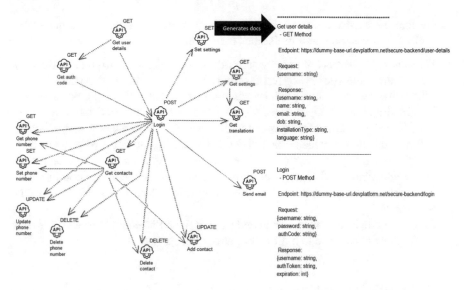

Fig. 8 The API ecosystem and generated documentation

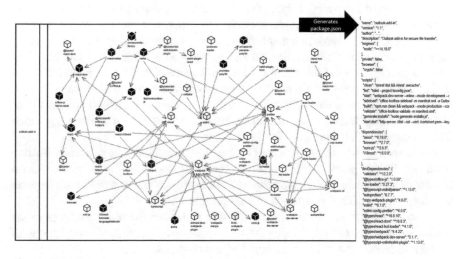

Fig. 9 The NPM dependencies and generated configuration file

Other projects where the proposed modeling tool was applied only involved the Workflow and Project Model since they were maintenance projects for legacy systems with no REST microservice view needed.

During the development of the model-driven scripts, the prototypes for the generated configuration files were always compared to the real package.json files, to assure that the sections, content, and formatting were accurate. It was noted that the following differences and limitations can appear:

- The generation works only one-way (model-to-JSON, model-to-documentation), the roundtrip approach being left for future iterations of the DSR cycle;
- When installed manually, modules are stored alphabetically in the package.json file, for simplicity. The generated file will contain the modules listed in the order of their creation. This misalignment in the order of the modules is insignificant;
- Different development teams have different formatting standards when it comes to indentation, empty lines, spaces before or after operators and punctuation marks. The mechanisms of the proposed modeling method generate the configuration file based on the preferences set within one selected development team in the company;
- Diagrammatic labels are not validated against the NPM ecosystem therefore any spelling errors can lead to a different package being installed.

6 Semantic Processing

With the help of inter-model links, the diagrams contribute to creating a semantic network of directed labelled graphs not unlike what has been recently called "Knowledge Graphs". This approach benefits from our prior converging work on employing RDF [18] as a means of serialization for any diagrams created in tools based on ADOxx metamodels (serialization patterns and relevant rules have been discussed in [20]). The generated graphs can be hosted by a graph database like GraphDB [19] and will thus enable semantic queries or reasoning rules from which both analytics and model-aware software engineering (a flavor of model-driven engineering which we introduced in [21]) can benefit.

In this section, we exemplify some of the queries enabled by the conceptualization described in this paper, which turns the modeling tool into the engine of novel engineering methods that can interoperate with project management tools beyond the already exemplified generation of configuration files.

Figure 10 shows the RDF content that was generated for some elements in the workflow model, more specifically for the "followedBy" connector and for one of the task instances, the "Get phone number" development task.

For both relations and modeling objects, the export generates unique URIs and some type declarations: e.g. *cv:Relation_class* represents the class of all the modeling connectors (e.g. arrows) and *:followedBy* is the custom relation class created in the metamodel for that specific connector, *cv:Instance_class* represents the class that contains all modeling nodes and *:Task* is the class corresponding to the concept present in the metamodel. Some connectors are treated as RDF nodes connected to where the connector starts (*cv:from_instance*) and to where it points (*cv:to_instance*) but a simple reasoning rule can also build out of it shortcut edges between the two ends of the connector, as shown in the patterns discussed in [20]. Modeling objects will have RDF properties corresponding to their ADOxx attributes (see the metamodel,

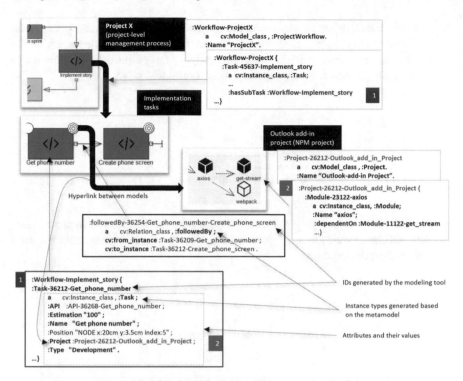

Fig. 10 RDF generation from inter-linked modeling layers

Fig. 3, for all the attributes). We can also see the *Position* attribute that captures the layout of the modeling elements on the canvas, which is not relevant for semantic queries, but can be made relevant for importing and recreating the visualization in other tools.

The following are examples of SPARQL [22] queries corresponding to "competency questions" that the semantic network derived from the modeling conceptualization can answer (i.e. can be posed by external systems using it as an interoperability interface or decision support):

1. Finding critical resources—e.g. the API with the highest number of other required services: we identify nodes related through a one-or-many chain of "relatedTo" relations, we group them based on the source and order by group count:

```
SELECT ?x (COUNT(DISTINCT(?y) AS ?noDependentAPIs)
WHERE {
?x :relatedTo+ ?y
}
GROUP BY ?x
ORDER BY DESC(?noDependentAPIs)
```

2. Finding critical dependencies—e.g. the projects with a dependency on a specific outdated module: in this case, we considered the RequestsModule for which the version number starts with 0.2 and we navigate the graph of dependencies to identify all projects that employ them directly or indirectly:

```
SELECT ?p ?x ?v
WHERE {
?x :isInside ?p.
?x :dependentOn+ :requestsModule.
:requestsModule :version ?v.
FILTER (STRSTARTS(?v, "0.2"))
}
```

3. Find all modules in a project that are required by the application in production: from all the modules that are used by a project we exclude those that are used only during development.

```
SELECT ?p ?x
WHERE {
?x :isInside ?p
MINUS {?x :devDevelopment "true"}
}
```

4. Extract a subgraph of all dependency paths between modules:

```
CONSTRUCT
WHERE
{
?x :dependentOn+ ?y
}
```

5. Calculate the total estimated cost for all the subtasks that correspond to development tasks: for those tasks that are of type "Development", we extract the name of the model that contains the subtasks and we calculate the sum of the values gathered for the :Estimation attribute.

```
SELECT ?task ?estimatedTotalTime
WHERE {
?task :Type "Development".
?task :hasSubtask ?taskmodel.
      SELECT (SUM(?tint) AS ?estimatedTotalTime)
      WHERE {
      GRAPH ?taskmodel {
             ?task :Estimation ?t.
             BIND (xsd:integer(?t) AS ?tint)
             }
      }
}
GROUP BY ?task
```

7 Related Work

Reference [23] provided early theorizing on a particular flavor of domain-specific modeling, labelled there as "technology-specific modeling"—where the concepts of a modeling language are not chosen to be specific to an application domain, but to a technological environment that needs to be managed with model-based support. The current work belongs to the same subclass of DSLs. Code generation has been a traditional goal of UML-based modeling, but technology-specific modeling can be tailored with the help of metamodeling for any kind of interfacing and technological context. The authors of [23] demonstrate this with a language for the design of ETL processes that are tailored for the in-house ETL engine of a company, having no reusability outside that company but bringing a certain productivity increase due to its tight coupling with the ETL engine.

A similar mindset motivated the current work, however it aims for wider reusability since the Node.js ecosystem is not company-specific but reasonably popular in Web development—the issue of managing dependencies in this ecosystem has been recognized for a long time in the community, with dependency auditing being discussed as a key challenge. We take the path of technology-specific modeling to also achieve a visual layer of a project portfolio for a Node.js-focused company, with a "code generation" approach that does not aim to produce running code, but instead machine-readable configurations that define the dependency map for a Node project.

Also employing the AMME framework and ADOxx as an implementation platform, [24] presented a modeling tool for visually building Resource Description Framework (RDF) data graphs—it shares with the current work tooling and methodology but it aims for another kind of technology-specific alignment.

The work presented in [25] showcases an intelligent software development platform that enables the design of AI applications with subsystems for "knowledge-based reasoning, spoken dialogue, image sensing, motion management, and machine learning", all combined into a workflow editor that enables users to modify in real-time the behavior for multiple robots and sensors, thus bringing the "technology-specific" aspect to the area of cyber-physical systems.

Reference [26] introduced a novel modeling method as an extension to the BPMN standard, facilitating the execution of HTTP requests from diagrammatic business process models, while also ensuring the business process-centric view a business analyst would expect from a diagrammatic model tool. Also, authors in [27] present a model-based approach for generation of RESTful APIs that enables collaboration among the development team members as it is designed as a web application. In our work, the process-centric view is tailored for the task types encountered and gleaned from personal experience in the company that inspired the hereby proposal. Further into the API management field, the work done in [28] introduces RESTalk, a tool that enables a more accurate representation of the client–server interactions. Even if, unlike the previous referenced work, that paper only extends the choreography diagram of the BPMN standard and does employ the AMME methodology, it also facilitates a new layer of abstraction for defining RESTful APIs, something that has been pursued for a long time in service-driven software architects, see also the emergence of the Swagger framework [29].

8   Conclusions and Future Works

To the best of our knowledge, this is the first paper proposing a modeling language specific for Node.js projects and for the NPM ecosystem. The proposed artifact can be used by non-technical stakeholders of a Node.js based project to better grasp and organize the development procedures and tasks in complement to a traditional management environment (e.g. Jira-based), and by specialized developers to integrate project details into development processes, to manage dependencies and even generate auxiliary files needed along project execution in different stages.

We showed that the conceptual models can not only be used to communicate knowledge among humans but can also benefit of semantic querying capabilities based on the underlying graph structure of created models and their inter-model hyperlinks.

Future plans aim to cover more diverse technologies—the pool of technologies can include most modular development environments, the authors also being familiar with at least Python's and PHP's package ecosystems.

Acknowledgements Further technical and theoretical aspects of the work are detailed in the master dissertation of B. S. Lixandru titled *A modeling method for managing Node projects and the complex ecosystem of NPM*, defended at University Babeş-Bolyai.

References

1. Thung, S. Request has been deprecated Retrieved March 16, 2022, from https://betterprogra mming.pub/request-has-been-deprecated-a76415b4910b.
2. Deno official website. Retrieved March 16, 2022, from https://deno.land.
3. Wieringa, R. J. (2014). Design science methodology for information systems and software engineering, Springer.https://doi.org/10.1007/978-3-662-43839-8
4. Karagiannis, D. (2015). Agile modeling method engineering. In *Proceedings of the 19th Panhellenic Conference on Informatics* (pp. 5–10). ACM. https://doi.org/10.1145/2801948. 2802040.
5. Hota, A. K., & Prabhu, D. M. (2014). NODE.JS: Lightweight, event driven I/O web development. Informatics. https://informatics.nic.in/article/287.
6. Lei, K., Ma, Y., & Tan, Z. (2014). Performance comparison and evaluation of web development technologies in php, python, and node.js. In 2014 IEEE 17th International Conference on Computational Science and Engineering (pp. 661–668). IEEE CS. https://doi.org/10.1109/ CSE.2014.142.
7. NPM Doc: Node Package Manager (npm) Documentation. Retrieved March 22, 2022, from https://docs.npmjs.com/about-npm.
8. Express.js official website. Retrieved March 16, 2022, from https://expressjs.com/.
9. Schmidt, D. C. (2006). Model-driven engineering. *Computer, 39*(2), 25–31. https://doi.ieeeco mputersociety.org/10.1109/MC.2006.58.
10. Karagiannis, D., Buchmann, R. A., Burzynski, P., Reimer, U., & Walch, M. (2016). Funda-mental conceptual modeling languages in OMiLAB. In *Domain-Specific Conceptual Modeling* (pp. 3–30). Springer. https://doi.org/10.1145/2976767.2987691.
11. Thalheim, B. (2012). Syntax, semantics and pragmatics of conceptual modeling. In *International Conference on Application of Natural Language to Information Systems* (pp. 1–10). Springer. https://doi.org/10.1007/978-3-642-31178-9_1.
12. Liddle, S. W. (2011). Model-driven software development. In *Handbook of Conceptual Modeling* (pp. 17–54). Springer. https://doi.org/10.1007/978-3-642-15865-0_2.
13. Buchmann, R. A. (2022). *The Purpose-Specificity Framework for Domain-Specific Conceptual Modeling, in Domain-Specific Conceptual Modeling: Concepts, Methods and ADOxx Tools* (pp. 67–92). Springer. https://doi.org/10.1007/978-3-030-93547-4_4.
14. Voelter, M., Benz, S., Dietrich, C., Engelmann, B., Helander, M., Kats, L. C., & Wachsmuth, G. H. (2013). DSL engineering-designing, implementing and using domain-specific languages. CreateSpace.
15. Buchmann, R. A., & Karagiannis, D. (2015). Agile modeling method engineering: Lessons learned in the ComVantage research project. In *IFIP Working Conference on the Practice of Enterprise Modeling* (pp. 356–373). Springer. https://doi.org/10.1007/978-3-319-25897-3_23.
16. BOC GmbH. (2022). The ADOxx metamodeling platform. Retrieved March 21, 2022, from https://www.adoxx.org.
17. BOC GmbH. (2022). The AdoScript programming language. Retrieved March 17, 2022, from https://www.adoxx.org/live/adoscript-language-constructs.
18. W3C: Resource Description Framework—official website. Retrieved June 24, 2022, from http:/ /www.w3.org/RDF.
19. Ontotext. GRAPHDB—offcial website. Retrieved September 17, 2022, from https://graphdb. ontotext.com/.
20. Karagiannis, D., & Buchmann, R. A. (2018). A proposal for deploying hybrid knowledge bases: The ADOxx-to-GraphDB interoperability case. In *Proceedings of the 51st Hawaii International Conference on System Sciences* (pp. 4055–4064). https://doi.org/10.24251/HICSS.2018.510.
21. Buchmann, R. A., Cinpoeru, M., Harkai, A., & Karagiannis, D. (2018). Model-aware software engineering. In *Proceedings of the 13th International Conference on Evaluation of Novel Approaches to Software Engineering* (pp. 233–240). https://doi.org/10.5220/000669410233 0240.

22. W3C: SPARQL 1.1 Query Language. Retrieved June 24, 2022, from http://www.w3.org/TR/2013/REC-sparql11-query-20130321.
23. Deme, A., & Buchmann, R. A. (2021). A technology-specific modeling method for data ETL processes. In *Proceedings of AMCIS 2021, Paper 1128*. Association for Information Systems. https://aisel.aisnet.org/amcis2021/sig_sand/sig_sand/2/.
24. Chiş-Raţiu, A., & Buchmann, R. (2018). Design and implementation of a diagrammatic tool for creating RDF graphs. In *2nd PrOse Workshop Co-Located with PoEM 2018, CEUR-WS* (Vol. 2238, pp. 37–48). https://ceur-ws.org/Vol-2238/paper4.pdf.
25. Morita, T., Nakamura, K., & Komatsushiro, H. (2018). PRINTEPS: An integrated intelligent application development platform based on stream reasoning and ROS. *The Review of Socionetwork Strategies, 12*, 71–96. https://doi.org/10.1007/s12626-018-0020-y
26. Chiş, A. (2021). A modeling method for model-driven API management. *Complex Systems Informatics and Modeling Quarterly, 25*, 1–18. https://doi.org/10.7250/csimq.2020-25.01
27. Ed-Douibi, H., Izquierdo, J. L. C., Gómez, A., Tisi, M., & Cabot, J. (2016). EMF-REST: Generation of RESTful APIs from models. In *Proceedings of the 31st Annual ACM Symposium on Applied Computing* (pp. 1446–1453). ACM. https://doi.org/10.1145/2851613.2851782.
28. Ivanchikj, A., Pautasso, C., & Schreier, S. (2018). Visual modeling of RESTful conversations with RESTalk. *Software and System Modeling, 17*, 1031–1051. https://doi.org/10.1145/2976767.2987691
29. The SwaggerHub API Development Tool. Retrieved March 16, 2022, from https://swagger.io/tools/swaggerhub/.

Employing Graph Databases for Business Process Management and Representation

Ştefan Uifălean, Ana-Maria Ghiran, and Robert Andrei Buchmann

Abstract There's growing interest in leveraging the structured and formal nature of business process modeling languages to make them available not only for human-oriented visualization and analysis, but also to machine-oriented knowledge representation. Standard serialization formats are predominantly XML-based, originating in times when XML was imposed as the mainstream interoperability format. Recent research on the interplay between knowledge representation and business process modeling has involved OWL or RDF for semantic enrichment and reasoning, which suggests an evolution towards treating business process models in formats that are better fit to their native structure—e.g., directed labelled graphs. In this paper we introduce a converter that translates the standards-compliant BPMN XML format to Neo4J labelled property graphs (LPG) thus providing an alternative to traditional XML-based serialization, while ensuring conceptual alignment with the standard serialization of BPMN 2.0. A demonstrator was built to highlight the benefits of such a parser and to test the conceptual coverage of BPMN models. The proposal enables graph-driven navigation of business process models in a knowledge-intensive context where procedural knowledge available as BPMN diagrams must be exposed to LPG-driven applications.

Keywords Labelled property graphs · Model-driven software engineering · BPMN 2.0 XML · Graph databases · Process queries

A prior version of this paper has been published in the ISD2022 Proceedings (https://aisel.aisnet.org/isd2014/proceedings2022/knowledge/2/).

Ş. Uifălean · A.-M. Ghiran · R. A. Buchmann (✉)
Babeş-Bolyai University, Cluj-Napoca, Romania
e-mail: robert.buchmann@econ.ubbcluj.ro

Ş. Uifălean
e-mail: stefan.uifalean@stud.ubbcluj.ro

A.-M. Ghiran
e-mail: anamaria.ghiran@econ.ubbcluj.ro

© The Author(s), under exclusive license to Springer Nature Switzerland AG 2023
G. C. Silaghi et al. (eds.), *Advances in Information Systems Development*,
Lecture Notes in Information Systems and Organisation 63,
https://doi.org/10.1007/978-3-031-32418-5_5

1   Introduction

This paper reports on a converter for transforming Business Process Model and Notation diagrams into Labelled Property Graphs.

Conceptual modeling tools export both semantic information and visual/positional data of diagrammatic elements for various purposes. For model-driven software engineering, as well as interoperability between diagrammatic tools, current standards mitigate differences with the help of various interchange formats. The BPMN standard facilitates both diagramming and execution of complex workflows by means of the WS-BPEL binding or the BPMN 2.0 XML serialization. Other standards popular in the past, e.g. XPDL, are also XML-based—for reasons perhaps historical. This means that a data structure that is fundamentally hierarchical (i.e. the XML DOM) is imposed on workflow descriptions that are fundamentally directed labelled graphs—and this is not limited to BPMN (see also XMI for UML interchange).

It is a design choice that deviates from the graph-like, relationship-driven nature of most visual diagrams, which is hinted at by their meta-metamodels—see [1] where "relationship" (although under different names) is identified as a first-class citizen. Even in diagramming sketches where no visual connectors are present, and only grouping or visual alignment are used, relationships are still implied by containment, relative positioning or interactive hyperlinking, as shown in the taxonomy of diagrammatic relations discussed by [2]. Other works have argued for a mapping between arrow-based visualizations and logic [3] naturally leading towards graph-based knowledge representations.

The Knowledge Graphs paradigm has employed machine-readable knowledge representations that are closer to how humans manage information—i.e., as networks of semantic associations on which reasoning mechanisms can be deployed and context can be navigated as far as relationship chains are relevant. Graph databases are the typical technology for storing and reasoning on such networks of associations; when storing diagrammatic content, they can expose knowledge that was diagrammatically captured to queries that focus on relationship navigation and discovery: path finding and navigation, subgraph extraction, node context extraction etc.

This article proposes a BPMN 2.0 compliant approach (i.e., preserving all information from the BPMN 2.0 XML standard) to representing business process models in a labelled property graph database, i.e., the LPG format promoted by Neo4J [4] with their CypherQL graph query language as means of navigating and retrieving graph information. We also deployed a proof-of-concept GUI to demonstrate graph navigation in concordance with the BPMN-based XML schema, leveraging a network visualization library (Vis.JS [5]) fed by a Spring Boot service. The result provides the usage experience of a "process stepper"—a typical learning tool for training employees, supporting process learning and understanding. In a more general sense, model-driven software engineering [6] may thus benefit from a new approach to interchange and interoperability that can be leveraged by process-aware systems, process analytics or workflow execution engines.

The remainder of the paper is organized as follows: Sect. 2 summarizes and comments on related work identified in the literature. Section 3 presents the work methodology and an overview of the solution artifact. Section 4 explains the conversion principles and patterns used by the converter. Section 5 describes an expository demonstrator, followed by implementation details in Sect. 6 and evaluation aspects in Sect. 7. The paper concludes by pointing out strengths and weaknesses.

2 Related Work

Managing process descriptions is not that different from other domains where LPG databases have been successfully employed—e.g. to capture protein participation and sequences in [7]. The treatment of graph database representation was also applied to UML [8] and LPGs recently started being considered also for event logs [9].

Modeling environments have been using various serialization formats for achieving interoperability, with various degrees of concordance. The legacy BPML 1.0 by OMG was for a while the preferred execution language. In [10] various other XML formats are discussed, revealing an XML-centric world of model-driven engineering and model interchange—the situation did not evolve much, due to the standardization efforts during that time. A modern pragmatic solution for model storage should move beyond the traditional execution and interchange goals, towards a knowledge representation goal that, besides supporting execution and interoperability, also enables semantic queries, rule-based reasoning or graph embedding.

Graph databases are predominantly available in two technological flavors—RDF and LPG. The RDF approach for knowledge modeling is the foundation for the Web of Data [11, 12], adopted by open knowledge bases such as DBpedia, or as a rich metadata format e.g., in Springer SciGraph [13]. An RDF serialization of BPMN models has been offered for a while in the BEE-UP tool [14], further leveraged in artifact-building research such as [15] where a dereferencing service was implemented for process browsing. The main limitation of that approach is that (a) it is built on a tool-specific meta-metamodel—i.e., not reusable outside BEE-UP; and (b) it is not fit for the increasingly popular Neo4J labelled property graph databases.

In our pragmatic approach, we take as input the BPMN 2.0 XML serialization based on its standard XML schema, therefore reusable for any BPMN tool that is compliant with that serialization (we employed Academic version of SAP Signavio Process Manager [16] for demonstration). We also move from RDF to the alternative LPG flavor of graph databases, where we can distinguish the relationship properties from the node properties, allowing to shift some of the data load from resources/nouns to relationships/predicates, which are commonly found in diagrammatic representations (e.g., probabilities or transition conditions on sequence flows of a process model). More recently, the RDF standard has also considered an extension to allow data to be associated with relationship instances (not only with relationship types)—see the RDF-star extension [17], but it hasn't been available during the development of the work presented here, and it is not yet part of the RDF standard (therefore still subject to imminent change). Once standardized, we plan to compare the benefits of having BPMN serializations in the two alternative formats—we are currently experimenting in parallel with an RDF approach to a BPMN flavor that was customized to describe front-end user experience [18].

The literature reports on various demonstrators of process-aware applications—e.g. in [19] a surgery workflow generates a checklist displayed in a dynamic HTML website, using a domain-specific output presentation that does not aim for general-purpose knowledge representation. The need to repurpose BPMN models for knowledge representation is gaining traction in the conceptual modeling community, see also the work in [20] which proposed on-the-fly ontology-based semantic enrichment of BPMN elements or [21] where a notion of semantic process modeling is introduced, referring to ontology-aided BPMN and EPC modeling. Earlier proposals of a semantic business process management [22] focused on the semantics of Web services consumed by processes.

An RDF approach to the generation of Knowledge Graphs from BPMN models was recently reported in [23] and more generic approaches to convert arbitrary diagrammatic content to graphs (not limited to BPMN, but applicable to BPMN as the BEE-UP tool [14] demonstrates) were proposed in [24] (for execution and data linking purposes, with an initial set of patterns introduced in [25]), and more recently in [26] (for model "smells" detection).

The work at hand takes a turn from the RDF-focused trend towards LPG databases and uses as input the standard XML schema of BPMN rather than a metamodeling platform—the project context where the work was developed aims for graph-based process automation, although other use cases found in the literature (e.g. smells detection, graph embeddings) may also investigate the benefits.

3   Prototype Summary and Research Method

This paper aims to set new grounds for a process execution approach enabled by a graph process repository. In the demonstration section, we emulate an execution engine by traversing a BPMN process model while also displaying a proximal execution context (all nodes directly connected to every process step) which can be flexibly extended. A Spring Boot-based service architecture ensures that process-aware behavior is fed on demand by that node execution context, which can potentially include graph data from outside the process model. For demonstration purposes, we also developed a visual layer based on Vis.JS and a process stepper (based on the graph browsing service, which was inspired by the dereferencing service described in [15]) to display the neighborhood for every node (i.e., process element), thus gradually revealing context during navigation.

From a software engineering point of view, we followed the Extreme Programming paradigm to design and implement an artifact. We guided our research effort according to the Design Science Research methodology [27] based on the needs of a project that must manage and navigate process paths flexibly in a technological environment that already employs graph databases for storing (organizational) contextual knowledge of those processes.

During the first stage of the project, the goal was to model content exported as BPMN 2.0 XML into a Neo4j store, including subprocess links to other diagrams. We also wanted to investigate the reasoning capabilities offered by Neo4j out-of-the-box, which can be emulated to some extent by queries acting as a form of production rules. Research that analyzed Labeled Property Graphs (LPG) as an equivalent to the standardized RDF reports advantages in query speed by using pre-aggregation [28], with the drawback of LPG not being tailored for the Linked Data distributed graph paradigm.

The traditional XML-based serializations are hierarchical and imply traversal using the DOM, although a process model is not really a tree-like structure. This makes DOM a redundant abstraction layer between how the process looks (is visually perceived and discussed by humans) and how it is stored/queried by machines. Authors of [29] stated that the XML-based interoperability is reduced in practice: "there are no tools or tests to check if model conforms to all restrictions"—moreover, the future of some XML-based standards is uncertain (e.g., XPDL).

In our pragmatic approach, we take as input the BPMN 2.0 XML serialization based on its standard XML schema, therefore reusable for any BPMN tool compliant with that serialization (we employed Signavio for demonstration).

Our converter loses the visual data and cannot be considered a true interchange tool—we focus on extracting the procedural knowledge content of BPMN diagrams and we enforce validation using the schema constraints of the XML serialization. Since we take input from the standard XML, the DOM tree is parsed to generate a graph node from each visual element, keeping only attributes of semantic value that may inform process execution or analytics, or visualization that does not care about the original graphical layout of the diagram. XML tags referring to BPMN relationships are further translated into Cypher relationships, most of them containing properties themselves, which are allowed by the LPG model (and less fit for RDF).

By creating a model base from the raw BPMN semantics, process descriptions can be queried and processed with graph-based algorithms, while also remaining human-readable [30]. The model can be executed remotely, as needed in robotic process execution [31]—this could be exploited by Robotic Process Automation, which currently also predominantly uses XML serializations (the XML-based user interface structure provides the "data objects" for UI process execution).

The usage flow of the graph-driven demonstrator starts with the app prompting a user to select the pool whose process is going to be simulated, then it initiates a "node browsing session" (designed in previous work on graph visualization [32]). At any step of the process traversal, the user is presented with the set of properties of the current process element and the proximal context of it—relationships incoming and outgoing from/to resources, subprocesses and flow elements. The programming goes beyond simply replicating the "token game" summarized in the standard [33] and generally employed by BPMN simulation tools, where the token is generated by a Start Event, passing through elements and relationships except a Message Flow, finally being consumed at any End Event. We explore all relations incoming and outgoing from a node, meaning the user can go beyond the normal sequence flow and access resources like documents, pools, or enter the resource describing a group. Therefore, we open the token game and actually let the user navigate every node described in the graph store, similar to a traditional Knowledge Graph exploration scenario.

Below the initial pool selection list, we rendered a network visualization of the conversations between process participants. By inference through successive queries, we found the source pool containing a conversation task and also the pool where the message flow leads (possibly into another workflow element that catches the message). This dereferencing from message sending activity type up to a process and containing pool was facilitated by a backwards induction through the clear CypherQL syntax and the resulting graph was assembled using Vis.JS in what resembles a Conversation Diagram.

The core implemented service methods have the purpose of retrieving an identified node and its relationships while interfacing with the graph database and the front-end visualization. The Middleware consists of a Spring Boot Java implementation of a classic MVC architecture, with a Data Access Layer (DAL) for the graph data and front-end rendering using the Thymeleaf Views. To bring the Neo4J data inside Spring Boot framework, we defined related POJO classes for each node type ("label" in Neo4J).

Current evaluation through the lens of Design Science has been limited to software testing and integration with contextual graph information that is still being developed within the project where the requirements for this serialization were raised. The client app for navigating graph contents was introduced to demonstrate the completeness of coverage for all elements present in exemplary BPMN models regardless of type and relationships.

4   Conversion Principles

Because our converter must map a BPMN 2.0 XML document to a intermediary Java abstractions (derived from the metamodel) that are further persisted in the graph using queries, the converter enforces validation using the schema definitions provided by the standard. If the converter service is given a schema-compliant serialization, an API constructs its DOM representation in-memory. Each XML tag is parsed using a custom algorithm to obtain a graph node for every visual element, with only a subset of indispensable attributes assigned as node's properties. Tags representing BPMN relationships are translated into Cypher relationships, some of them containing properties as well. The Java "business logic" implements rules illustrated in Table 1. Any Neo4J entity—Node or Relationship—has labels (colored ellipses on last column) equivaling to Class hierarchy types of BPMN elements. Underneath are properties of the entity instance, fundamental ones being id (auto-assigned by Neo4J engine), name and documentation).

Table 1 Exemplary conversion patterns

Principle explanation	BPMN pattern	LPG pattern
Splitting/merging **Gateway** becomes *node* with outgoing/ incoming sequence flow *relationships* linking to succedent *nodes*	Script filtering. Task 3. Attributes (Sequence Flow): Name — Script filtering; Element ID — sid-6AEC5031[…]. Task: Task type — Script; Name — Task 3; Element ID — […]; Process ID — […]. Inclusive Gateway: Name — INCLUSIVE SPLIT; Element ID — sid-026BB783[…]; Process ID — sid-6697516F[…]; Gateway type — OR. INCLUSIVE SPLIT	Relationship Properties. SEQUENCE_FLOW. id — 35; name — Script filtering. Task 3. id — 195; name — Task 3; type — SCRIPT. INCLUSIVE SPLIT. id — 1AA; direction — DIVERGING; name — INCLUSIVE SPLIT
Data object and **start message event** inside **lane** contained in **pool** become 4 *nodes* plus intermediary process *node* and 4 different containment *relationships*	Orchestrator. Thread 1. Data. Client request received. Data Object: Name — Data; Is collection — false; Element ID — […]. Start Message Event: Name — Client request received; Trigger — Message	Data. id — 233; hasCollection — false; Marker — name — Data. id — 200; name — Client request received; triggerList — [MESSAGE]
Boundary event remains an intermediate event *node* linked to its task through one *relationship*	Task 4. Timeout. Intermediate Timer Event: Name — Timeout; Trigger — Timer; Cancel activity — true	Task 4. IS_ATTACHED. id — 168; cancelActivity — true; name — Timeout; triggerList — [TIMER]
Collapsed **Subprocess** remains an activity *node* but the actual linked Embedded process is inserted inside the graph through an intermediary process *node*	Subprocess 1. Task 2. Task 1. Collapsed Subprocess: Subprocess reference — Subprocess 1; Name — Subprocess 1; Loop type — Standard; Documentation — […]; Subprocess type — Embedded	id — 182; documentation — For each request component execute a subprocess; loopMarkerType — LOOP; name — Subprocess 1
Message flow becomes *relationship* with property *name* (if defined) or *message* (**message** data object must be attached with name attribute set)	Service response received. Message Flow: Name. 3rd p. Response message. Message: Name — 3rd p. Response message. 3rd party Service	MESSAGE_FLOW. id — 8; message — 3rd p. Response message

Figure 1 highlights some selected BPMN elements in the XML serialization, including the attribute referencing the BPMN 2.0 schema definition's namespace. The process elements consisting in a named Task and End Event have *name* attributes capturing their diagrammatic textual labels. These process elements have *outgoing* and *incoming* child elements that refer to the same relationship ID, which is a sequence flow, permitting us to construct the relationship at the same time with the source node, or retrieve it later based on its unique ID in case it has multiple attributes

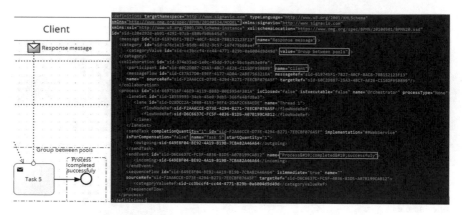

Fig. 1 XML serialization of BPMN elements

(thus benefiting from the LPG relationship properties). The lane containment relationships as depicted in the code side for both "Task 5" and "Process completed successfully" are referred through the *flowNodeRef* attributes with each ID as value. The Message Flow in the model diagram is retrieved embedding the two referenced nodes in the form of children *sourceRef* (pointing to "Task 5") and *targetRef* (with "Client" pool ID). The mapped instances—two nodes and a relationship—are built upon these patterns along with attaching the "Response message" content to the relationship as property. Lastly, the sequence flow relationship embeds a tag for a category ID reference, which points to the "Group between pools" containment element.

To query the XSD-compliant tree XPath was used. We handle conceptual model's re-construction in a well-defined hierarchy by iterating over each category tag and searching for the elements that refer to it. Typical to XML markup representation, dependencies like relationships and many properties rely on ID referencing. This principle is also what makes queries that cross between disparate graphs possible in RDF but we wanted to transform essential objects inside triplets into properties and separate the aggregations used by the XSD tree-like referencing into relationships with their own properties. Thus, we favored a more natural representation in the form of LPG through a redesigned, more relationship-centric schema that is natural while resembling the original diagrammatic visual model.

5   Demonstrative Application

Figures 2 and 3 describe a BPMN model before and after the conversion. We have created the diagram (of a distributed service ecosystem) using Signavio Process Manager, exported the standard XML serialization and passed as input to the endpoint that performs the conversion. In Fig. 3 nodes that do not show any name tag are

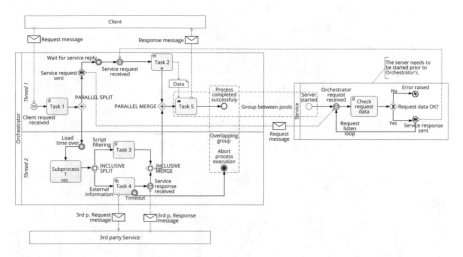

Fig. 2 Top-level BPMN model of example

instances of label/type Process which are grouping constructs that intermediate between a Pool and its Lanes or a SubProcess and its first Start Event. Additionally, the graphical tool will not show names for nodes that did not have any name attribute at the time of modeling—e.g., a single-laned process (still those will have internal IDs).

In a preliminary version of the artifact, we designed the navigation app to go in a single forward direction resulting a process stepper loyal to a Token Game simulation. That means that from a subprocess element to its start event and from its end event back to the subprocess element there is no Succedent relationship. Covering this functionality determined small changes in terms of schema at graph store level to match the only-outgoing initial dereferencing of neighbors. For this reason, we artificially introduced at graph creation time a JUMP_TO relationships for bridging this gap. In the current iteration, this was overhauled by opening the token game to navigation in any direction.

We encountered some technical limitations. If we draw a couple of Message "envelopes" with the same name, Signavio exported only a single XML corresponding element (a message with that text). The solution was to model the message text as an attribute of the Message Flow relationship, rather than splitting the relationship and adding a Message node. The value of the message property can be the same in different relationship instances. Another issue is due to the limitations of the subprocess XML Schema when exporting a top-process using the option "include linked subprocesses". From inside the linked model only non-collapsed pools will be exported into XML, although collapsible pools can be drawn. Upon closer inspection we have found the reason behind this behavior. Top-process has a <collaboration> header tag with children being at least one pool wrapped inside a <participant> tag, that can have one or none <processRef> attributes of type Process, so no subProcess elements can be linked to any pool. Instead, Subprocess is serialized directly inline

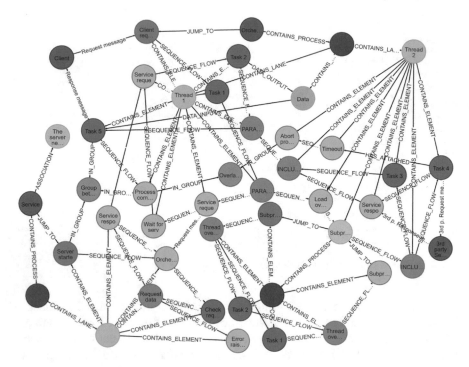

Fig. 3 Converted BPMN as Neo4J graph visualization

as a FlowElement (like a complex task) inside that pool's process containing only
lanesets with the actual mini-flow; the only participants serialized in the top header
tag <collaboration> are the ones in the top-process. It might be because in BPMN a
subprocess is thought of as a series of actions done only by that participant (pool)
inside the top-process that are taken out of that model in order to unclog it or do
exception handling, but it isn't concerned with interaction with the other participants. The standard points, indeed, that subprocesses are just a complex type of Task
divided into small Tasks. Our modeling service works according to this standard
behavior with a small change in that the subProcess FlowElement has a relation with
an intermediate Process element artificially introduced to group the subprocess flow.

Figure 3 is generated by a built-in visualizer for LPG. The process stepping
demonstrator is depicted in Fig. 4. The left side shows the process stepper demo
gradually revealing each step of the process with its immediate context (messages,
resources etc.). Some additionally inferred information is isolated in the right panel—
e.g., the "social network" of how pools communicate (similar to a Conversation
Diagram but inferred from the process/collaboration model).

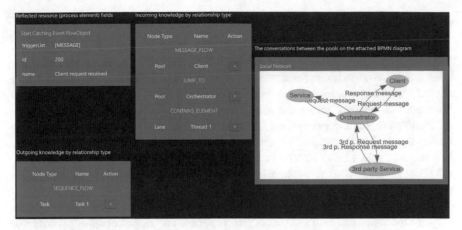

Fig. 4 Process stepper" demo app (left) and inferred "social network" of pools (right)

6 Implementation Details

Implementation-wise, we set up three controllers—Modeling, Pool, Resource—, each with an endpoint binding to the basic services. ModelingService performs the parsing of the BPMN model XML into a tree, clears the entire graph repository, does conversion from tree to Spring Data Neo4J POJO (Plain Old Java Object) classes that are immediately persisted into graph repository when given as attributes to the repository.save() command. It adds one new type of relationship (JUMP_TO) on the resulting graph through trivial reasoning—we derive such useful relationships not explicitly present in the model, facilitating the "process stepping" traversal in the front-end.

At the parsing stage, one difficulty arises to pick a relevant attribute as identifier. In the XML definition, this kind of metainformation is provided in the XSD (XML Schema Definition) file. As a result of setting validation inside the parser (code courtesy to the reference [34]), the parser takes into consideration the XSD declarations in the XML file.

The conversion algorithm applies a well-defined parsing order:

1. Nested iterations over each pool, lane, and flow node children ensure that the first nodes extracted are the Flow Elements;
2. Then their parent lanes;
3. Followed by additional FlowObjects inside each previously persisted SubProcess node; the reason these are executed after the first FlowObjects is because we designed each iteration object after the pools and lanes as a call to a monolithic algorithm;
4. Then data association connectors, sequence flow connectors;
5. After the root loop is closed, it converts message flows, annotation associations;

6. The last are the group concept and corresponding relationships.

This emulates a depth first-style traversal, the order of conversion being critical for the graph building. If we would make a slight change in the order of execution, the code would produce unexpected graphs—this is because of the hierarchical nature of XML files and because of the graph building precedence. To clarify, a message flow can't be created before the actual pools are created—some effort was spent on identifying such dependencies to come up with an Object-Oriented mapping having a good binding while also simplifying the XSD traversal. The original XML Schema hierarchy of data structures, being bulky, was compacted without negatively affecting semantics—e.g., exploiting the attribute categoryValueRef in correlation with the schema of the Group concept.

We needed to explicitly map BPMN's modeling language class diagram to an Object-Oriented form with a subset of the properties and essential concepts covered, while corelating with the mapped tree-based XSD-compliant serialization which got compacted into the final class hierarchy. In the following we present some relevant extracts. The representation of a BPMN model using Java consists of a hierarchy of POJO classes that maps to the BPMN 2.0 schema/metamodel, as shown in Fig. 5.

We wanted to preserve and also to allow for extending the XSD schema, with inheritance levels suggested by the standard metamodel. The root class is Node, bearing the structure:

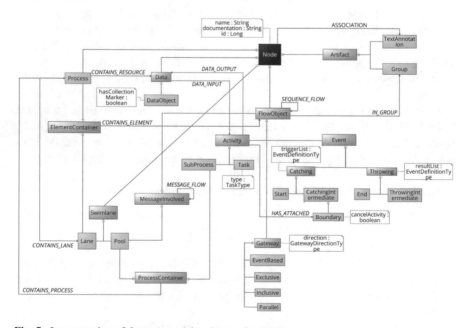

Fig. 5 Java mapping of the metamodel to the graph schema

```
@NodeEntity
@NoArgsConstructor
public abstract class Node {
    @Id @GeneratedValue @Getter private Long id;
    @Getter @Setter private String name;
    @Getter @Setter private String documentation;
    @Relationship(type = "ASSOCIATION", direction = Relation-
ship.OUTGOING)
    @Getter @Setter private ASSOCIATION outgoingAssociation;
    @Relationship(type = "IN_GROUP", direction = Relation-
ship.OUTGOING)
    @Getter @Setter private List<IN_GROUP> outgoingInGroupList;
}
```

Any element on the model is translated in our graph as a Node at its root, with fields name, documentation and two relationships that any derived elements would have: one that links to a TextAnnotation separate element, and one that links to a Group element. We decided not to initialize any field at instance creation, dealing with the scenario that the modeler may omit filling in some property values as, for instance, element description.

Using Reflection provided by the powerful RTTI (RunTime Type Identification) feature in Java, an object of the identified class is constructed and initialized; the class name is found using a dictionary that maps XSD tag name to actual Java class name. This is attached to a template method. The template method subclasses were hardcoded to correspond to different conversion scenarios, and their basic structure includes an additional design pattern: Strategy. The converted object is instantiated, but the server chooses which name of Strategy to choose based on reflecting upon the type of the object created as a result of the XML parsing.

The described ModelingService creates the Neo4j graph, and additional ModelingRepository method calls allow the graph database to infer relationships that are useful to client-level navigation code e.g., JUMP_TO, by means of the following queries:

```
@Query("MATCH (root)-->(proc:Process)-[*1..2]
                -> (start:Start)
    CREATE (root)-[:JUMP_TO]->(start)") void inferPastProcess();

@Query("MATCH (sbpr:SubProcess)-->
            (proc:Process) -->(end:End)

        CREATE (end)-[:JUMP_TO]->(sbpr)") void inferBackToSubPro-
cess();
```

The first query overhauls the intermediary node that acts as a "container" parent for a sequence of Flow Nodes (it stands between a Pool and Lanes, respectively a SubProcess and Flow Elements). Since these Process nodes do not contain any information, and they do not specify which contained node is to be traversed first we provide an alternative "Sequence Flow" substitute that also acts as shortcut to an actual Flow Element. We create a similar shortcut connector from the terminal End

Event node back to the SubProcess task "host"—from where a Sequence Flow will lead the process traversal further down the described model.

The client app demonstrator makes use of View Reflection using Thymeleaf in tandem with SPEL (Spring Expression Language). We thus make part of the view layer processing generic resulting in a single view file of the referenced node being reflected upon and its neighbors fetched in a uniform way. Thus, only the fields describing a particular resource instance are auto generated at runtime. The structure of the Front-End could thereafter be reduced to only a few modular View components, each representing a particular feature:

- *default.html* is the general layout of the UI, divided with the help of HTML5 container tags and *Thymeleaf Standard Layout System;*
- *pools.html* accessible through the "Pool View" hyperlink in navigation header is rendered when starting resource traversal and requires the user to select an initial BPMN resource of type Pool;
- *resource.html* does the heavy lifting, as it is served (by the Controller and under-lying middleware layers) a model containing the current element and its immediate context.

The model sent to pools.html from the Controller contains all Pool elements. SDN (Spring Data Neo4J [35]) automatically creates a query under-the-hood and communicates with Neo4j using the proprietary Bolt protocol. In the actual rendering, SPEL applies some in-view business logic, mainly identifying the Collapsed Pools and rendering an anchor-less tag, else a particular tag with anchor. The resource.html logic is segmented in three files for self, incoming and outgoing information. Using Thymeleaf intermediate variables we render names of neighbors grouped by category and assemble hyperlinks to them which call the Resource Controller endpoint. We also use Reflection inside the view template to populate the page with the source element's properties. Because different resource types have different properties, we eliminate the need to make redundant views for each resource type to be rendered and the incoming and outgoing relationships are fetched from the Controller without Reflection, so performance is not critically affected. In Appendix we provide a code snippet of the resource_self and resource_outgoing modules detailing this property rendering, with fieldUtils and outgoingEntry objects providing access to the contextual information (attributes and outgoing relationships).

7 Evaluation

Performance-wise, there is a cost to using an Object-To-Graph mapper (OGM). Most OGM operations, including Query Result binding are implemented under-the-hood and on Java reflection at full capacity resulting in a decrease in response time, but are versatile in OO manipulation. Therefore, we constructed an abstraction from the BPMN file in Object-Oriented manner, in-memory, and by annotating the classes we specified how the SDN should map between instances of these classes and the graph

Table 2 Average time for graph resource acquisition benchmark

Elapsed time for	Node with	
	1 relationship (ms)	>6 relationships (ms)
Direct bolt resource query	2	3
Loading full resource page in browser	830	863

entity instances. We passed the actual responsibility of constructing the queries to SDN, using our in-memory Java representation. We try to balance higher processor waiting time with lower memory footprint. The response is controlled mapper classes instance initialization, by selectively initializing the properties of nodes (only if they have a non-null value in the XML). The benefit of implementing the prototype in this way is perceived in terms of responsiveness and structural flexibility.

Abstracting interactions with graph data is done through Spring Boot, with the advantage of the framework providing a common workflow for general MVC application development. Thanks to the integration with Neo4j, the DAL code strictly resides to functionalities about POJO classes and hides configuration details.

One strength of our solution is that it provides a Java Reflection-based best practice for the design and development of relationship-centric information systems which may be exploited where relationships must be revealed gradually without knowing them in advance, something we demonstrated by opening up the BPMN token game towards a knowledge graph navigation approach. Further development of complex business logic on the API end is facilitated thanks to the decoupling of concerns, achieved by following principles of [36].

We analyzed the time to fetch content from the model base. A lower-level call on Bolt protocol from the Neo4j tool took 3 ms to retrieve a node linked by more than 6 relationships. Viewing that node context in the browser implies more time loading all the properties, 1st level neighbors, and finally rendering the data in HTML. With all these, the duration measured by calculating the request time was also below 1 s. For a node with only 1 neighbor/relationship, the results are lightly smaller, as can be seen in Table 2, and also the overhead of passing our query logic through the complex middleware is reasonable.

8 Conclusions

This paper introduces a BPMN-to-LPG (Neo4J) converter that takes input from the standard BPMN 2.0 XML serialization thus it is generalizable to any BPMN-compliant tool, unlike existing diagram-to-graph converters reported by the literature which have been tailored for metamodeling platforms or targeted the production of RDF. It acts as a bridge between the process execution paradigm and the knowledge representation paradigm, since even Neo4J graphs can also be enriched by RDF(S) and OWL domain models as shown in [37].

This was motivated by a Design Science project context where graph representations of business process models must become part of an encompassing organizational knowledge graph to support novel knowledge management approaches (not detailed in this paper's scope). A demonstrator client app was built to showcase how the graph-based process content can be streamlined to end user-oriented functionality, which will also be necessary in the context project.

The key quality we wanted to achieve is universality and standard compliance. Any process modeled using the BPMN standard can be turned into a model base that can be further exploited for this flavor of Model-Driven Software Engineering or process analytics that need to make use of a graph view on a business process. Neo4j proved to be a reliable database system that exploits relationship-centric data modeling and intuitive data traversal or reasoning rules through graph queries. The Spring ecosystem removed the burden of writing low-level code to interface the demo app with Neo4J and the middleware, also minimizing the client app user interface by exploiting the Reflection pattern in Java and fragment insertion in Thymeleaf.

Requirements for model interchange have not been raised in the current iteration (the focus is on linking process structures to organizational context), however to generalize the value of the proposal for a roundtrip approach we plan to also provide a reverse conversion in the future.

Acknowledgements The present work has received financial support through the project: Integrated system for automating business processes using artificial intelligence, POC/163/1/3/ 121075—a Project Cofinanced by the European Regional Development Fund (ERDF) through the Competitiveness Operational Programme 2014-2020.

Appendix

Source code sample of the *resource_self.html* file:

```
<html xmlns:th="http://www.thymeleaf.org">
<article th:fragment="GenericGenerator" th:with="cls = ${re-
source.getClass()}">
  <p>Reflected resource (process element) fields</p>
  <div class="card blue-grey darken-1">
    <div class="card-content white-text">
      <span class="card-title" th:text="${resourceClassnames}"></span>
      <table class="responsive-table highlight">
        <tbody>
        <!--/* Since default Reflection API retrieves only public
scoped members in superclasses use separate lib */-->
        <!--/*@thymesVar
            id="fieldUtils" type="org.apache.commons.lang3.re-
flect.FieldUtils"*/-->
        <th:block th:each="field : ${fieldUtils.getAllFields(cls)}">
          <th:block th:if="${
            !field.isAnnotationPresent(T(org.neo4j.ogm.annotation.Re-
lationship))}"
                    th:with="val = ${fieldUtils.readField(field, re-
source, true)}">
            <tr th:if="${val}">
              <td th:text="${field.getName()}"/>
              <td th:text="${val}"/>
            </tr>
          </th:block>
        </th:block>
        </tbody>
      </table>
    </div>
  </div>
</article>
</html>
```

Source code sample of the *resource_outgoing.html* file:

```html
<html xmlns:th="http://www.thymeleaf.org">
<article th:fragment="Iterator">
  <p>Outgoing knowledge by relationship type</p>
  <div class="card blue-grey darken-1">
    <div class="card-content white-text">
      <table class="responsive-table centered highlight">
        <tr>
          <td>Node Type</td>
          <td>Name</td>
          <td>Action</td>
        </tr>
        <th:block th:each="outgoingEntry: ${outRelTypeStringToNodeL-
ist}">
          <tr>
            <td colspan="3"><span class="card-title" th:text="${out-
goingEntry.key}"/></td>
          </tr>
          <th:block th:each="outgoingNode: ${outgoingEntry.value}">
            <tr>
              <td>
                <span th:text="${outgoingNode.getClass().getSimple-
Name()}"></span> <!-- Reflection API call -->
              </td>
              <td>
                <span th:text="${outgoingNode.getName()}"/>
              </td>
              <td>
                <a class="btn link" th:href="|/resource/${out-
goingNode.getId()}|">
                  <i class="material-icons">navigate_next</i>
                </a>
              </td>
            </tr>
          </th:block>
        </th:block>
      </table>
    </div>
  </div>
</article>
</html>
```

References

1. Kern, H., Hummel, A., & Kühne, S. (2011). Towards a comparative analysis of meta-metamodels. In *Proceedings of the compilation of the co-located workshops on DSM'11, TMC'11, AGERE! 2011, AOOPES'11, NEAT'11, & VMIL'11* (pp. 7–12). Association for Computing Machinery. https://doi.org/10.1145/2095050.2095053.
2. Buchmann, R. A., & Karagiannis, D. (2017). Modelling mobile app requirements for semantic traceability. *Requirements Engineering, 22*, 41–75. https://doi.org/10.1007/s00766-015-0235-1

3. Diskin, Z., Kadish, B., Piessens, F., & Johnson, M. (2000). Universal arrow foundations for visual modeling. In: M. Anderson, P. Cheng, & V. Haarslev (Eds.), *Theory and Application of Diagrams* (pp. 345–360). Springer. https://doi.org/10.1007/3-540-44590-0_30.

4. Neo4j Graph Data Platform—The leader in graph databases. Retrieved April 08, 2022, from https://neo4j.com/.

5. vis.js. Retrieved April 10, 2022, from https://visjs.org/.

6. Brambilla, M., Cabot, J., & Wimmer, M. (2017). *Model-Driven Software Engineering in Practice* (2nd ed.). Morgan & Claypool Publishers. https://doi.org/10.2200/S00751ED2V01Y20 1701SWE004.

7. Lysenko, A., Roznovăţ, I. A., Saqi, M., Mazein, A., Rawlings, C. J., & Auffray, C. (2016). Representing and querying disease networks using graph databases. In *BioData Mining* (Vol. 9, paper 23). https://doi.org/10.1186/s13040-016-0102-8.

8. Daniel, G., Sunyé, G., & Cabot, J. (2016). UMLtoGraphDB: Mapping conceptual schemas to graph databases. In: I. Comyn-Wattiau, K. Tanaka, I.-Y. Song, S. Yamamoto, & M. Saeki (Eds.), *Conceptual Modeling* (pp. 430–444). Springer. https://doi.org/10.1007/978-3-319-46397-1_33.

9. Esser, S., & Fahland, D. (2021). Multi-dimensional event data in graph databases. *Journal on Data Semantics, 10*, 109–141. https://doi.org/10.1007/s13740-021-00122-1

10. Shapiro, R. (2002) A technical comparison of XPDL, BPML and BPEL4WS, https://www.bptrends.com/bpt/wp-content/publicationfiles/Comparison%20of%20XPDL%20and%20BPML_BPEL%2012-8-0211.pdf.

11. Berners-Lee, T. (1998) What the semantic web can represent. Retrieved April 08, 2022, from https://www.w3.org/DesignIssues/RDFnot.html.

12. Bizer, C., Lehmann, J., Kobilarov, G., Auer, S., Becker, C., Cyganiak, R., & Hellmann, S. (2009). DBpedia—A crystallization point for the Web of Data. *Journal of Web Semantics., 7*, 154–165. https://doi.org/10.1016/j.websem.2009.07.002

13. SciGraph Springer Nature. Retrieved April 10, 2022, from https://www.springernature.com/gp/researchers/scigraph.

14. Bee-Up for Education. Retrieved April 10, 2022, from https://www.omilab.org/activities/bee-up/.

15. Cinpoeru, M. (2017). Dereferencing Service for navigating enterprise knowledge structures from diagrammatic representations. In W. Abramowicz (Ed.), *Business Information Systems Workshops* (pp. 85–96). Springer. https://doi.org/10.1007/978-3-319-69023-0_9.

16. SAP Signavio Process Manager—BPM Platform for Process Modeling. Retrieved December 06, 2022, from https://www.signavio.com/products/process-manager/.

17. RDF-star and SPARQL-star. Retrieved April 10, 2022, from https://w3c.github.io/rdf-star/cg-spec/editors_draft.html.

18. Uifălean Ş., Ghiran, A. M., & Buchmann, R. A. (2022). User experience modeling method for a vision of knowledge graph-based process automation. In: *Proceedings of the 30th International Conference on Information Systems Development (ISD2022)*. Cluj-Napoca, Romania: Association for Information Systems (AIS) eLibrary. https://aisel.aisnet.org/isd2014/proceedings2022/knowledge/12/.

19. Ryniak, C., & Burgert, O. (2020). Automatic generation of checklists from business process model and notation (BPMN) models for surgical assist systems. *Current Directions in Biomedical Engineering, 6*(1). https://doi.org/10.1515/cdbme-2020-0005.

20. Laurenzi, E., Hinkelmann, K., & van der Merwe, A. (2018). An agile and ontology-aided modeling environment. In: R. A. Buchmann, D. Karagiannis, & M. Kirikova (Eds.), *The Practice of Enterprise Modeling* (pp. 221–237). Springer. https://doi.org/10.1007/978-3-030-02302-7_14.

21. Thomas, O., & Fellmann, M. (2009). Semantic process modeling—Design and implementation of an ontology-based representation of business processes. *Business & Information Systems Engineering, 1*, 438–451. https://doi.org/10.1007/s12599-009-0078-8

22. Hepp, M., Leymann, F., Domingue, J., Wahler, A., & Fensel, D. (2005). Semantic business process management: A vision towards using semantic Web services for business process

management. In *IEEE International Conference on e-Business Engineering (ICEBE'05)* (pp. 535–540). IEEE. https://doi.org/10.1109/ICEBE.2005.110.

23. Bachhofner, S., Kiesling, E., Revoredo, K., Waibel, P., & Polleres, A. (2022). Automated process knowledge graph construction from BPMN models. In C. Strauss, A. Cuzzocrea, G. Kotsis, A. M. Tjoa, & I. Khalil (Eds.), *Database and Expert Systems Applications* (pp. 32–47). Springer. https://doi.org/10.1007/978-3-031-12423-5_3.

24. Karagiannis, D., & Buchmann, R. A. (2018). A proposal for deploying hybrid knowledge bases: The ADOxx-to-GraphDB interoperability case. In *Proceedings of the 51st Hawaii International Conference on System Sciences* (pp. 4055–4064). https://doi.org/10.24251/HICSS.2018.510.

25. Buchmann, R. A., & Karagiannis, D. (2015). Pattern-based transformation of diagrammatic conceptual models for semantic enrichment in the web of data. *Proceedings of KES 2015, Procedia Computer Science, 60*, 150–159. https://doi.org/10.1016/j.procs.2015.08.114.

26. Smajevic, M., & Bork, D. (2021). From conceptual models to knowledge graphs: A generic model transformation platform. In *2021 ACM/IEEE International Conference on Model Driven Engineering Languages and Systems Companion (MODELS-C)* (pp. 610–614). https://doi.org/ 10.1109/MODELS-C53483.2021.00093.

27. Wieringa, R. J. (2014). *Design Science Methodology for Information Systems and Software Engineering.* Springer.https://doi.org/10.1007/978-3-662-43839-8

28. Ravat, F., Song, J., Teste, O., & Trojahn, C. (2020). Efficient querying of multidimensional RDF data with aggregates: Comparing NoSQL, RDF and relational data stores. *International Journal of Information Management., 54*, 102089. https://doi.org/10.1016/j.ijinfomgt.2020. 102089

29. Mertins, K., Bénaben, F., Poler, R., & Bourrières, J.-P. (Eds.). (2014). *Enterprise Interoperability VI: Interoperability for Agility, Resilience and Plasticity of Collaborations.* Springer. https://doi.org/10.1007/978-3-319-04948-9.

30. Dijkman, R. M., Dumas, M., García-Bañuelos, L. (2011). Business process graphs : Similarity search and matching. In A. Sakr, & E. Pardede (Eds.), *Graph Data Management: Techniques and Applications* (pp. 421–439). Hershey: IGI Global. https://doi.org/10.4018/978-1-61350-053-8.ch018.

31. Sadik, A. R., Goerick, C., & Muehlig, M. (2019). Modeling and simulation of a multi-robot system architecture. In *2019 International Conference on Mechatronics, Robotics and Systems Engineering (MoRSE)* (pp. 8–14). IEEE. https://doi.org/10.1109/MoRSE48060.2019. 8998662.

32. Uifălean, Ş., Silaghi, G. C., & Buchmann, R. A. (2019). A graph database approach to managing data with unpredictable schema in academic information systems development. In *Proceedings of the 18th International Conference on Informatics in Economy* (pp. 141–146). Bucharest: Bucharest University of Economic Studies Press. https://doi.org/10.12948/ie2019.03.10.

33. About the Business Process Model and Notation Specification Version 2.0.2. Retrieved July 05, 2022, from https://www.omg.org/spec/BPMN/About-BPMN/.

34. Validate XML using a XSD (XML Schema)—Real's Java How-to. Retrieved April 10, 2022, from https://www.rgagnon.com/javadetails/java-0669.html.

35. Spring Data Neo4j—Developer Guides. Retrieved April 10, 2022, from https://neo4j.com/developer/spring-data-neo4j/.

36. Martin, R. C. (2017). *Clean Architecture: A Craftsman's Guide to Software Structure and Design.* Prentice Hall.

37. Importing Ontologies—Neosemantics. Retrieved April 10, 2022, from https://neo4j.com/labs/neosemantics/4.0/importing-ontologies/.

IT Alignment as a Roadmap for Digital Transformation Success

Gideon Mekonnen Jonathan, Lazar Rusu, and Erik Perjons

Abstract Digital transformation undertaken in many public organisations often fail to result in the anticipated results. Given the recognition of the important role of IT alignment as one of the prerequisites for digital transformation, this study explores how public organisations can improve the degree of IT alignment. Thus, a case study is conducted in four sub-cities within a city administration, applying interviews and internal documents as multiple sources of data. The findings indicate that public organisations are likely to succeed in their digital transformation attempts if they can appropriately manage IT alignment-related factors. These factors identified— organisational structure, organisational culture, organisational agility, leadership skills, human resource management, digital metrics, external domain alignment, and stakeholder relationships—are categorised and presented as managerial or organisational. The contributions of the study for research and practice are presented.

Keywords Digital transformation · IT alignment · Public organisations · Public value theory · Theory of technology enactment

1 Introduction

Organisations across sectors and industries are embarking on the digital transformation journey. This comes in response to the dynamic business environment that has made it necessary for organisations to venture into the use of emerging technologies. This has resulted in, among others, the application of new digital technologies to design new and innovative business models, shorter product life cycles, highly cus-

G. Mekonnen Jonathan (✉) · L. Rusu · E. Perjons
Department of Computer and Systems Sciences (DSV), Stockholm University, Kista, Sweden
e-mail: gideon@dsv.su.se

L. Rusu
e-mail: lrusu@dsv.su.se

E. Perjons
e-mail: perjons@dsv.su.se

© The Author(s), under exclusive license to Springer Nature Switzerland AG 2023   93
G. C. Silaghi et al. (eds.), *Advances in Information Systems Development*,
Lecture Notes in Information Systems and Organisation 63,
https://doi.org/10.1007/978-3-031-32418-5_6

tomised or differentiated products, value-added services, and synchronised product-service combinations. However, researchers argue that there is still the lack of clarity on how organisations approach the organisation-wide changes to enable successful digital transformation. Thus, despite the continuous research and debate among practitioners, managing digital transformation to fruition remains a daunting task for leaders.

A closer look into the academic literature also indicates that digital transformation is still a protean concept [19, 34]. More recently, however, there is a growing consensus among scholars that digital transformation is a multifaceted phenomenon. According to Jedynak et al. [14], technology itself is just one piece of the complex puzzle that needs to be solved if organisations are to achieve their overall objective in the new digital world. Thus, digital transformation refers to *"the IT-enabled change in organisations through the digitalisation of products, services, core processes, customer touch points and business models"* [13]. To this end, the work towards a successful digital transformation should incorporate an appropriate strategy formulation [3], introduction of new technologies and the necessary organisational changes including organisational structure [33], business processes [34], and organisational culture [22]. To accomplish this and improve the value derived from the investment in digital technologies, the significance of digital transformation and how it is managed is often discussed at various levels, and across industries [10]. At a higher level, digital transformation is concerned with the application of new and emerging technologies to further the interest of societies at large. The use of new digital technologies shapes the communication between various stakeholders and determines the economic, social and political environment [10]. For these changes to happen, the digital transformation journey involves a long list of changes in various industries resulting in profound changes in a society [28]. At the organisational level, digital transformation is viewed as a response to environmental changes with the aim of exploiting new opportunities and improving performance while maintaining stability [19].

According to the extant literature, the extent in which organisations achieve digital transformation success in enabling value creation is dependent on how the various organisational changes are in agreement with the introduction of new technologies [10, 26] as well as the fit between the IT- and overall organisational strategies [2, 34]. This phenomenon, referred to as IT alignment, has been one of the top agenda for researchers and practitioners across industries [20, 21]. IT alignment—defined as the *"application of information technology in an appropriate and timely way, in harmony with business strategies, goals and needs"* [25, p. 3]—is recognised as one of the determinants of successful digital transformation [10, 19]. Given the significance of IT alignment during the digitalisation era, there are calls for further studies investigating the relationship between IT alignment and digital transformation (e.g., [16, 20, 37]). However, a closer look into prior studies reveals that public organisations were not adequately represented in these studies [29, 32]. We argue that this paucity of knowledge needs to be addressed for two reasons. First, IT alignment is found to be more challenging in highly pluralistic organisational settings, such as organisations in the public sector [36]. Second, the difference between organisations in the private and public sectors calls for nuanced empirical investigation of digital transformation [32]. Thus, our interest is to explore how organisations' attempt to reach and maintain IT alignment contributes to successful digital transformation in the public sector. The aim of this study, therefore, is to identify IT alignment related success factors and their significance for digital transformation. Therefore, our study attempts to answer the following research question: *Which factors related to IT alignment are important to enable successful digital transformation in a public organisation?*

The remainder of the paper is structured as follows. The next section presents a brief literature review related to digital transformation and IT alignment in the public sector. The subsequent section outlines the research methodology—the research strategy adopted as well as the data collection and analysis methods. The fourth section discusses the results of the empirical data. Finally, the conclusion summarises our findings and the implications for research and practice, together with the limitations of this study and proposition for future research.

2 Literature Review

2.1 *Digital Transformation in Public Organisations*

It has been acknowledged that digital technologies have had significant implications on how organisations operate across industries and not only disrupted but also challenged the traditional business models, organisational structures, and well-established operations [32]. Organisations that were slow to recognise the transformative powers of emerging technologies lost their competitiveness for their rivals. Within the public sector, the significant role of digital transformation in improving the delivery of public services is recognised in the literature [6, 29, 31]. However, the debate surrounding how to plan and execute successful digital transformation still continues. This confusion is also reflected in the various theories applied in prior studies. To start with, the technological determinism theory applied in prior studies [1] is criticised for not acknowledging the role of various organisational factors in the success of digital transformation. For instance, Luna-Reyes and Gil-Garcia [27] argue that the provision of public services that can satisfy citizens requires a transformed public sector-not just the introduction of new technologies. This transformation involves redesigning the internal processes and making continuous organisational adjustments. This is consistent with Fountain's theory [11] of technology enactment (TTE) recognising the significance of various organisational factors determining the way specific meanings are assigned to technologies. Thus, TTE was found appropriate for exploring how IT could be used in public organisations. For instance, TTE suggests that the success of digital transformation initiatives in the public sector depends on the social, cultural and institutional arrangements, including stakeholder relationships [27].

Since digital transformation is a process, organisations need to make continuous assessments and adjustments. Thus, leaders have to account for the benefits of their investment in new digital technologies. In this regard, the original work of Moore [30]—public value theory—has been mentioned in prior IS studies. Researchers argue that this theory has provided us with the foundation for assessing digital transformation and the success of digital government initiatives. This is a departure from the New Public Management (NPM) narratives, where public organisations are expected to be run as business-like enterprises, mostly relying on economic concepts [9]. In connection with NPM, digital transformation was seen as a means to improve administrative efficiency [31]. However, following the unfortunate lack of success of the NPM, there is a growing quest for public value creation among researchers and practitioners [6]. Thus, the public value theory is used to support the argument that public organisations stand to benefit from the complex digital transformation journey [31]. This organisation-wide transformation (i.e., digital transformation) is expected to transform public service delivery [13, 33] and create value that might not be measured in economic terms [31].

2.2 Managing Digital Transformation

In the public sector context, digital transformation is considered to be a full-fledged and well-coordinated set of changes in policies, processes and services resulting in added values for citizens and those who work in public organisations [29]. The application of digital technologies is meant to benefit the internal as well as the external users of the services enabled through digital transformation. Even though the potential of important improvements it brings to the sector has been presented, Meijer and Bekkers [28] argue that the focus of prior studies has been on the advances of the available technologies with little attention to the management of organisational factors. Particularly, what is missing from the prior digital transformation studies is the recognition of the importance of the management of fundamental change processes. These changes within a public organisation affect the design, production and delivery of public services [29]. Scholars argue that the management of digital transformation in public organisational context should be based on the acknowledgement of specific conditions of public organisations. For instance, according to Plesner et al. [32], digital transformation can be best understood if public organisations are studied with a consideration for the bureaucratic formal structure as well as the accountability issues.

Regardless of sector or industry, transformation of any sort involves a list of small and big changes. In the case of digital transformation, the new changes involve the adoption of new digital technologies to replace old tools which were in use for some time. These changes also require that people need to assume new roles and responsibilities. As emerging technologies are being introduced continuously, it is imperative that employees at various levels also need to acquire new sets of skills to discharge their responsibilities appropriately [19]. However, most importantly, the realisation of the benefits of digital transformation can be accomplished only when an organisation manages to make a coordinated approach. This approach needs to be driven by a well-formulated strategy based on a unified view of organisational objectives as well as the pathway towards a common organisational goal [29, 31]. On the other hand, formulation and execution of an objective strategy in a public organisation was found to be difficult [8]. As a sector with pluralistic context, characterised by multiple stakeholders with diverse or opposing objectives, many digital transformation initiatives have suffered [28, 29, 31]. However, the recognition of the significance of a common vision and organisational goal will make the digital transformation journey more manageable.

2.3 IT Alignment and Digital Transformation in Public Organisations

Prior studies attempted to explore the complexity of digital transformation, dismantling the puzzling interplay between IT and various organisational arrangements [19]. The objective was to find appropriate ways that could enable the realisation of the benefits of digital transformation. A phenomenon that is often brought up in such studies is IT alignment. In fact, the relationship between IT alignment and digital transformation has been gaining the attention of researchers in recent years (e.g., [10, 19, 20]). This development is no surprise given the result of prior studies acknowledging the important role IT alignment plays in digital transformation. A review of IS studies indicate that there are three areas where IT alignment can help organisations in their digital transformation attempts [18]. These were identified as the necessary prerequisites to enable successful digital transformation [13, 34]. First, IT alignment helps organisations improve the value they derive from their new digital technologies. The rationale is that the fit between organisational objectives and the use of new technologies improves organisational performance [26]. Second, as digital transformation requires a continuous organisational adaptation, IT alignment helps enable the necessary organisational agility [37]. Third, IT alignment was found to facilitate the integration of new technologies into the existing IT infrastructures, organisational structures and business processes [18].

With multiple stakeholders and varying interests as well as arrangements with inherent administrative and political tensions, public organisations are more complex than private organisations [32, 36]. This complexity, in turn, has implications for how organisations plan their digital transformation journey and formulate their IT- and organisational strategies that can satisfy the interests of the diverse stakeholders [32, 36]. Recent case studies (e.g., [24]) also revealed that the introducing digital technologies to solve complex public administrative tasks had raised many unanswered questions. For instance, researchers [28, 29] pointed out the lack of studies recognising the relevance of organisational and managerial elements of digital transformation. On the other hand, the extant literature indicates that organisational and managerial approaches should be selected based on the acknowledgement of specific conditions of public organisations [24, 36].

Despite the extensive research throughout the past years, various developments in the business environment as well as the emergence of new technologies has made IT alignment a challenging enterprise. According to some accounts, IT executives spend about half of their time in their attempt to reach IT-aligned positions [20]. A review of IS studies revealed that organisational structure, organisational culture, leadership skills, as well as external domain alignment were found to be among the most important factors influencing IT alignment in organisations undertaking digital transformation [18]. Besides, within the public organisations' context, the important role of stakeholder relationships is acknowledged [4]. As the focus of public management shifts to the creation of integrated public value, the success of digital transformation is measured by whether public organisations satisfy the interest of stakeholders [31]. Researchers have also found that stakeholder relationship is vital as leaders attempt to align their IT strategies with the organisational goal in the digitalisation era. Given the dynamic technological landscape and the ongoing digital transformation in the public sector, we argue that it is time to revisit the various factors influencing IT alignment.

3   Research Methodology

3.1   Research Strategy and Case Study Setting

To explore how IT-aligned position contributes to the success of digital transformation, a case study research strategy is deemed appropriate. Case studies are best suited when researchers are interested in exploring a complex phenomenon in a natural setting [38]. Given the complex organisational structure and a long list of stakeholders with varying interests in public organisations, we argue that case studies provide the opportunity to further our understanding of the relationships between IT alignment and digital transformation.

The case study was conducted at Addis Ababa City Administration which is comprised of ten sub-city administrations—organised in 28 districts and 328 neighbourhood units (also referred to as kebeles). The City Administration is recognised to be among the public administrations highly investing in digital transformation in the country. Even though each of the ten sub-city administrations is organised as separate organisations, their operations are similar, except the sub-cities are mandated to deliver public services to residents in their geographic area. The vision and strategic plan of the city guide the operations of the sub-cities. Leaders of the various functional units of the sub-cities report to the corresponding directors at the central city administration. Among the ten sub-cities we approached, four of them responded favourably to our request to take part in our study. Our research process is depicted in Fig. 1.

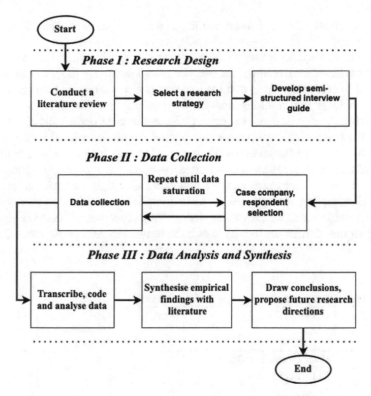

Fig. 1 The research process

3.2 Data Collection Method

In order to investigate the role of IT alignment in digital transformation within a public organisation, an interpretative approach was adopted. This approach is in line with the aim of our study focusing on gathering data as provided by participants aiming to capture the holistic view and unique situation in the natural environment [35]. One of the advantages of case studies is that it provides multiple ways of data collection methods fitting the line of enquiry. However, Yin [38] suggests the practice of triangulating data sources to improve the credibility of findings of case studies. Thus, the data collection was carried out through interviews and analysis of internal documents as well as publicly available information from websites. Besides, a case study protocol was developed to guide the data collection and data analysis procedures.

First, as the primary method of enquiry, we conducted semi-structured interviews with participants who are involved in the decision making of the IT alignment and various digital transformation initiatives. Consistent with prior IT alignment studies [15, 25], we approached leaders from the IT and administration side. Probability sampling was deemed inappropriate for our study given our aim is an in-depth insight, not a generalisation, of a phenomenon in the wider population. Thus, as a starting point of a purposive sampling, we adopted criteria of selection of experts. Purposive sampling is a sampling strategy where researchers decide criteria for selection of participants based on the aim of the study or prior knowledge [35]. Hence, we were interested to recruiting those who have deeper understanding of IT alignment and digital transformation resulting from their experience and functional status within their respective organisations. To ensure we have selected samples that could provide us with the richest information, we investigated the organisational structure of the case organisation. In the second stage of our selection, the HR head as well as the IT and administrative leaders was consulted to establish the involvement of potential participants in decisions pertaining IT alignment and digital transformation initiatives. This sampling strategy enabled us to compile the multiple point of views on strategy formulation as well as the decision-making processes related to IT alignment and digital transformation. Table 1 shows the list of research participants and their profile.

Table 1 List of participants with their position and domain

Code	Position	Domain	Work experience (years)	Interview length (min)
ITL1	Chief Information Officer	IT	12	55
ITL2	Chief Information Officer	IT	7	60
ITL3	Deputy Chief Information Officer	IT	11	60
ITL4	Chief Digitalisation Officer	IT	9	50
ITL5	Chief Digitalisation Officer	IT	12	50
ITL1	IT Infrastructure Lead	IT	4	55
ITL2	IT Infrastructure Lead	IT	3	65
ITL3	Lead Network Administrator	IT	5	55
ITL4	Information security Lead	IT	2	55
ITL5	Information Security Lead	IT	3	60
ITL6	System Administration Lead	IT	4	45
Adm1	Development planning Head	Admin.	8	55
Adm2	Housing Administration Head	Admin.	5	50
Adm3	Health Services Head	Admin.	10	65
Adm4	Health Services Head	Admin.	13	55
Adm5	Local Law Enforcement Head	Admin.	7	55
Adm6	Local Law Enforcement Head	Admin.	12	60
Adm7	Education Bureau Head	Admin.	11	55
Adm8	Economic planning Head	Admin.	12	50
Adm9	Population Register Head	Admin.	6	65
Adm10	Population Register Head	Admin.	9	55

According to the literature, the rigour of a research which is based on interviews is a function of the quality and number of interviews conducted. For instance, the literature suggests a minimum of numbers of interviews to sufficiently capture the insights from respondents. However, there is a growing consensus among researchers that not only the number of interviews but the point of data saturation needs to be the criteria for deciding whether the collected data is adequate or not [12]. Accordingly, not more than the 21 interviews were necessary for this study since no new themes were emerging, indicating the point of data saturation. Both IT and administrative experts were selected from the four public organisations under the Addis Ababa City Administration of the capital of Ethiopia, Addis Ababa.

Interview guides were used to conduct the semi-structured interviews with respondents from the administration and IT departments to ensure reliability and ease of comparing the results of the interviews. The questions were derived from the extant literature on IT alignment and digital transformation. The formulation of the questions was different taking the functional roles of the respondents into consideration. For instance, the CIOs were asked to provide their insights and opinions on the role of IT in their respective organisations, how their counterparts view IT and how they collaborate with other departments as well as how their relationship with the whole organisation plays a role in the success of the digital transformation. On the other hand, leaders from the administration departments were asked questions pertaining their perception of the role of IT for their organisation. There were also questions regarding the interaction between the IT unit and the rest of the organisation, and how this influences digital transformation. The interview guide consisted of a total of 15 questions formulated in two versions, i.e., one for leaders from the IT unit and another for people from the administration departments. The interview questions were organised under the following four themes:

Part 1: General questions about the interviewees' background and functional role.
Part 2: Questions about the various aspects of IT alignment including strategy formulation, organisational structure, and relationship between IT and administration departments.
Part 3: Questions about the various digital transformation efforts within the city administration.
Part 4: Questions about the participants perception on the relationship between IT alignment and digital transformation.

Except six of the participants who were interviewed using online video tool (Zoom), the remaining interviews were conducted face-to-face at the vicinity of the City Administration. Right after the interviews, the participants were asked to suggest the names of potential interviewees. The recorded interviews were transcribed verbatim for ease of data analysis. To make sure what has been said during the interviews is captured accurately, the transcription of each interview was sent to the participants for comments. Only three of the interviewees made some corrections.

Yin [38] argues that the application of multiple sources of evidence i.e., triangulation, improves the reliability of the findings of case studies. To this end, the data collected through interviews and questionnaire was supplemented with secondary data. Internal organisational documents provided by the participants and publicly available data from websites were used for the study.

3.3 Data Analysis Method

For the data analysis procedure, we adopted a thematic analysis approach. This analysis method is widely adopted among qualitative researchers as it provides flexibility while enabling rich and detailed account of data [5]. Researchers also argue that thematic analysis can be used in study areas where complex phenomena are explored. For instance, prior IT alignment and digital transformation have also applied thematic analysis (e.g., [10, 29]). For our study, the use of thematic analysis method was deemed appropriate as our aim was exploratory in nature focusing on the relationship between IT alignment and digital transformation, in a complex organisational setting.

Baraun and Clarke [5] outline six phases of thematic analysis, i.e., familiarising with data, generating initial code, searching for themes, reviewing themes, defining and naming themes, and producing the report. The procedure involves the search and identification of common threads. The themes emerge as researchers carefully read and familiarise themselves with the raw data. To help us in describing the phenomenon under investigation, one of the two forms of coding might be applied- inductive or deductive. Inductive coding describes the process of theme generating from a raw data without relying on prior theoretical and epistemological underpinning. On the other hand, deductive coding is a procedure whereby a researcher starts generating themes based on existing theories or frameworks. Even though, inductive coding is common among exploratory studies, we argue that a hybrid approach incorporating both inductive and deductive theme generation can improve the rigour of our qualitative study. Thus, we adopted both inductive and deductive coding in our analysis. First, we developed the initial codes and sub-themes from our transcribed data following the inductive approach. Later, we mapped and grouped these themes deductively using a priori template. The conceptual research framework (i.e., based on prior IT alignment and digital transformation literature) shown in Fig. 2 was used to formulate the priori template. As recommended by Walsham [35], the whole data analysis process was run as an iterative process.

4 Results and Discussion

The results as well as the discussions presented here are our analysis from the coding of the interviews we conducted. To respond to our research question, the starting point for our analysis is the role of IT alignment for a successful digital transformation. Thus, our focus is on exploring the various factors that are relevant to enable IT aligned position at the case organisation. We structure our results in eight subsections

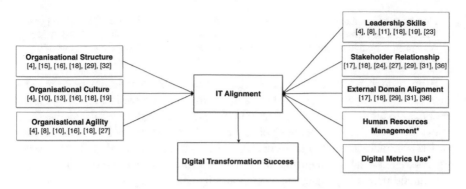

Fig. 2 IT alignment-related factors in a public organisation undertaking digital transformation

according to the coding and analysis of the empirical data. We were able to identify various factors that are important to improve IT alignment at our case organisation (see **Fig.** 2). These factors were grouped into eight categories. For instance, during the interviews, our respondents pointed out that flexibility of organisational structure and work processes were important to improve the appropriate use of IT according to the current organisational goal. These were grouped and presented as "*organisational agility*" in the paper.

As shown above, we traced back most of the factors, in the extant IS literature—organisational structure, organisational culture, organisational agility, external domain alignment, leadership skills and stakeholder relationships. Besides, our empirical data also revealed the significance of digital metrics and human resource management in improving IT alignment in a public organisation undertaking digital transformation (marked with *). In the subsequent sections, we discuss the significance of these factors for digital transformation success.

4.1 Organisational Structure

To facilitate the implementation of the digital transformation in the city administration, the organisational structure was modified on various occasions. For instance, the interviewees from the IT and administration sides (IT1, IT2, IT5, Adm1, Adm2, Adm8) were adamant that several of the IT roles and the respective responsibilities (e.g., the office of Chief Digitalisation Officer) were created or changed to facilitate the digital transformation initiatives at the city administration. Other changes introduced recently include the reporting structure where the Information Security Leads are now under the direct supervision of the CIO at the central city administration rather than the CIOs at the sub-city level. Similar changes were also made in the administrative departments to facilitate the execution of many digitalisation projects. In the words of Adm10:

> I lost track of count how many times we changed the structure of our sub city. I can't tell you who would be under my supervision or which projects are the responsibility of my office. As a professional in a public office, my responsibility is to act within the constraints of my office.

Even though making changes to organisational structure is desirable and not uncommon [4, 16], we found the statements from our participants interesting for two reasons. First, the internal document we were provided with (formal organisational chart) did not reflect the changes pointed to us. However, we found an explanation for the contradiction in the literature. According to Plesner et al. [32], the formal organisational structure in the public organisation is less likely to remain unchanged to maintain public legitimacy and accountability. However, people will find various ways of alternative "informal" ways of going around the rigid bureaucratic structure to get their work done. Studies on IT alignment within a public organisation (e.g., [15]) have also confirmed the presence of informal organisational structures with favourable implications for the application of IT. The analysis of the interviews also suggests that the informal arrangements have contributed to some of the success of the implementations of new systems in the city administration.

According to Adm1, there is an ongoing discussion with heads of departments to decide which forms of the organisation's arrangements should be maintained or altered to speed up the digital transformation in the city administration. A closer look into the responses also indicates that organisational structure is closely related to the other factors that were found to be important. This finding is consistent with prior studies (e.g., [4, 15, 18, 27]) confirming the significance of appropriate organisational structure for IT alignment and digital transformation.

4.2 Organisational Culture

The critical role of organisational culture in digital transformation was brought up by almost all of our participants. Specifically, the existence of sub-cultures within the city administration is a concern shared. Leaders from the IT side argue that organisational culture at the organisation has become so dire that many of the new systems launched at the city administration were not being used by administrative employees. According to IT1 and IT2, while resistance to change and attitudes towards technology are often the reasons, lack of skills and training were often cited as factors affecting the use of technology in the city administration. In relation to the top management involvement, IT leaders are hesitant on whether the city administration is ready to promote, for instance, data-driven decision-making and technology-supported changes to the existing work processes. Administrative leaders (Adm3, Adm5, and Adm10) admit that their organisation has many red tapes, rigid procedures and relatively stable organisational structure and a formal division of labour. In their opinion, this has resulted in a perpetuation of conservative organisational culture that might be a source of scepticism towards the adoption of new technologies and embracing change. Our analysis also indicates that the organisational culture of the city administration has implications for the success of the digital transformation. Thus, we argue that the city administration needs to work towards an organisational culture that promotes development of new digital skill sets, embracing open communications, risk-taking behaviour, and a positive attitude towards digital transformation. Our findings are on par with the IS literature on IT alignment and digital transformation supporting organisational cultures that promote organisational change [18, 19].

4.3 *Organisational Agility*

Similar to the debates in the extant literature (e.g., [4, 8, 10]), our participants have differing views on the relationship between organisational agility and IT alignment and how this relationship affects the success of the digital transformation. However, the dilemma is not whether there is a positive relationship between agility and IT alignment but how organisational agility could be implemented in a public organisation. According to the respondents from the IT side (IT1, IT2, IT4, IT6), organisational agility (flexibility in organisational structure and work processes) is necessary to reach IT alignment. The argument is that the flexibility of the "informal" organisational structure created an "agile-like" arrangement that was helpful to speed up some of the digital transformation works. Particularly, this has resulted in the creation of multidisciplinary teams from various departments to solve organisation-wide problems.

On the other hand, the respondents from the administration side seem to have mixed views on the effectiveness of organisational agility in general and digital transformation in particular. For instance, while the development planning head (Adm1) supports some form of flexibility in work processes, others (Adm4, Adm7, Adm8, Adm9) prefer relatively consistent structure and processes. However, when asked to reflect on the digital transformation projects, our respondents agree that cross-departmental collaborations and agile teams have resulted in relatively more timely and effective IT solutions. These responses reveal a few closely related issues that need to be addressed to help the city administration succeed in its digital transformation. The IT side (IT1, IT2, and IT6) argues that the flexibility of the IT infrastructure and organisational structure is critical. The administration side (Adm 3, Adm7, and Adm9) views the adaptability of the workforce as of paramount importance since the city administration is introducing new technologies. The statements suggest that promoting less formal and more flexible arrangements supports digital transformation. To this end, we concur with the Bitzer et al. [4] on forming agile structures comprising interdisciplinary teams. Such teams are invaluable in improving, for instance, the IT decision-making processes [10, 18].

4.4   Leadership Skills

Similar to the findings of prior studies (e.g., [5, 8, 18]), our analysis of the interview data indicates that skills of leaders are associated with many of the factors recognised to influence the success of digital transformation. This is also a factor that was mentioned in relation to IT strategy formulation and IT governance. For instance, the administrative leaders (e.g., Adm1, Adm5, Adm10) admit that those in the administration leadership do not believe they possess the skill sets to contribute to IT strategic planning. According to the participants, many digitalisation initiatives could benefit from appointing leaders with the digital leadership skills necessary to formulate robust IT strategic plans. Even though the participants from IT (IT1, IT2, IT3, IT5) concur that IT leaders should take the lion's share of the responsibility for the IT strategic planning, the support from top leaders in the administration is critical.

On the other hand, participants agree that the biggest challenge they have during this digital transformation journey is to make informed decisions on the priorities. Two of our interviewees (Adm1, Adm8), who happen to be in the committee mandated to make high-level IT decisions, admit that their selection is not based on governing the digital transformation. Instead of members with administration and IT acumen, the committee comprises highly placed bureaucrats representing most of the administration. This had implications for the IT Governance arrangement for two reasons. First, many IT teams have been waiting for decisions to be made for long time (IT8, IT9, IT10). Second, the final say on IT priorities is almost always influenced by those who do not possess the right knowledge (IT7, IT9) meant not optimal choices were made. However, the two are not mutually exclusive. In contrast with the private sector, which is driven by economic gains and tangible organisational goals, organisations in the public sector need to make their priorities based on other criteria. The two CDOs we interviewed argue that navigating through the bureaucracies and red tapes to coordinate the prioritisation and implementation of the digital transformation plans is their utmost challenge. This is not only related to the governance mechanism in place, but also the ability of leaders. According to ITL4,

> …The IT governance mechanism in place is regulated by the institutional and political arrangements. If you are the IT leader in the private sector, you probably need to discuss with the board of directors who would have the best interest of the stakeholders. In our case, we have various interest groups that have interests and their priorities. So, we need to be very craftful to make the decision-making arrangements be utilised the most effective way, overcoming the most formal and bureaucratic practice.

Our findings confirm what researchers have been saying about the significance of leadership skills. First, to support the formulation of a robust IT strategy supporting the digital transformation journey, there are few leadership skill sets expected from both sides. Among others, emotional intelligence, as well as conversational competency, are essential to support in forging a favourable relationship that comes in handy, enabling the formulation of IT strategy acceptable by several stakeholders [18]. Second, the decision-making process in relation to the adoption of new technologies within the public organisations is dependent on the existing rules and regulations which are stricter in bureaucratic settings [11, 23]. Thus, it behoves leaders of such organisations not only to be aware of the leeway but also to possess skills that support them to forge a working relationship with those mandated to oversee the applicable regulations.

4.5   Human Resources Management

Even though our participants recognise the significance of human resource management for the success of digital transformation, their responses (mainly from the IT leaders' side) seem to suggest a lack of sufficient investment related to human resources acquisitions as well as skills development. The general view from the administration and IT sides is that the lack of skilled personnel is unfavourably affecting the utilisation of new digital technologies at the city administration. According to IT4 and IT5, the city administration is struggling to recruit employees essential to improve the utilisation of new technologies in the work processes. For instance, it was found that there is a lack of people with expertise in robotic process automation (RPA), information security, cloud computing and network administration. In his own words, one of the CIOs (ITL1) says:

> It has been always a struggle convincing our leaders to open up their wallets. From what I gathered, the politicians promise almost anything when they are in front of the camera and our leaders tend to believe them. For us it is a big problem to live up to the expectation from the public since we almost always get money to buy new technologies…but not to hire or train the people we have. It is frustrating…

The claim is supported by the IT infrastructure leads and information security lead. IT6 and IT8 also complained about the high turnover within their organisation, which is much higher than in the private sector. Even though the problem is acknowledged, many administration heads (Adm1, Adm3, Adm8, Adm10) believe a lot has been done to solve the issue. According to them, the public administration bureaucracy does not provide a leeway to adjust the pay scale and other related benefits. Our analysis indicates that the organisation currently does not seem to have a consistent and formalised skills development arrangement to support digital transformation. As researchers [8, 14, 19] put it, organisations undertaking digital transformation needs to sketch clear recruitment, remuneration as well as training and development programmes to succeed in their digitalisation attempts. Digital transformation could only succeed when an organisation ensures investment in measures that could help the administrative and IT personnel continuously acquire and develop appropriate skills [10]. Our finding is also consistent with what prior studies have found. For instance, according to Jedynak et al. [14], the issue of human resource management in relation to digital transformation is not a topic that attracted appropriate attention from researchers and practitioners. The observation is not surprising given the continuous attention rendered to the technological aspects of digital transformation. We argue that this lack of appreciation for human resource issues (from the administration side) undermines the essential role of individuals as well as teams in enabling the adoption and exploitation of new technologies.

4.6   Digital Metrics

The internal documents we obtained indicate that the objectives of digital transformation at the city administration were to enable data-driven decision-making and create added value. Participants from the IT side argue that it is through digital performance metrics that they can assess whether these objectives are being met. Two reasons are pointed out. First, digital performance metrics would help the organisation ensure the efficiency and speed of public services delivered to citizens. This could be done either by measuring the gains by eliminating most of the repetitive tasks and automating them; or by looking into the amount of time and space saved for other tasks that require employees' actions. Second, digital metrics are also important for managing the digital transformation journey. As a continuous process, digital transformation initiatives need to be monitored, and actions might require adjustments. Leaders from both sides indicate that commonly agreed measures could help them take corrective actions. Among others, internal and external bench-marking, service level agreements, and integration of services were mentioned as essential to manage the successful digital transformation.

Unfortunately, in reality, the city administration does not seem to follow through with what is on paper. As Adm1 pointed out, while he is convinced of the favourable outcomes of digital transformation, the IT leaders did not do their homework in making a case for most of the initiatives. In his own words,

> Through the years, we have developed some sort of measurement for what we produce in our department. It is not just us; all our departments have their way of measuring the outputs, be it service or product. Of course, it is different between us, but I know how much of the budget I spent and how much worth of service I produced. When it comes to IT services, we still need to see how much of our expenditure has improved our efficiency…

As a public institution with greater scrutiny, investment decision on new technologies needs to be tied to outcomes that could be "observed or measured". The IT leaders disagree that it is the sole responsibility of their units to measure the success of digital transformation. The major issue, according to IT3, is that the organisation itself does not have a set of outcomes that can be assessed objectively. Thus, the responsibility of accounting for the improvement of services needs to be shared, recognising the role of metrics measuring the contribution of IT. Luftman et al. [26] also recommend collaboration between IT and the remaining departments in developing demonstrable measures. Thus, we argue that it is in the organisation's best interest to encourage the participation of various stakeholders in developing metrics to measure the added value resulting from digital transformation. Accounting for the value gained is critical as public organisations make continuous adjustments to improve their digital transformation success [14, 31].

4.7   External Domain Alignment

Our participants recognise that digital transformation at their organisation is, by default, aimed at solving complex problems beyond the boundaries of the city administration. Thus, the IT leaders (IT1, IT2, IT7, IT9) and those in the administration (Adm3, Adm4, Adm10) argue that the success of the transformation initiatives requires inter-organisational collaboration and information-sharing with other public agencies. Accordingly, the relationship between these organisations is important because the ultimate objective of digital transformation is to support the provision of integrated services that make the lives of citizens easier. For that to happen, the responses suggest that several IT infrastructure and compatibility issues need to be solved. Among others, the compatibility of software, hardware and communication networks between the city administration and partner organisations was necessary.

On the other hand, conflicting organisational goals, divergent political attitudes, lack of trust, legal issues, and diversity of organisational culture were found to be challenging as the city administration attempted to align the new technologies with its overall organisational goal. The literature suggests that, in addition to maintaining IT alignment within their organisation, leaders need to take measures to cope with the external environment. This concept, referred to as external domain alignment (i.e., IT alignment with due consideration for the organisational objectives and IT application of related organisations and their customers), is one of the significant factors that determine the success of digital transformation in organisations [7, 18].

4.8   Stakeholder Relationships

Our participants acknowledge that digital transformation is a collaborative work involving internal and external stakeholders. According to IT4 and IT5, various digital transformation projects across the city administration have benefited from good stakeholder relationships in many ways. First, through consultation with their stakeholders (users), the city administration could improve the services delivered to citizens and businesses. The relationship with other public organisations has also brought about the possibility of delivery of integrated services to citizens. A smooth relationship with external service providers has also helped the organisation better understand and adapt to changes in the external environment. In addition to the political and legal developments, the external service providers have provided the city administration with invaluable information on the current and emerging technologies. IT1, IT2, and IT6 also highlighted the importance of top management assuming the leading role in promoting good stakeholder relationships. In the words of IT2,

> As IT personnel, we are preoccupied with designing and developing new systems, acquiring and integration of new technologies as well as training and maintenance. Mostly, our contact is with staff within the organisation. So, we need all the help we could get to better understand the needs of our citizens...

The analysis of our responses indicates that user engagement, and collaboration with external service providers and other agencies are important for the success of digital transformation in a public organisation. Prior studies on digital transformation (e.g., [10, 31]) and IT alignment (e.g., [17, 36]) put stakeholder relationship as one of the important factors determining the appropriate utilisation of new technologies. Thus, we argue that by encouraging the participation of stakeholders, public organisations will be able to succeed in providing solutions that meet their stakeholders' needs.

5 Conclusions

Owing to the perceived importance for organisations in many sectors, the IT alignment and digital transformation phenomena have attracted the attention of researchers and practitioners. However, the focus of prior studies has been on private organisations. To respond to the call for further research, the aim of our study was twofold- (1) to explore the role of IT alignment for digital transformation, and (2) establish how public organisations reach and maintain IT alignment enabling successful digital transformation.

The result of our study, based on the technology enactment- and public value theories, highlights the significance of formulating a robust road map for digital transformation. We argue that this road map needs to be founded on recognising the role of organisation-wide changes and making continuous digital value assessments as well as adjustments to organisational structure and internal processes. Our focus on the factors related to IT alignment (i.e., *organisational structure, organisational culture, organisational agility, leadership skills, external domain alignment, digital metrics, HR management, and stakeholder relationships*) indicates that organisations' attempt towards IT-aligned position can be beneficial for digital transformation. In addition to confirming the results of prior studies, our findings revealed the important role of digital metrics and HR management practices in reaching IT-aligned position in a public organisation, even more than in organisations in the private sector. The rigid organisational structure and decision-making arrangements do leave not much space for flexibility. However, recognising the internal and external factors affecting their work towards integrating new digital technologies is of paramount importance. Our findings identified areas that need to be monitored and acted upon to enable successful digital transformation in public organisations. For instance, we highlighted the important role of continuous monitoring of the organisational culture, and informal organisational structure to improve IT alignment. Our findings also underscore the significance of stakeholder relationships and organisational agility. However, given the challenges arising from strict organisational arrangements, we recognise the role of informal practices that could be applied to meet the demand for digital transformation initiatives.

Our study is subject to some limitations that need to be taken into consideration when the results are interpreted. First, we recognise that our decision to rely on a

single case study restricts our findings to the context of the selected public administration (e.g., organisational size, digital transformation stage). Based on the analysis
of the extant literature, we argue that the case organisation exhibits the strategic and
structural choices of those public organisations undertaking digital transformation.
However, we encourage future studies at the same or similar organisation as the
internal and external situations are bound to change. Second, as public organisations
operate under dynamic environment (i.e., changes in the economic, political and
technological landscape), we endorse future research accounting for these changes.
Third, the findings of our study reflect the snapshots of what the case organisation is
doing to reach and maintain IT alignment to enable the success of its digital transformation endeavour. Future longitudinal studies might reveal how an organisation
can realise the success of digital transformation through time as various changes
are made to improve IT alignment. Fourth, our research conceptualised (Fig. 2) that
IT alignment in the public sector is primarily influenced by organisational structure, stakeholder relationship and organisational agility. Future studies could focus
on other contextual factors that could influence IT alignment in relation to digital
transformation success.

Acknowledgements This study is partially funded by the Swedish Research School of Management and Information Technology (MIT).

References

1. Aurigi, A. (2005). Competing urban visions and the shaping of the digital city. *Knowledge, Technology & Policy, 18*(1), 12–26.
2. Benbya, H., Leidner, D. E., & Preston, D. (2019). MIS quarterly research curation on infor-
mation systems alignment. *MIS Quarterly (Research Curations)*, 1–19.
3. Bharadwaj, A., El Sawy, O. A., Pavlou, P. A., & Venkatraman, N. V. (2013). Digital business
strategy: Toward a next generation of insights. *MIS Quarterly*, 471–482.
4. Bitzer, M., Hinsen, S., Jöhnk, J., & Urbach, N. (2021). Everything is IT, but IT is not Everything-
What Incumbents Do to Manage Their Digital Transformation Towards Continuous Change. In
Proceedings of the 42nd International Conference on Information Systems (ICIS) (pp. 12–15).
AIS.
5. Braun, V., & Clarke, V. (2006). Using thematic analysis in psychology. *Qualitative Research
in Psychology, 3,* 77–101.
6. Cordella, A., & Bonina, C. M. (2012). A public value perspective for ICT enabled public sector
reforms: A theoretical reflection. *Government Information Quarterly, 29*(4), 512–520.
7. Dawes, S. S., Gharawi, M., & Burke, B. (2011). Knowledge and information sharing in transna-
tional knowledge networks: A contextual perspective. In *Proceedings of the 44th Hawaii International Conference on System Sciences (HICSS)* (pp. 1–10). IEEE.
8. Deiser, R. (2018). *Digital transformation challenges in large and complex organisations*. Clare-
mont.
9. Di Mauro, A., Cominola, A., Castelletti, A., & Di Nardo, A. (2020). Urban water consumption
at multiple spatial and temporal scales. A review of existing data sets. *Water, 13*(1), 36.
10. Fischer, M., Imgrund, F., Janiesch, C., & Winkelmann, A. (2020). Strategy archetypes for digital
transformation: Defining meta objectives using business process management. *Information &
Management, 57*(5), 103262.

11. Fountain, J. E. (2001). The virtual state: Transforming American government? *National Civic Review, 90*(3), 241–252.
12. Francis, J. J., Johnston, M., Robertson, C., Glidewell, L., Entwistle, V., Eccles, M. P., & Grimshaw, J. M. (2010). What is an adequate sample size? Operationalising data saturation for theory-based interview studies. *Psychology and Health, 25*(10), 1229–1245.
13. Heilig, L., Lalla-Ruiz, E., & Voß, S. (2017). Digital transformation in maritime ports: Analysis and a game theoretic framework. *Netnomics: Economic Research and Electronic Networking, 18*(2), 227–254.
14. Jedynak, M., Czakon, W., Kuźniarska, A., & Mania, K.: Digital transformation of organisations: What do we know and where to go next?. *Journal of Organisational Change Management, 34*(3), 629–652.
15. Jonathan, G. M., Rusu, L., & Perjons, E. (2020). Organisational structure's influence on IT alignment: The case of a public organisation. In *Proceedings of the 16th European, Mediterranean, and Middle Eastern Conference on Information Systems (EMCIS)* (pp. 471–485). Springer.
16. Jonathan, G. M., Rusu, L., & Perjons, E.: Business-IT alignment in the era of digital transformation: Quo vadis?. In *Proceedings of Hawaii International Conference on System Sciences (HICSS)* (pp. 5563–5572). AIS.
17. Jonathan, G. M., Rusu, L., Perjons, E., & Kuika Watat, J. (2021). The relationship between organisational agility and IT alignment in public organisations. In *Proceedings of the 32nd Australasian Conferences on Information Systems (ACIS)* (p. 28). AIS.
18. Jonathan, G. M., Rusu, L., & Van Grembergen, W. (2021). Business-IT alignment and digital transformation: Setting a research agenda. In *Proceedings of the 29th International Conference on Information Systems Development (ISD)*. AIS.
19. Jöhnk, J., Oesterle, S., Olig, P., & Rövekamp, P. (2022). Managing the complexity of digital transformation: How multiple concurrent initiatives foster hybrid ambidexterity. *Electronic Markets, 3*.
20. Kahre, C., Hoffmann, D., & Ahlemann, F. (2017). Beyond business-IT alignment-digital business strategies as a paradigmatic shift: A review and research agenda. In *Proceedings of the 50th Hawaii International Conference on System Sciences (HICSS)* (pp. 4706–4715). AIS.
21. Kappelman, L., Maurer, C., McLean, E. R., Kim, K., Johnson, V. L., Snyder, M., & Torres, R. (2021). The 2020 SIM IT issues and trends study. *MIS Quarterly Executive, 20*(1), 8.
22. Karimi, J., & Walter, Z. (2015). The role of dynamic capabilities in responding to digital disruption: A factor-based study of the newspaper industry. *Journal of Management Information Systems, 32*(1), 39–81.
23. Kraemer, K. L., & King, J. L. (2006). Information technology and administrative reform: Will e-government be different? *International Journal of Electronic Government Research, 2*(1), 1–20.
24. Lindgren, I., Toll, D., & Melin, U. (2021). Automation as a driver of digital transformation in local government: Exploring stakeholder views on an automation initiative in a Swedish municipality. In *DG.O'21: DG.O2021: The 22nd Annual International Conference on Digital Government Research* (pp. 463–472). ACM.
25. Luftman, J. (2000). Assessing business-IT alignment maturity. *Communications of the Association for Information Systems, 4*(1), 1–51.
26. Luftman, J., Lyytinen, K., & Zvi, T. B. (2017). Enhancing the measurement of information technology (IT) business alignment and its influence on company performance. *Journal of Information Technology, 32*(1), 26–46.
27. Luna-Reyes, L. F., & Gil-Garcia, J. R. (2014). Digital government transformation and internet portals: The co-evolution of technology, organisations, and institutions. *Government Information Quarterly, 31*(4), 545–555.
28. Meijer, A., & Bekkers, V. (2015). A metatheory of e-government: Creating some order in a fragmented research field. *Government Information Quarterly, 32*(3), 237–245.
29. Mergel, I. (2018). Open innovation in the public sector: Drivers and barriers for the adoption of challenge.gov. *Public Management Review, 20*(5), 726–745.

30. Moore, M. H. (1995). *Creating public value: Strategic management in government*. Harvard University Press.
31. Panagiotopoulos, P., Klievink, B., & Cordella, A. (2019). Public value creation in digital government. *Government Information Quarterly, 36*(4), 101421.
32. Plesner, U., Justesen, L., & Glerup, C. (2018). The transformation of work in digitised public sector. *Journal of Organisational Change Management, 31*(5), 1176–1190.
33. Selander, L., & Jarvenpaa, S. L. (2016). Digital action repertoires and transforming a social movement organisation. *MIS Quarterly, 40*(2), 331–352.
34. Vial, G. (2019). Understanding digital transformation: A review and a research agenda. *Journal of Strategic Information Systems, 28*(2), 118–144.
35. Walsham, G. (2006). Doing interpretive research. *European Journal of Information Systems, 15*(3), 320–330.
36. Winkler, T. (2013). IT governance mechanisms and administration/IT alignment in the public sector: A conceptual model and case validation. In *Wirtschaftsinformatik Proceedings* (pp. 831–845). AIS.
37. Yeow, A., Soh, C., & Hansen, R. (2018). Aligning with new digital strategy: A dynamic capabilities approach. *The Journal of Strategic Information Systems, 27*(1), 43–58.
38. Yin, R. K. (2017). *Case study research and applications*. Sage.

On What Kind of Applications Can Clustering Be Used for Inferring MVC Architectural Layers?

Dragoş Dobrean and Laura Dioşan

Abstract Mobile applications are one of the most used pieces of software nowadays, as they continue to expand, the architecture of those software systems becomes more important. In the fast-paced domain of the mobile world, the applications need to be developed rapidly and they need to work on a wide range of devices. Moreover, those applications need to be maintained for long periods and they need to be flexible enough to work and interact with new hardware. Model View Controller (MVC) is one of the most widely used architectural patterns for building those kinds of applications. In this paper, we are analysing how an ML technique, in fact clustering, can be used for detecting autonomously the conformance of various mobile codebases to the MVC pattern. With our method *CARL*, we pave the way for creating a tool that automatically validates a mobile codebase from an architectural point of view. We have analyzed *CARL*'s performance on 8 iOS codebases distributed into 3 different classes based on their size (small, medium, large) and it has an accuracy of **81%**, an average Mean Silhouette coefficient of **0.81**, and an average Precision computed for each layer of **83%**.

Keywords Software architecture recovery · Mobile SDK · Clustering

1 Introduction and Context

Mobile applications are one of the most important software products nowadays used by hundreds of millions of people [17]. These applications need to be flexible to change as the entire domain is fast-paced, there is a constant flux of new hardware and software updates that these applications need to take advantage of, to stay rel-

D. Dobrean (✉) · L. Dioşan
Computer Science Department, Babes-Bolyai University, Mihail Kogălniceanu 1, Cluj-Napoca 400347, Cluj, Romania
e-mail: dragos.dobrean@ubbcluj.ro

L. Dioşan
e-mail: laura.diosan@ubbcluj.ro

© The Author(s), under exclusive license to Springer Nature Switzerland AG 2023
G. C. Silaghi et al. (eds.), *Advances in Information Systems Development*,
Lecture Notes in Information Systems and Organisation 63,
https://doi.org/10.1007/978-3-031-32418-5_7

evant. The software architecture used for building such products plays a major role in their success, as its heavily related to the flexibility and maintainability of these software product [3, 24, 25]. By respecting an architectural pattern the codebase becomes more testable and more extensible in the areas which are important for the business. In addition to this, having a well-defined architecture in place helps the new or inexperienced developers write new code more easily by having clear architectural guidelines in place. Moreover if implemented correctly the architectural pattern makes the entire codebase more open and accommodating to changes (hardware and software).

With this study, we pave the way for building an architecture checker system (that highlights architectural issues, early in the development phase) and examining if there is a correlation between the number of components, size of the codebase, and the performance of our approach. An automatic system that detects architectural layers and issues in the mobile codebase can be integrated into CI/CD pipelines for improving the architectural health of those projects or used as a quality gate. In a previous work [11], the architectural layers of mobile codebases were detected by some heuristics, but they have quite a few downsides. It needs to have the correct heuristics in place to yield good results. However, those might vary from one codebase to another and needs developer interaction (for configuring the heuristics), that could also introduce some bias. Furthermore, the detection approach will have to be adjusted every time the codebase evolves to another architectural pattern or when a new architectural layer/sublayer is introduced.

Thus, arose the need for an automatic and non-deterministic approach, in which machine learning techniques are used for automatically distributing the components of a mobile codebase into architectural layers. *CARL* is using information from the mobile SDKs as they contain more types of components, than web SDKs for instance and the majority of the mobile applications use them for building the UI interfaces. The proposed approach could also work on other platforms such as desktop applications. However, for this study, we are continuing to analyze mobile SDKs as they are richer and the vast majority of the mobile projects are using them. In this paper, we strengthen our findings regarding *CARL*, which is an unsupervised approach, involving a clustering step. Related work in applying clustering techniques for detecting architectural layers already exists [15, 20]. However, none of those approaches takes into consideration the SDK information or is specifically designed for mobile applications.

We are extending our findings by better validating our approach and checking on what types of mobile applications does this method work better. We have enriched the validation phase by adding more codebases (we have added 5 new projects) and split them into 3 categories (small, medium, and large applications, based on the number of components). Moreover, we are enhancing the analysis mechanism by adding external metrics (Silhouette and Davies-Bouldin indexes for measuring the clustering performance and homogeneity, and completeness scores for measuring the integrity of our approach). Furthermore, we address the evaluation of our approach as well as its applicability and efficiency on different types of applications with new research questions. Last but not least, we look at the correlation between the number of components in a codebase and the performance of our approach, to identify classes of applications in which our method works best.

The main **research challenges** are: assesing the performance of our detection method *CARL* on different-sized codebases and investigating if there is a correlation between the size of the codebase and the performance of *CARL*.

The following Section presents the background for our work using text mining and unsupervised ML methods in architecture reconstruction and detection as well as insights about the analyzed architectural pattern Model View Controller (MVC). Section 3 talks about our approach *CARL*, the evaluation process is outlined in Sect. 4 together with the conducted experiments. In Sect. 5 we present the downsides of our approach, and at the end of the paper (Sect. 6) we talk about our conclusions and some directions for further work.

2 Background

For the purpose of this work, our focus was on one of the most prolific presentational architectural patterns, MVC [9], one of the most widely and commonly used architectural pattern that represents the foundation for more specialised architectural patterns such as Model View Presenter or Model View View Model. MVC is a software architecture frequently used in client applications that separates the elements of the codebase in 3 layers: Model (business logic), View (user input/output) and Controller (mediator between the Model and the View). MVC continues to be one of the most used architectural patterns on mobile platforms, a survey conducted in 2019 and filled by over 2000 developers showed that over 66% of the developers use MVC as an architectural pattern, being the most popular of all the architectural choices [34].

Architecture reconstruction methods are two-folded: identification of architectural modules (by clustering) and identification of architectural rules among modules. Several approaches were proposed to support the architecture reconstruction process based on static analysis. A part of these approaches exploit the structural information extracted from the codebase [7, 23], another part exploit the lexical information [8], while some recent approaches exploit both of them [15, 20]. Furthermore, few of them consider the architectural style of the system under analysis. Because our empirical validation is performed in the context of three iOS applications and Apple's flavour of MVC which can be viewed as a linear layered architectural pattern, we describe in what follows several approaches that take into account the particularities of the layered-based architecture. Similar to the general systems case, the approaches developed for analysing the layer-style projects take into account either the structural features of the codebase [19, 36] or the hybrid (structural and lexical) features [4, 28].

Even if these approaches are able to identify the codebase's components that belong to each layer, in the case of mobile applications they cannot be properly applied. For instance, the methods developed in [33] produce clusters with a nested structure that does not fit the MVC architecture that can be viewed as a layered-architecture. To our knowledge, there are not any approaches that use the information from SDK for inferring the architectural layers of a codebase, hence why we could not compare our method against another proposal. Tools such as ARCADE [6] are not developed for mobile platforms and they are not fit for purpose when applying them to mobile development languages such as Swift or Kotlin.

Vocabulary The following definitions are used throughout the remainder of the paper: **component**—the building block of software architectures and patterns [18]; it can be a programming language structure such as class, struct, another system or subsystem (e.g. CarBookingViewController—class, User—model entity, struct); **layer**—a set of components which perform the same role in the software system [29] (e.g. Model layer from MVC—responsible for the business logic of the application, Coordinator layer—responsible for keeping the state of the application and deciding when and how to alter it); **module**—a set of components that are related, fulfill the same general purpose; **class** (of applications)—a category of applications based on the number of components.

3 CARL—A Smart Framework for Automatic Detection of Architectural Layers in Mobile Codebases

Mobile applications are usually client—presentational applications, they commonly use monolithic architectures and are frequently self-contained. The purpose of *CARL* is to identify the architectural layers in those codebases based on the scope of the composing components. Such a system could be a real help for both the developers which would be constrained to write better code as well as for the management team which could see in real time the architectural health of the codebase.

The applicability of *CARL* was studied and explained in one of our previous articles [13], our research has shown that over 60% of the students struggle with architectural issues, and over 94% of them make those mistakes, unknowingly in the projects they hand in (according to their instructors). In terms of professional developers, all the responders to our survey stated they encounter architectural issues at least once a month. Over 90% of the participants in our study agreed that a tool like *CARL* would help them write better code.

We base our research on the idea that components from the same architectural layer should have similarities (the same purpose, the same interface, or they achieve the same system goal). In order to detect those similarities and not to restrict our research to a single platform or a single programming language, *CARL* performs a static code analysis and groups the elements from the codebase on layers by exploring a multi-modal knowledge extracted from: API contracts, public/private method and properties definition, inheritance mechanism.

CARL's mechanism involves more stages. In the first phase, *CARL* identifies the program elements (classes, procedures, data structures, etc.) contained in the source code and constructs the abstract representation that reflects the dependencies between these elements. This phase can be done with certain tools, specific for different programming languages and development environments (such as SourceKitten for Swift, or kotlinx.ast for Kotlin). The second stage of the process is to extract information related to the source code architecture. A directed graph is constructed based on the result from the previous stage. This graph reflects the relationships between the program elements. The first two steps of *CARL* are similar to those of *mACS* [11] and more details about them can be found in [12].

The next step, that of architecture's identification, uses an unsupervised learning technique, in which structural and lexical information associated with different program elements is used and which results in a clustering of the elements into the basic categories of an architectural model. ML algorithms are one of the most powerful tools we have for finding patterns in data. Since every project is different we have decided to use an unsupervised and autonomous algorithm for finding relations between the elements of the codebase. Unsupervised denotes from an ML perspective that the algorithm needs no prior knowledge for finding patterns in data, while autonomous means there is no developer interaction needed while using the proposed approach. These two attributes (unsupervised and autonomous) enhance *CARL* to be a smart system/framework.

In terms of Machine Learning, the investigated association component-layer is considered a clusterisation problem: grouping components into clusters without an a-priori knowledge of the category they belong to. The clustering process follows three important steps:

- extract relevant information (features) from the raw data source; in our case, each codebase represents an instance of the dataset;
- use all the features or just some of them to analyse the similarities among components and to build a clustering model; the output generated in this step is, in fact, a division of the data;
- validate the obtained clusters by using evaluation standards.

For the clustering part of our approach, we have discovered using a trial and error approach that Agglomerative Clustering [5, 27] works best for splitting the components of the codebase into architectural layers, and this is what *CARL* uses.

For pilotating our approach, we have conducted a preliminary study where, based on the available information extracted from the codebase, we searched the combination of features which would yield the best results in terms of correctly splitting the codebase into architectural layers [12]. For this part of the investigation, we have used a validation application from which different sets of features were been extracted. This case study is actually an iOS E-Commerce application which has over 20.000 lines of code and uses MVC architecture (this application was also included in the experiments we conducted in the current paper). Two senior iOS developers with over 5 years of development experience had constructed the ground truth by manually labelling the components of the validation application. They tagged the components of the codebase separately and afterwards, they cross checked the differences and agreed on the correct architectural layer where a component should be

Table 1 Analysis of all five versions of *CARL* on the validation application

	Model		View		Controller		Accuracy
	Precision	Recall	Precision	Recall	Precision	Recall	
CARL-F_1	0.50	0.01	0.22	1,00	1,00	0.10	0.24
CARL-F_2	0.49	0.93	0.17	0.09	1,00	0.08	0.46
CARL-F_3	0.62	0.75	0.33	0.53	0.65	0.22	0.52
CARL-F_4	0.70	0.93	0.84	0.83	0.99	0.56	0.78
CARL-F_5	0.76	0.99	1.00	1.00	0.99	0.57	0.85

placed. In their analysis the definition of a codebase component (interface, inheritance, name) had a higher importance than the body of the functions since the code written in a component can present various design and architectural smells, since the purpose of *CARL* is to place the components in the right architectural layers not to highlight architectural drift.

The preliminary study [12] resulted in 5 different approaches which incrementally improved the accuracy of the clusterization process on the validation application as seen on Table 1:

- **CARL** F_1 (*Number of dependencies*): how many dependencies a component has with each of the other codebase's components; we use $F_1(c_i)$, for all components c_i ($i \in \{1, 2, \ldots, n\}$) of the codebase;
- **CARL** F_2 (*Presence of dependencies*): the type of dependencies that it has with each of the other codebase's components;
- **CARL** F_3 (*Name distance*): how many dependencies it has with each of the other codebase's components and the distances between the name of the current component and the names of the other codebase's components; the name distances are computed by using specific text mining methods [22].
- **CARL** F_4 (*Keywords presence*): the features F_3 are enriched by the keyword-based features;
- **CARL** F_5 (*SDK inheritance*): the features F_4 are enriched by the SDK's inheritance-based features.

For all these feature subsets, the same agglomerative clustering algorithm is applied in order to detect the clusters which encode architectural layers. In the initial study the focus was on analysing MVC architectures; ergo, the number of clusters were set to 3 (Model, View and Controller). After the clustering process is completed, *CARL* assigns responsibilities to the layers based on the types of their components and their inheritance (e.g. the cluster with the most items that inherits from UIViewController is marked as Controller layer).

The best subset of features identified in the preliminary study is used in a second more complex one, when eight application are investigated (see the details in Sect. 4.3). Finally, the findings are analysed and possible improvements are suggested. For the rest of the study we are focusing only on the iOS platform and we are analysing Swift codebases. However, our proposed approach can be easily extrapolated to other platforms which use SDKs for building user interfaces and are presentational software products.

4   Numerical Experiments

We validate our approach by applying it to various MVC iOS codebases. MVC was studied by both practitioners and academia [9] and paves the way for analyzing more specialized architectural patterns that descend from MVC (MVVM, MVP, etc.). Our analysis was focused on the iOS platform; however, the same process can be applied to any other platform which uses MVC and SDKs for building UI interfaces. We extend our previous study [12] with new research questions. In this study we are interested in the effectiveness of our approach on more different sized codebases, we examine the performance of the clustering process and inspect its applicability and efficiency on 3 classes of applications (small, medium, large) of the process by answering the following research questions:

- RQ1—How effective is the proposed categorization method compared to manual inspections?[1]
- RQ2—What is the clustering process performance when using the proposed approach?[2]
- RQ3—On what class of applications does this method work best?
- RQ4—What is the reliability of *CARL* when compared to *mACS*?
- RQ5—What is the extensibility and maintainability of the codebases by using CARL for inferring architectural layers?

4.1   Analysed Codebases

We have enriched our analysis with five new codebases: Firefox, Game, Stock, Education and Apple's Demo for AR/VR applications. The analysis was conducted on applications from different domains, different sizes, different development styles (private, open-source, Apple's example). For this study, we were interested in analyzing mobile codebases that follow the rules of the MVC architecture, as it one of the most used architectural patterns of those types of software products [34]. To our knowledge, there does not exist a selection of repositories used for analyzing iOS applications. iOS was chosen as opposed to Android as it implements MVC more consistently and Apple encourages the developers to be aware and respect architectural patterns, especially MVC [1].

---

[1] Metrics like accuracy, precision, and recall will be used for this purpose.

[2] The performance can be evaluated through metrics like homogeneity, completeness, Silhouette Coefficient score, Davies-Bouldin index.

Table 2 Description of investigated applications together with the split by number of components

Application	Blank	Comment	Code	#comp	Class
Demo [2]	785	424	3364	27	Small
Game [private]	839	331	2113	37	Small
Stock [private]	1539	751	5502	96	Medium
Education [private]	1868	922	4764	105	Medium
Wikipedia [35]	6933	1473	35640	253	Medium
Trust [32],	4772	3809	23919	403	Large
E-Commerce [private]	7861	3169	20525	433	Large
Firefox [26]	23392	18648	100111	514	Large

Table 2 presents the characteristics of the codebases: blank—refers to empty lines, comment—represents comments in the code, code states the number of code lines, while components represent the total number of components in the codebase. In addition to this, we've also split the codebases into 3 different classes, small (Demo and Game), medium (Stock, Education, Wikipedia, and Trust), and large (E-Commerce, Firefox). We've split the codebases into classes based on the number of components because we are interested in whether or not *CARL* is able to correctly place all the components in the right architectural layers, not on the complexity of the components and how big they are (number of lines).

4.2 Evaluation Metrics

During the validation, we are interested in both the correctness and the integrity of the categorization process. Three metrics are of interest in the correctness validation: accuracy, precision, and recall [14], while the integrity is measured through some specific clustering scores: homogeneity and completeness [30]. Besides, we were also interested in the performance of the clustering process, and we have used ML-specific metrics for analyzing this Silhouette Coefficient (Silh. Coef.) score [31] and Davies-Bouldin Index (Davies) [10].

The Silhouette Coefficient score indicates how well are the components placed, while the Davies-Bouldin Index expresses whether or not the layers were correctly constructed. The homogeneity score denotes if a layer contains **only** members that are correctly placed, while the completeness score expresses the degree to which all the members of a layer are assigned by the categorization method to **the same** layer.

The accuracy, precision, and recall metrics are calculated for every architectural layer. For instance, if a codebase has 100 components in the Model layer (in the ground-truth) and *CARL* manages to correctly identify X, then the accuracy is X%. In the same manner, we calculate the precision and recall against the number of elements in each layer.

The ground truth was constructed by manually inspecting each component of the codebases by two senior iOS developers (with over 5 years experience on the iOS platform) who reached a consensus regarding the type of each component. Moreover, for the private projects, we also had developer documentation and internal architectural guidelines to aid the process, since those projects were developed by a mobile specialized software company.

Besides these metrics, we also have two ones oriented for evaluating how well-suited the system is for expected changes: Cumulative Component Dependency (CCD) and Average Component Dependency (ACD) [16, 18].

- *The CCD is the sum, over all the components in a subsystem, of the number of components needed in order to test each component incrementally* [18].
- The ACD is defined as the ration between the CCD of the subsystem and the number of components of the analysed subsystem [18]. $ACD = \frac{CCD(Subsystem)}{\#Components}$.

The CCD indicates the cost of developing, testing, and maintaining a subsystem. When developing a new feature or modifying an already existing one in a large number of cases the changes will impact more components of the subsystem, that is why the cost is better reflected by using the ACD metric. Note that architectural change metrics (e.g. architecture-to-architecture, MoJoFM, cluster-to-cluster [21]) can not be used to establish which rules are violated since the conceptual/intended architectures of the analyzed systems are unknown.

4.3   Empirical Evaluation

After the experiments were ran we analysed the data and answered the research questions based on the results obtained. This subsection presents our findings.

RQ1—How effective is the proposed categorisation method compared to manual inspections?

Using *CARL-F_5* approach we have obtained an average accuracy of **81.17%** on all the analysed codebases. We have observed that on one of the most complex and largest projects—Firefox—we have obtained an accuracy of **91.17%**. In the case of the worst performing codebases analysed with our method, we have found out that the elements did not have a consistent naming convention. They did not contain many elements which had similarities between names or contained one of the used keywords.

Our method works better in the cases where the codebase is consistent in respects to naming conventions for each architectural layer. Table 3 presents the results of the proposed method on all the analysed codebases.

From Tables 2 and 3 we can easily deduce that proposed approach works on both large projects as well as smaller ones: we have good accuracies for large projects

Table 3 *CARL-F₅* results in terms of detection quality

Codebase	Model		View		Controller		Accuracy
	Precision	Recall	Precision	Recall	Precision	Recall	
Firefox	0.92	0.95	1.00	0.99	0.73	0.64	0.91
Wikipedia	0.78	0.83	1.00	0.54	0.83	0.98	0.82
Trust	0.79	0.69	0.38	0.66	0.62	0.57	0.66
E-comm	0.76	0.99	1.00	1.00	0.99	0.57	0.85
Game	0.87	0.95	0.75	1.00	1.00	0.75	0.88
Stock	0.64	0.98	1.00	0.59	1.00	0.61	0.76
Education	0.55	0.98	0.50	0.05	0.95	0.44	0.62
Demo	0.96	1.00	1.00	0.75	1.00	1.00	0.96

(Firefox) as well as for the smaller ones (Game). Our approach however, is greatly impacted by the coding standards and the consistencies of the project. The Education codebase had a recall of only *0.05* which is extremely low. We have analysed the codebase to find the cause and we have discovered that the components did not have a coding standard and a naming convention in place. Also the number of elements in the codebase was small—ergo the clustering algorithm has problems in correctly splitting the elements. The scores chosen for the features detection in the preliminary study [12] might need to be adjusted for some of the analysed codebases, in order for those to yield better results. A better scoring mechanism should be implemented in order to remove the variability of the results.

RQ2—What is the clustering process performance when using the proposed approach?

Apple's AR/VR example (Demo project) codebase performed best from a clustering performance perspective when we applied the proposed method. Table 4 shows the clustering performance on all the codebases, and we can see that Apple's appli-

Table 4 *CARL-F₅* results in terms of cohesion and coupling of identified clusters. Homogeneity and completeness of the analysed codebases

Codebase	Mean silhouette coefficient	Davies-Bouldin index	Homogeneity score	Completeness score
Firefox	0.78	0.44	0.60	0.62
Wikipedia	0.74	0.43	0.50	0.56
Trust	0.73	0.42	0.19	0.17
E-comm	0.78	0.32	0.66	0.73
Game	0.89	0.32	0.73	0.78
Stock	0.82	0.37	0.40	0.49
Education	0.78	0.32	0.16	0.30
Demo	0.95	0.05	0.80	0.90

cation scored nearly perfect on the Mean Silhouette Coefficient as well as in the case of the Davis-Bouldin Index. The Mean Silhouette Coefficient was better for small codebases in which there were fewer types of components as the distinction between the three clusters (corresponding to the Model, View and Controller layer) was more pronounced. In the case of larger codebases where we had many components that fulfilled various micro purposes in each layer, the performance of the clustering algorithm decreased. The Davies-Bouldin Index was also worst in the case of large codebases compared to the smaller ones. This is mainly due to the fact that in small codebases, just like in the case of the Mean Silhouette Coefficient, the clustering algorithm created better clusters (which have a higher density and a larger distance from the other clusters).

CARL achieved good homogeneity and completeness scores on both small (Demo, Game) codebases as well as on larger ones (Firefox, E-comm). The results are in-sync with the ones from Table 3 where accuracy, precision, recall were computed. The homogeneity and completeness score of the worst performing codebases (Trust, Education) are also caused by the naming conventions or the lack of conventions used in the codebase. Those had fewer components that had similarities between the names and did sometimes contain multiple keywords for the same element.

RQ3—On what class of applications does this method work best?

CARL works well on all classes of codebases, when compared to the manual inspection of the codebases the best accuracy was obtained on one of the smallest codebases (Demo 0.96) followed closely by one of the largest codebases (Firefox 0.91) however similarly good values were also obtained for smaller codebases (Demo, Game 0.88).

Table 5 shows the average of the results on each class of codebases, from an accuracy point of view, the method works best on small and large-sized applications. Those results are in sync with the ones obtained at a layer level (precision and recall) and with Homogeneity and Completeness scores. While the method might separate better codebases that have fewer elements, as the differences between them are more prominent, it's important to notice that *CARL* also works well on large-sized codebases. The class of applications with the worst performance is the medium one, in this case, the separation of concerns is not that well defined, and coding standards are not always in place, hence our feature selection does not yield good results on

Table 5 Average (on applications classes) precision, recall, accuracy, homogeneity, completeness, adjusted rand index, mean silhouette coefficient, and Davies Bouldin index of *CARL* F_5 on the analyzed codebases against the ground truth.

Size	Average		Accuracy	Homog.	Compl.	ARI	Silh. Coef.	Davies
	Precision	Recall						
Small	0.93 ± 0.11	0.90 ± 0.13	0.93	0.77	0.84	0.80	0.92	0.18
Medium	0.81 ± 0.15	0.67 ± 0.24	0.74	0.35	0.45	0.33	0.78	0.37
Large	0.80 ± 0.16	0.78 ± 0.15	0.81	0.48	0.51	0.50	0.76	0.40

those. If the coding standards are not well implemented in the codebase, especially in one of a medium-size where the clustering doesn't have a lot of components to work with, *CARL* may not achieve the best results.

In terms of ML metrics, the Adjusted Rand Index (ARI), Davies Bouldin index, and Mean Shillouete Coefficient, those results (see Table 5) are in sync with the ones obtained when compared the results with the ground-truth. The clustering algorithm performed best on the small class of applications, followed by the large one. This is mainly because in smaller codebases the clusters are more pronounced, the components from a cluster have many more particularities than the items in the other clusters.

The results of our approach *CARL* are promising. However, for achieving a better clusterization performance on large and especially medium-sized codebases and other architectural patterns the proposed approach needs to be enriched with more features for the clusterization process and analyze them with respect to the entropy of the analyzed codebase. *CARL* can be efficient and scalable on both small and large projects, as long as the naming conventions and the coding standards are respected all over the codebase.

For measuring the correlation between the number of components and the performance of our proposed approach, we've used Pearson's Correlation Coefficient.

In terms of the correlation between accuracy and the number of components, as shown in Table 6, there is a perfect negative relationship in the case of small codebases, and a high positive relationship in the case of the large-sized applications. Those results are in sync with the ones obtained for precision and recall at a layer level. While in the case of large-sized codebases the results are not perfect, the values obtained indicate good performance for those types of applications. In the case of large applications, the results might not be perfect as the number of components is much higher and their roles are not as well defined as in the case of small applications. In addition to this, in the case of large codebases, the coding standards and naming conventions are often not consistent throughout the entire codebase which makes the detection mechanism less accurate, nevertheless, we have discovered strong correlations between the number of components and the accuracy of the method which indicates that our method is well suited for those kinds of codebases as well.

Table 6 Pearson's Correlation Coefficient between the number of components and the detection quality of *CARL* F_5

Size	Model		View		Controller		Accuracy
	Precision	Recall	Precision	Recall	Precision	Recall	
All	0.16	−0.35	0.02	0.37	−0.69	−0.31	−0.43
Small	−1.00	−1.00	−1.00	1.00	0.00	−1.00	−1.00
Medium	0.90	−1.00	0.46	0.38	−0.97	0.93	0.70
Large	0.90	0.52	0.71	0.69	0.03	0.97	0.85

In terms of correlation between the number of components and the precision for the Controller, the layer was the least valuable metric as the values indicate that there is no correlation between those two.

RQ4—What is the reliability of *CARL* when compared to *mACS*?

Table 7 presents the topological structure of the codebases after applying *CARL*. The table contains the number of components in each layer, together with the total number of relationships between the layers (#ExtDepends) and the number of unique ones (#DiffExtDepend). *CARL* managed to split the codebase in a way that there are fewer architectural violations for the Firefox, Wikipedia, Demo, and Game codebases when compared to *mACS* CoordCateg. approach. In the comparison with *mACS* CoordCateg, we have noticed an increase in the number of external dependencies (#CompleteExtDepend) for the Model layer and a decrease for the View and Controller layers. That means that the components inferred as Model by *CARL* had more external dependencies with the other layers. In addition to this, the components from the View layers also exhibited an increase in the number of external dependencies. Judging by the number of external dependencies and the relationship between the number of dependencies among the layers, *CARL* concluded that the components of the Model and View are more coupled than in the case of *mACS*. When compared to *mACS* SimpleCateg. approach, *CARL* identified much fewer violations of the architectural rules, while the results for the number of external dependencies have the same distribution and are roughly the same for both approaches, with small differences between the codebases and the layers.

RQ5—What is the extensibility and maintainability of the codebases by using *CARL* for inferring architectural layers?

The same metrics were used for analyzing the extensibility and maintainability of the codebases after applying *CARL* as in the case of *mACS*—CCD and ACD. Table 8 show the CCD and ACD metrics for each architectural layer (Model, View,

Table 7 Analysis of codebases dependencies—*CARL*

#ExtDepends / #DiffExtDepend								
Dependency	Firefox	Wiki.	Trust	E-comm.	Game	Stock	Educ.	Demo
View-Model	27/9	7/3	160/27	72/27	1/1	0/0	0/0	1/1
View-Ctrl	0/0	0/0	2/1	0/0	0/0	0/0	0/0	0/0
Model-View	22/10	0/0	16/10	1/1	0/0	17/3	5/1	0/0
Model-Ctrl	66/10	6/3	120/29	418/64	0/0	64/14	46/10	0/0
Ctrl-Model	290/44	86/33	124/23	292/63	38/6	51/14	71/20	9/6
Ctrl-View	126/26	31/13	77/48	148/29	2/2	41/10	0/0	5/3
#CompleteExtDepends								
Model	3281	1077	1332	1927	122	442	471	278
View	752	182	903	337	42	114	20	13
Ctrl	1897	3077	1066	1826	204	475	264	106

Table 8 CCD and ACD metrics for the analysed codebases—*CARL*

Codebase	Metric	Model	View	Controller	Total
Firefox	CCD	7713	1448	2682	11843
	ACD	15	12	16	14
Wikipedia	CCD	1187	338	4868	6393
	ACD	6	7	19	11
Trust	CCD	4092	1125	1603	6820
	ACD	12	9	11	11
E-comm	CCD	5179	684	2107	7970
	ACD	13	6	21	13
Game	CCD	108	28	85	221
	ACD	3	3	7	4
Stock	CCD	1173	112	463	1748
	ACD	11	5	12	9
Education	CCD	798	12	313	1123
	ACD	7	2	13	7
Demo	CCD	148	6	41	195
	ACD	4	1	6	4

Controller) as well as for the entire system. From a complexity point of view, the least complex system was Demo while the most complex one was Firefox. Those results are in sync with the ones obtained by *mACS*. In case of the E-Commerce application, *CARL* achieved results comparable with *mACS* SimpleCateg. approach. For all the other codebases, the results are fairly similar. The largest codebases have the highest CCD and ACD values as their codebases are more complex. When comparing *CARL* with *mACS*, the results obtained by *CARL* are higher than on both *mACS* approaches. The way *CARL* split the codebases resulted in layers that are harder to test and maintain as they contain more complexity.

5 Threats to Validity

After the analysis we have found out that our proposed method presents the following threats of validity. **Internal**: we discovered the features sets based on a trial and error approach; however, a different set of features which was not tested might yield better results. In order to have more details about this aspect, entropy could be used for measuring the importance of a feature. **External**: the experiments were ran on the iOS platform and on the Swift language, there might be other SDKs and languages which have particularities which we have not addressed in this paper. Moreover, we have focused this preliminary research only on the MVC pattern without taking much into consideration more complex architectural patterns and their particularities.

Conclusion: the analysed codebases might also be responsible for some bias and more experiments should be executed.

6 Conclusion and Further Work

With our study, we have increased the confidence in applying AI techniques for the detection of software architectures on mobile devices. Our proposed approach *CARL* works well on codebases that respect coding standards and development best practices, in its current state, small and large-sized codebases. *CARL* is an unsupervised method that needs no prior knowledge to work with a system and is fully autonomous. It paves the way for identifying architectural issues in the codebase by taking care of one of the most important aspects, the mapping between the codebase elements and the architectural layer they reside in.

We plan to further increase the accuracy of the system by running more experiments to find better-suited features that can be feed to the clusterization process as well as trying to leverage the behavioral aspects of the analyzed architectures. Later, we want to test the approach on more specialized architectures, which have more than three layers, and see in what other kinds of software architectures could *CARL* be applied. In the end, we intend to use this system for improving the architectural health of the mobile codebases by highlighting architectural issues early in the development phase *mobile ArchCheckSys* [11]. Furthermore, such a system can be successfully used for educational purposes, as it can aid beginners to write better-architectured code.

References

1. Apple. (2012). Model-view-controller. https://developer.apple.com/library/archive/documentation/General/Conceptual/CocoaEncyclopedia/Model-View-Controller/Model-View-Controller.html
2. Apple. (2019). Placing objects and handling 3d interaction. https://apple.co/3eHS164
3. Avgeriou, P., Kruchten, P., Ozkaya, I., & Seaman, C. (2016). Managing technical debt in software engineering (dagstuhl seminar 16162). In *Dagstuhl reports* (Vol. 6). Schloss Dagstuhl-Leibniz-Zentrum fuer Informatik.
4. Belle, A. B., El Boussaidi, G., & Kpodjedo, S. (2016). Combining lexical and structural information to reconstruct software layers. *IST, 74,* 1–16.
5. Bishop, C. M. (2006). *Pattern recognition and machine learning.* Springer.
6. Boudali, H., et al. (2008). Arcade-a formal, extensible, model-based dependability evaluation framework. In *13th IEEE ICECCS* (pp. 243–248). IEEE.
7. Cai, Y., et al. (2013). Leveraging design rules to improve SA recovery. In *ACM Sigsoft Conference on Quality of Software Architectures* (pp. 133–142). ACM.
8. Corazza, A., Di Martino, S., Maggio, V., & Scanniello, G. (2011). Investigating the use of lexical information for software system clustering. In *2011 15th European Conference on Software Maintenance and Reengineering* (pp. 35–44). IEEE.

9. Daoudi, A., et al. (2019). An exploratory study of MVC-based architectural patterns in android apps. In *ACM/SIGAPP SAC* (pp 1711–1720). ACM.
10. Davies, D. L., & Bouldin, D. W. (1979). A cluster separation measure. *IEEE Transactions on Pattern Analysis and Machine Intelligence, 2,* 224–227.
11. Dobrean, D., & Dioşan, L. (2019). *An analysis system for mobile applications MVC software architectures* (pp. 178–185). INSTICC, SciTePress.
12. Dobrean, D., & Dioşan, L. (2020). Detecting model view controller architectural layers using clustering in mobile codebases. In *ICSOFT* (pp. 1–6).
13. Dobrean, D., & Dioşan, L. (2021). Importance of software architectures in mobile projects. In *2021 IEEE 15th International Symposium on Applied Computational Intelligence and Informatics (SACI)* (pp. 000281–000286). IEEE.
14. Fawcett, T. (2006). An introduction to roc analysis. *Pattern Recognition Letters, 27*(8), 861–874.
15. Garcia, J., Ivkovic, I., & Medvidovic, N. (2013). A comparative analysis of software architecture recovery techniques. In *ICASE* (pp. 486–496). IEEE Press.
16. Ghorbani, N., Garcia, J., & Malek, S. (2019). Detection and repair of architectural inconsistencies in Java. In *Proceedings of the 41st International Conference on Software Engineering* (pp. 560–571). IEEE Press.
17. Intelligence, G. (2019). 2019 report. https://www.gsmaintelligence.com
18. Lakos, J. (1996). Large-scale c++ software design. *Reading, MA, 173*, 217–271.
19. Laval, J., Anquetil, N., Bhatti, U., & Ducasse, S. (2013). Ozone: Layer identification in the presence of cyclic dependencies. *SCP, 78*(8), 1055–1072.
20. Le, D. M. (2018). *Architectural evolution and decay in software systems.* Ph.D. Thesis, University of Southern California.
21. Le, D. M., Behnamghader, P., Garcia, J., Link, D., Shahbazian, A., & Medvidovic, N. (2015). An empirical study of architectural change in open-source software systems. In *2015 IEEE/ACM 12th Working Conference on MSR* (pp. 235–245). IEEE.
22. Levenshtein, V. I. (1966). Binary codes capable of correcting deletions, insertions, and reversals. In *Soviet physics doklady* (Vol. 10, pp. 707–710).
23. Lutellier, T., et al. (2015). Comparing SA recovery techniques using accurate dependencies. In *ICSE* (Vol. 2, pp. 69–78). IEEE.
24. Martini, A., & Bosch, J. (2015). The danger of architectural technical debt: Contagious debt and vicious circles. In *2015 12th Working IEEE/IFIP Conference on Software Architecture* (pp. 1–10). IEEE.
25. Martini, A., Bosch, J., & Chaudron, M. (2015). Investigating architectural technical debt accumulation and refactoring over time: A multiple-case study. *Information and Software Technology, 67,* 237–253.
26. Mozilla. (2018). Firefox iOS application. https://github.com/mozilla-mobile/firefox-ios
27. Murtagh, F. (1983). A survey of recent advances in hierarchical clustering algorithms. *The Computer Journal, 26*(4), 354–359.
28. Rathee, A., & Chhabra, J. K. (2017). Software remodularization by estimating structural and conceptual relations among classes and using hierarchical clustering. In *ICAICR* (pp. 94–106). Springer.
29. Richards, M. (2015). *Software architecture patterns.* O'Reilly Media, Incorporated.
30. Rosenberg, A., & Hirschberg, J. (2007). V-measure: A conditional entropy-based external cluster evaluation measure. In *EMNLP-CoNLL* (pp. 410–420).
31. Rousseeuw, P. J. (1987). Silhouettes: A graphical aid to the interpretation and validation of cluster analysis. *Journal of Computational and Applied Mathematics, 20,* 53–65.
32. Trust. (2018). Trust wallet iOS application. https://github.com/TrustWallet/trust-wallet-ios
33. Tzerpos, V., & Holt, R. C. (2000). ACCD: An algorithm for comprehension-driven clustering. In *Proceedings of 7th Working Conference on Reverse Engineering* (pp. 258–267). IEEE.
34. Verwer, D. (2020). The ios developer community survey. https://iosdevsurvey.com/2019/01-apple-platform-development/

35. Wikimedia. (2018). Wikipedia ios application. https://github.com/wikimedia/wikipedia-ios/tree/master
36. Zapalowski, V., Nunes, I., & Nunes, D. J. (2014). Revealing the relationship between architectural elements and source code characteristics. In *Proceedings of the 22nd International Conference on Program Comprehension* (pp. 14–25). ACM.

Police Interventions as a Context-Aware System. A Case of a Contextual Data Modelling

Radosław Klimek

Abstract Smart systems which operate in Intelligent Environments (IE) are complex. They analyse the large volumes of various contextual data on-line and often in real time to obtain, autonomously and reliably, the required pro-activeness of a system which operates pervasively. We proposed both a development framework for context-aware systems and a context-based decision making scheme for the system of managing police interventions, focusing on providing support for police patrols in life threatening situations. This system, owing to the symultaneous collection of rich contextual information from many police officers, which constitute the mobile network, as well as the complex processes of contextual reasoning, takes automatic decisions on supporting officers in emergency. We implemented the initial, yet not trivial, simulations of the system behaviour within the whole city. The results obtained prove the feasibility of the framework.

Keywords Pervasive Sensing · Gathering and Modelling Contextual Data · Decision Making · Police Interventions

1 Introduction

Smart systems, especially in connection with IoT (Internet of Things), AmI (Ambient Intelligence) or AI (Artificial Intelligence), and operating in IE (Intelligent Environments), may be a source of misunderstandings both on the part of the designers (difficulties) and the users (threats) of such systems. The difficulties and threats mentioned may be overcome by introducing appropriate methodologies and frameworks that will allow for better development of context-aware systems and consequently making decisions in the complex multi-agent environment.

The most general idea of the system supporting police interventions proposed herein, colloquially referred to as a *smart gun*, consists in the system searching

R. Klimek (✉)
AGH University of Science and Technology, al. Mickiewicza 30, 30-059 Krakow, Poland
e-mail: rklimek@agh.edu.pl

© The Author(s), under exclusive license to Springer Nature Switzerland AG 2023
G. C. Silaghi et al. (eds.), *Advances in Information Systems Development*,
Lecture Notes in Information Systems and Organisation 63,
https://doi.org/10.1007/978-3-031-32418-5_8

autonomously for support among police patrols located in the surroundings in the event of sudden and unplanned firing by a police officer during a regular intervention. Thus, a police officer is released from activities connected with communication and such a police officer can be focused on the firing situation and he/she can be certain that the support of colleagues will be soon provided automatically.

Our objective and contribution is to introduce an appropriate framework for the modelling and developments of context-aware and pervasively sensing systems which provide smart decisions as a result of the pervasively acquired contextual data, its online filtration and processing, including weighted MaxSAT solving. We will argue in favour of our approach showing the practical implementation of a non-trivial system supporting police services. The architecture of multi-agent system oriented at contextual data processing was proposed, where the agentification was carried out together with its behavioural model. We conducted the first few simulation experiments; these are the experiments on the scale of the entire city. The system increases the self-awareness of the environment and the processes of decision-making automation in IE.

2 Context Understanding and Modelling

According to a classic definition [5], a *context* is a collection of circumstances and facts surrounding a given object. Context awareness is a driver for smart human-system interactions, see also [9, 12–14], when providing different context categories for the context-aware features, which are necessary when considering pro-active actions on the basis of the contextual data. The introduction of subsequent notions will be illustrated with references to our system through the following phases: category identification (CI) $\rightarrow$ operational relationships (OR) $\rightarrow$ attributing $\rightarrow$ assigning.

2.1 Categorisation

Category identification (CI) means the conceptual data division into respective categories, see Fig. 1, in order to obtain the subsets of elements which are semantically disjunctive:

- *Individuality*—the circumstances in which an object is present, something in which it is involved, here: being on/off duty, also a patrol which is incomplete as a result of firing;
- *Time*—the circumstances related to the current and passing time, here: the time of an incident, i.e. a day or a night, current time, the prolonging duration of an incident;
- *Location*—the position of an object, its geolocation, as well as spatial relation, here: geolocation, also a bad/good (not safe/safe) district, i.e. with a higher/lower risk;

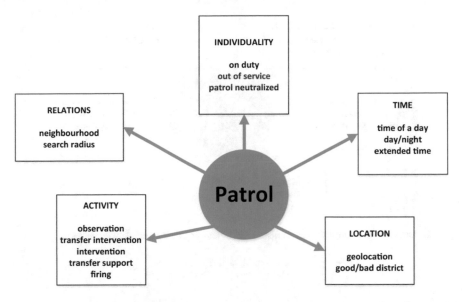

Fig. 1 The categorisation of the entire system contextual data in relation to a single police patrol

- *Activity*—information on activities which an object is involved in, here: the patrol statuses: observation, going for an intervention, intervention, going to provide support, firing;
- *Relations*—a relation towards other objects in the environment under consideration, here: searching radii both for intervention and support, different times of a day/night, etc.

Identified contextual data resulting from the categories proposed, see Fig. 1, affect considerably the decision-making processes of MC agent, see Sect. 3.

2.2 Operational Relationships

Operational relationships OR, see also Fig. 2, allow to plan activities on contextual data in the system under design using the following *R6 rule*:

- *Represent*—leaving the data unchanged, leaving the data as it is after its readout, for instance: current time readout, patrol geolocation;
- *Resolve*—data conversion, filtering or aggregating, to forms which are proper and readable in terms of the system needs;
- *Retain*—preserving unchanged data in a form obtained in a previous phase, data collection phase, here: e.g. current system time;
- *Reinforce*—data collection, perhaps merging and thus obtaining a new emphasising perspective, here: time/time stamp with patrol geolocation;

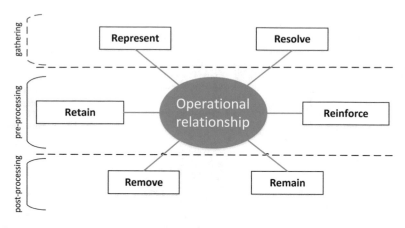

Fig. 2 Operational relationship as an operational model of contextual data conversion

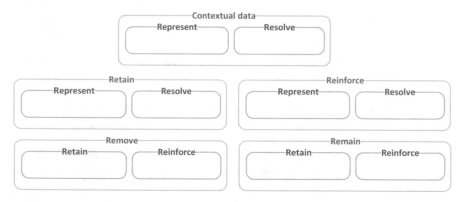

Fig. 3 The interrelation between the individual sets and subsets of contextual data, or a schema for a top-down selecting of successive disjoint subsets, see also Fig. 4

- *Remove*—data removal and not storing it, such data is not used until new values are read out, here: e.g. a current patrol distance from a location where it is to provide support;
- *Remain*—leaving data in the system until it is overwritten by the readout in a new data acquisition cycle, here: e.g. geolocation intervention locations.

Figure 3 presents the interrelations between the respective sets of contextual data. Furthermore, this allows to plan and track the processes of contextual data conversion. We assume that given subsets are pairwise non-intersecting.

2.3 Attributing

The next step is to attribute the information obtained concerning contextual data and its hierarchy. *Attributing* involves, firstly, assigning variables to the individual leaves of the tree shown in Fig. 4. The next step is *assigning* variables to the agents of the adopted MAS (the MAS architecture is proposed in Sect. 3). It means that individual agents operate on these variables. Both attributing and assigning allow us to build a rich picture of the MAS system operations, in particular, taking contextual data into account.

   To sum up the entire section: it allows for better understanding and management of contextual data, with consideration of said agent model. First, we identify the categories of contextual data, then we plan specific variables for each of them, however, multiple variables may be associated with each category. We evaluate how the OR (R6) model affects these variables (attributing), i.e. how particular variables will be processed in the system. In the end, we identify which variables will be required by particular agents (assigning). It gives us a good picture of contextual data processing in the entire context-aware system.

3 Multi-agent System

We propose the following division of agents constituting the entire multi-agent system (MAS) and its architecture. *Agentification* means the creation of specialised software objects which combines the autonomy and the specialisation of tasks. It allows

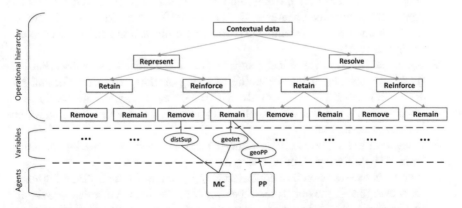

Fig. 4 Attributing contextual data and its hierarchy basing on the previous relations, see Figs. 3 and 4, and assigning individual variables to leaves. (For example, variables $geoInt$ ≡ geolocation of the intervention location; $distSup$ ≡ distance from the support location of a current patrol; $geoPP$ ≡ geolocation of the police patrol.) Then, assigning variables to agents. (The MAS architecture is shown in Fig. 5)

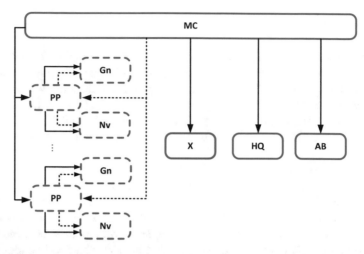

Fig. 5 Basic agent architecture, illustrated by only two PP agents, and agent relationships (solid ovals show permanent agents and dashed ovals show agents which may exist temporarily. Solid and dashed lines show agent constructions and destructions, respectively)

us to disperse well and balance the system activities. This agentification issue is close to the IoT (Internet of Things), which is discussed in some articles, see the articles by Maamar et al. [18], and by Kwan et al. [16]. Our approach, when considering an urban ecosystem, covers partially the proposed methodology for the agentification of things. Figure 5 presents the architecture of the proposed agent system.

MC   management centre, an agent initiating the system and other agents, and subsequently implementing the ongoing management, appoints and dismisses PP agents, it collects data on interventions from all PP, it stores and models incoming contextual data, it submits the demands for dispatching ambulances to the firing site to AB,

PP   police patrol, or police officer's smartwatch, it establishes its geolocation and sends it cyclically, at the beginning of being on duty, it creates Gn and Nv agents, it receives signals from MC with the order for regular intervention.

Gn   police officer's gun, it sends signals to PP, informing on the fact of firing, which is its fundamental role,

Nv   navigation in the police officer's car, it receives a new, indicated geolocation from PP with the order for directing the patrol to the spot,

X   it collects messages on the monitored area incoming from all PP and it hands them over to MC, the only role of the agent is to mediate in message providing, In the future, the entire system may be optimised in terms of increasing its capacity through many X agents,

HQ   police headquarters, command system, is capable of affecting the current situation by changing the values of given parameters affecting MC decisions, e.g. increasing or decreasing the number of patrols when providing support, changing the number of ambulances reaching the place, etc.

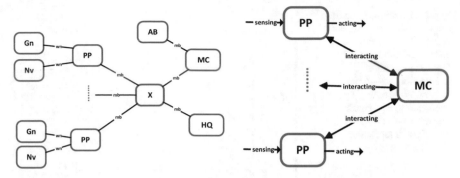

Fig. 6 The agent environment, left: the topology and types of communications ("wn" means a local wireless network and "mb" means use of a message broker), right: the model of agents' interactions

AB the centre of management and ambulances fulfilling the demand of MC.

The architecture presented may be developed in the future, for instance MC may be extended and decomposed by the separation of tasks. As already mentioned, Fig. 4 illustrates the assignment of context variables to individual agents.

Figure 6 shows the agent environments. Communication takes place either via the wireless local network (short-range radio, Bluetooth, etc.) or with the use of a message broker (e.g. Kafka, Rabbit, etc.). The logical model includes both the context sensing and action, but also the agents' communication.

We applied one simplification, although not a significant one. Usually, a patrol consists of two police officers—however, at this moment, we assume, for one patrol, the existence of one PP agent, patrol commander, one Nv agent, patrol car equipment, and Gn agent. In fact, police officers may have more than one gun.

4 Behavioural Model

4.1 Police Patrol

Let us present the behavioural model of the system based on the state diagrams in respect of police patrols, see Fig. 7. Each patrol can have one of the following states:

- **Observation** or **patrolling**—A patrol moving around a neighbourhood, usually moving slowly, stopping occasionally, observing the area patrolled until it is called for intervention or a firing incident;
- **Transfer intervention**—A patrol going to an (regular) intervention—upon the MC call, a patrol goes to an intervention to an indicated location; such a drive may be interrupted only by a call for support, if this takes place, there is switching to

Fig. 7 A state machine for a
single police patrol PP, basic
states only. (Observation is
both initial and final state.
Signals: oi—order
intervention, os—order
support, ri—reach
intervention, rs—reach
support, f—on fire,
fi—finish intervention,
ff—finish firing)

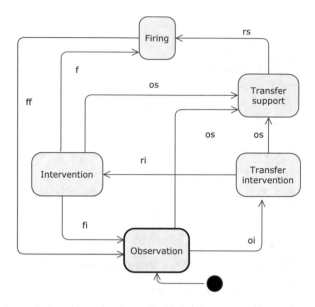

the support state, and the intended intervention still remains in the MC in the pool
of interventions requiring solving;

- **Intervention**—A patrol during an (regular) intervention—it may be interrupted
  only by a call for support in a firing incident, and the intended intervention goes
  back to the MC to the pool of interventions requiring solving;
- **Transfer support**—A patrol going to support—upon the MC call, a patrol goes to
  support to the indicated geolocation; such a patrol drive may be interrupted only by
  calling off, in the meantime, the assumed number of patrols in the support, if such
  calling off takes place, observing is started, but if a patrol going to support reaches
  its intended geolocation, it switches automatically to the during firing state;
- **Firing**—Patrol during firing or chasing—only during a regular intervention, it
  may change into a firing incident; a trigger here is firing a shot by one of the police
  officers; a patrol intervening originally becomes a firing host then;

A proper city map of the system operation procedure, with the patrol positions
marked, is available at the headquarters from the HQ agent; whereas, Fig. 7 presents
a state machine for each patrol on a patrol duty in the monitored area.

The other rules binding in the system are as follows:

- only one patrol indicated by the MC may go to an intervention;
- support in a firing incident may be provided by a certain number of patrols; nonethe-
  less, during a drive, a specific excess number of patrols may be called for support,
  and this redundancy is an effect of various calculations, including the distance of
  the patrols called from a target place, anticipated increased traffic hindering the
  drive, etc. – it is better to call more patrols, and the prospective excess may be called

off when the intended number is reached on the spot. Our context consideration extends [15] and Algorithm 1 shows how to get the list of supporting agents.

Algorithm 1 Negotiating fire support

Input: $geoInt$ ▷ geolocation of the intervention location, see also Fig. 4
Output: $supList$ ▷ list of agents to provide support
1: $Cx_t = P_t \cup X_t \cup Y_t$;   ▷ establish context Cx for the time t
2: $sizeSup := 1$;   ▷ public variables processed in lines 2–6
3: **for** every $var \in Y_t$ **do**   ▷ the size of support required
4:     $sizeSup := sizeSup \cdot (var.map)$ ▷ each variable is mapped
5: **end for**
6: $sizeSup := round(rdF \cdot C \cdot sizeSup)$;   ▷ redundancy factor rdF, const C set by HQ
7: $formula := \emptyset$;   ▷ private variables processed in lines 7–18
8: **for** every agent $\in P_t$ **do**
9:     **for** every $var \in X_t$ **do**
10:        Add var to the weighted MaxSAT problem in $formula$
11:     **end for**
12: **end for**
13: $supList := weightedMaxSAT(formula)$;
14: **if** $supList.len > sizeSup$ **then**   ▷ to obtain $supList.len = sizeSup$ in both cases
15:     Remove from $supList$ agents farthest from $geoInt$
16: **else**
17:     Add agents from $(P_t \setminus supList)$ closest to $geoInt$
18: **end if**

Regarding line 1: P_t is a set of negotiating agents, here $P_t = \{MC, PP_1, PP_2, \ldots\}$, Y_t is a set of *public* pieces of context data (variables), e.g. $Y_t = \{districtSafety, timeOfDay, dayOfWeek\}$, and X_t is a set of *private* pieces of context data (variables), e.g. $X_t = \{geoPP, currentState, serviceTime\}$. Lines 2–6 show public variables processing to determine the size of support required ($sizeSup$). Lines 7–18 show private variables processing to designate a specific set of agents ($supList$). Each variable in line 4 is mapped to correspond-ing numeric values, which in turn is set by HQ before or while the system is run-ning. For example, for variable $districtSafety$, the values of the following triple ($NotSafe, RatherSafe, Safe$) are mapped to numbers (2.5, 1.5, 1.0), respec-tively. Other public variables are processed in a similar way. Once the final value of $sizeSup$ is determined, see line 6, through the public contextual data analysis, it remains to designate the specific PP agents. This is solved as a weighted MaxSAT problem, see lines 7–18, where private pieces of contextual data are weights in the task, see also [11]. For example, a short distance to the shooting site (i.e. small difference between $geoInt$ and $geoPP$) has a high weight, $currentState = Observation$ is high, with $currentState = TransferIntervention$ rather low and $currentState = Intervention$ very low. Because the size of the designated optimal set of PP may be different than $sizeSup$, it is corrected, see lines 14–18, according to a simple distance criterion. We have already shown the effectiveness of the SAT solvers usage in article [8].

4.2 Outline of the Remaining Rules

The other behavioural rules are outlined briefly below:

- Selection for an ordinary intervention: the MC selects an observing patrol which is closest to the location of the planned intervention and calls it for going to an intervention. If in the assumed radius/area, there is no observing/available patrol, we wait until patrols are released from the current interventions so that they could undertake a new/subsequent intervention. A selection radius may be conditioned on a district (good/bad) and day time (day/night). The HQ may increase/decrease additionally these set searching parameters.
- during a firing incident, a police officer from the patrol may get injured, then such a patrol does not come back to its service;

The following, see Fig. 8, is marked on the city map in different colours: patrols in different states, patrols excluded after the loss of a police officer, ambulances, drones.

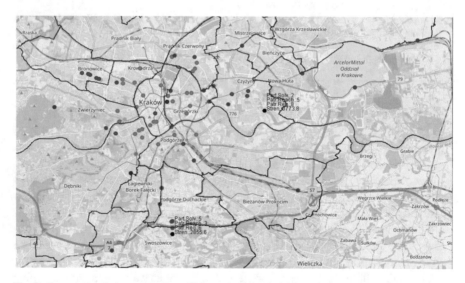

Fig. 8 System simulation screenshot. (Coloured points: dark blue—HQ; green—observing patrols; dark green—patrols returning to the HQ after finishing their service; orange—transfer to intervention; red—transfer to firing; blue—patrols after the termination of intervention, absent on the screen; violet—patrols after the termination of firing; white—neutralized, absent on the screen; pink—patrols which choose the route of further movement; red—a simple intervention that did not turn into a shootout; black—firing)

5 Simulation Results

5.1 Basic Assumptions

Figure 9 shows the environment in which the experiments were performed. Said environment consists of two basic components, namely, a system supporting the work of the police and an environment imitating the urban environment in the sense of generating interventions, turning some of them into shootings, etc. The basic guidelines concerning simulation rules are given below. Patrols move slowly in the observation mode, stopping occasionally. When a patrol is called to intervene, then a drive takes place based on the familiarity with parameters for the navigation subsystem, indicating a driving route, from the patrol starting point to the target point of intervention, the drive time is randomised concerning the distance. The intervention duration is chosen at random. The probability of a regular intervention changing into a firing incident is chosen at random; moreover, the time is selected at random, after which a standard intervention is likely to change, if applicable, into a firing incident; firing or chasing duration is randomised as well. All the above parameters are predefined but can be changed within their ranges before starting the simulation. The parameters characterizing the operation of the police patrols, and thus the course of the simulation, result from our knowledge and intuition, and in the future they can be consulted with the polices.

5.2 Course of the Simulation

The system was subject to simulation in order to verify the model created and its assumptions [17]. The simulation maps the real 24 h in a shorter period, i.e. events during the simulation happen faster (speed-up) than it would be in the real world. Figure 8 presents an exemplary panel of the simulation observer; it is similar to the panel found in the command centre, which is available for the HQ agent. The coloured points denote an event generated; the black colour refers to the most dangerous event connected with a firing incident, that is with the highest priority; the green colour indicates regular observations, and red points represent regular interventions.

The simulator enables the creation of many diagrams depicting a situation on the monitored area. An example here is Fig. 10 which presents police officers on duty on the monitored area and their involvement in the entire simulation process. Yet this

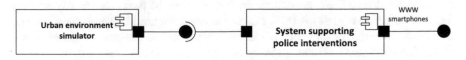

Fig. 9 Police supporting system and the urban simulator as separate components

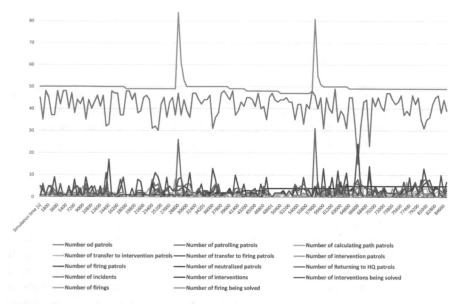

Fig. 10 The analysis of the police officers' involvement in the simulation. (Vertical axis—the current number of police officers, horizontal axis—subsequent simulation steps)

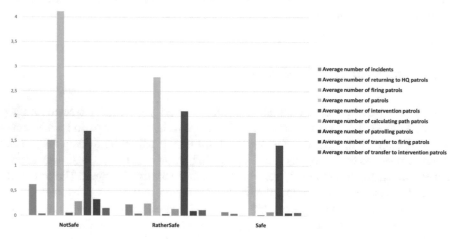

Fig. 11 Interventions in different city districts, worse districts are presented from left to right

figure shows many different events, see the caption in the bottom. The two peaks observed are due to a change of patrols, that is, some of them are already leaving the shift, and a new group is taking up the service. Figure 11 shows the course of the simulation with consideration of different city districts. The results show that the simulation is reliable and reflects reality well, that is in bad districts we have a greater number of shootings but also there are more patrols in such locations. Figure 12 shows

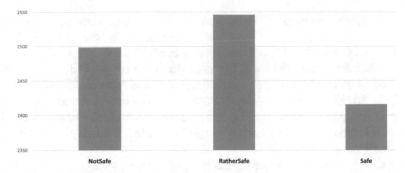

Fig. 12 Average values of the cumulative spatial proximity for districts

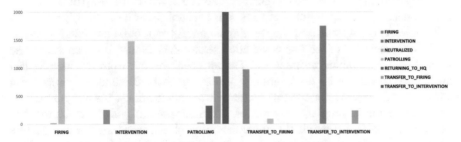

Fig. 13 Context transition, or state changes during the simulation. (Vertical axis—the current state, horizontal axis—number of state changes)

the average values of the total spatial proximity for the different categories of city districts. *Spatial proximity* means proximity and approaching by objects on the space under consideration. This shows the influence of contextual data on the system and decision making. On the other hand, the cumulative value of spatial proximity in bad districts is lower, which should come as no surprise as there are more patrols there, that is, more patrols are directed there.

Figure 13 shows how the patrol states changed during the course of the simulation, which gives a good image of the simulation assumption implementations. After the intervention, patrols most often undergo observing/patrolling. From patrolling, we most often turn to interventions. An intervention always transfer to firing, unless the call was redundant. The transfer to intervention is sometimes interrupted by the transfer to firing due to a sudden need for support.

6 Related Works

The concept of a context and contextual data is known and it was mentioned for the first time by Dey and Abowd [6]. Whereas, Zimmermann et al. [21] introduce the categories of a context, which is to cope with the complexity of contextual data and to facilitate understanding. We introduced a similar categorisation for contextual data but matching the reality of the system aiding police interventions, cf. [8, 21]. The article by Cheng et al. [4] also analyses the endeavours of research communities to understand the context. Whereas, the article by Bettini et al. [2] discusses context modelling techniques, introduces abstraction levels and other requirements. Perera et al. [19] survey context awareness from an IoT perspective. It addresses a great variety of techniques, methods and solutions related to context awareness and IoT. The article helped us to understand the background when introducing IoT for context-aware basics.

Biegel and Cahill [3] proposed the development framework to gather data from separate sensors, to represent a context and to reason about a context. It was designed for ad-hoc wireless environments. Our approach takes the relationship between contextual data and its operational aspects into account. Ferreira et al. [7] presented a framework to gather reasons concerning a context on mobile devices. By means of the encapsulation of the implementation sensor data details, it is exposed to the sensed context enabling abstractions. The approach results from the mobile data specificity and it can be used partially in our approach. Bardram [1] proposed a Java-based framework for creating context-aware applications. It supports runtime architecture and its programming model. From our point of view, this approach is oriented excessively towards the implementation phase, whereas, our approach is focused on the design stage. Perhaps, in the future, it will be advisable to combine both approaches. The smart gun idea is not completely new [20] but it is limited only to the identification of an authorised user. Such an approach is related to pattern recognition when biometric data is used. This article follows [10].

7 Conclusions

In order to ensure pro-activeness, the system processes complex contextual data; we proposed its categorisation corresponding to the field under design, and the entire framework with the data identified, so that it would be possible to obtain the clear image of its meaning in the system under design, to differentiate the individual roles, to plan the effective and efficient processes of contextual reasoning. We proposed a multi-agent system as the best environment for processing such contextual data.

The initially implemented simulation environment proves the feasibility of our proposal for context modelling and decision making in an environment with a rich set of contextual variables. We have not come across any significant efficiency limitations for average parameter values; perhaps, the planned stress tests will show some significant limitations of the system.

Further works will also consist in developing this environment to supply the full system analytics, to be able to affect the simulation process by any means, and also to research the phenomena characteristic for smart systems which operate in a smart city. It is also possible to introduce other actors, such as police squad groups in dangerous districts.

References

1. Bardram, J. E. (2005). The java context awareness framework (JCAF)—a service infrastructure and programming framework for context-aware applications. In H. W. Gellersen, R. Want, & A. Schmidt (Eds.), *Pervasive Computing* (pp. 98–115). Berlin Heidelberg, Berlin, Heidelberg: Springer.
2. Bettini, C., Brdiczka, O., Henricksen, K., Indulska, J., Nicklas, D., Ranganathan, A., & Riboni, D. (2010). A survey of context modelling and reasoning techniques. *Pervasive and Mobile Computing, 6*(2), 161–180. https://doi.org/10.1016/j.pmcj.2009.06.002
3. Biegel, G., & Cahill, V. (2004). A framework for developing mobile, context-aware applications. In *Proceedings of the 2nd IEEE Annual Conference on Pervasive Computing and Communications* (pp. 361–365). https://doi.org/10.1109/PERCOM.2004.1276875
4. Cheng, Z. A., Dimoka, A., & Pavlou, P. A. (2016). Context may be king, but generalizability is the emperor! *Journal of Information Technology, 31*(3), 257–264. https://doi.org/10.1057/s41265-016-0005-7
5. Dey, A. K. (2001). Understanding and using context. *Personal Ubiquitous Computing, 5*(1), 4–7. https://doi.org/10.1007/s007790170019
6. Dey, A. K., & Abowd, G. D. (2000). Towards a better understanding of context and context-awareness. In *Workshop on the What, Who, Where, When, and How of Context-Awareness (CHI 2000).* http://www.cc.gatech.edu/fce/contexttoolkit/
7. Ferreira, D., Kostakos, V., & Dey, A. K. (2015). AWARE: Mobile context instrumentation framework. *Frontiers in ICT, 2*, 6. https://doi.org/10.3389/fict.2015.00006
8. Klimek, R. (2018). Exploration of human activities using message streaming brokers and automated logical reasoning for ambient-assisted services. *IEEE Access, 6*, 27127–27155. https://doi.org/10.1109/ACCESS.2018.2834532
9. Klimek, R. (2020). Sensor-enabled context-aware and pro-active queue management systems in intelligent environments. *Sensors, 20*(20), 1–29. https://doi.org/10.3390/s20205837
10. Klimek, R. (2022). Police interventions as a context-aware system. A case of a contextual data modelling. In R. Buchmann, et al. (Eds.), *Proceedings of 30-th International Conference on Information Systems Development (ISD 2022)*, 31 August–2 September, 2022, Cluj-Napoca, Romania (p. 12).
11. Klimek, R., & Kotulski, L. (2014). Proposal of a multiagent-based smart environment for the IoT. In J. C. Augusto, T. Zhang (Eds.), *Workshop Proceedings of the 10th International Conference on Intelligent Environments*, Shanghai, China, 30th June–1st of July 2014. *Ambient Intelligence and Smart Environments* (Vol. 18, pp. 37–44). IOS Press. https://doi.org/10.3233/978-1-61499-411-4-37
12. Klimek, R., & Kotulski, L. (2015). Towards a better understanding and behavior recognition of inhabitants in smart cities. a public transport case. In L. Rutkowski, et al. (Eds.), *Proceedings of 14th International Conference on Artificial Intelligence and Soft Computing (ICAISC 2015)*, 14–18 June, 2015, Zakopane, Poland. *Lecture Notes in Artificial Intelligence* (Vol. 9120, pp. 237–246). Springer. https://doi.org/10.1007/978-3-319-19369-4_22
13. Klimek, R., & Rogus, G. (2014). Modeling context-aware and agent-ready systems for the outdoor smart lighting. In L. Rutkowski, et al. (Eds.), *Proceedings of 13th International Conference on Artificial Intelligence and Soft Computing (ICAISC 2014)*, 1–5 June, 2014, Zakopane, Poland. *Lecture Notes in Artificial Intelligence* (Vol. 8468, pp. 269–280). Springer. https://doi.org/10.1007/978-3-319-07176-3_23
14. Klimek, R., & Rogus, G. (2015). Proposal of a context-aware smart home ecosystem. In L. Rutkowski, et al. (Eds.), *Proceedings of 14th International Conference on Artificial Intelligence and Soft Computing (ICAISC 2015)*, 14–18 June, 2015, Zakopane, Poland. *Lecture Notes in Artificial Intelligence* (Vol. 9120, pp. 412–423). Springer. https://doi.org/10.1007/978-3-319-19369-4_37
15. Kröhling, D. E., Chiotti, O., & Martínez, E. C. (2021). A context-aware approach to automated negotiation using reinforcement learning. *Advanced Engineering Informatics, 47*. https://doi.org/10.1016/j.aei.2020.101229

16. Kwan, J., Gangat, Y., Payet, D., & Courdier, R. (2016). An agentified use of the internet of things. In *IEEE International Conference on Internet of Things (iThings) and IEEE Green Computing and Communications (GreenCom) and IEEE Cyber, Physical and Social Computing (CPSCom) and IEEE Smart Data (SmartData)* (pp. 311–316). https://doi.org/10.1109/iThings-GreenCom-CPSCom-SmartData.2016.76

17. Lepianka, S. (2022). System for simulating police interventions in a smart city. Engineering diploma thesis, supervisor: Radosław Klimek, AGH University of Science and Technology.

18. Maamar, Z., Faci, N., Boukadi, K., Ugljanin, E., Sellami, M., Baker, T., & Angarita, R. (2018). How to agentify the internet-of-things? In *12th International Conference on Research Challenges in Information Science (RCIS)* (pp. 1–6). https://doi.org/10.1109/RCIS.2018.8406665

19. Perera, C., Zaslavsky, A. B., Christen, P., & Georgakopoulos, D. (2014). Context aware computing for the internet of things: A survey. *IEEE Communications Surveys and Tutorials, 16*(1), 414–454.

20. Weiss, D. R. (1994). Smart gun technologies: One method of eliminating unauthorized firearm use. In *1994 Proceedings of IEEE International Carnahan Conference on Security Technology* (pp. 169–172).

21. Zimmermann, A., Lorenz, A., & Oppermann, R. (2007). An operational definition of context. In *Proceedings of the 6th International and Interdisciplinary Conference on Modeling and Using Context, CONTEXT'07*, Roskilde, Denmark. *Lecture Notes in Artificial Intelligence* (Vol. 4635, pp. 558–571). Springer.

Relevance Judgment Convergence Degree—A Measure of Assessors Inconsistency for Information Retrieval Datasets

Dengya Zhu, Shastri L. Nimmagadda, Kok Wai Wong, and Torsten Reiners

Abstract The quality of training/testing datasets is critical when a model is trained and evaluated by the annotated datasets. In Information Retrieval (IR), documents are annotated by human experts if they are relevant or not to a given query. Relevance judgment of human assessors is inherently subjective and dynamic. However, a small group of experts' relevance judgment results are usually taken as ground truth to "objectively" evaluate the performance of an IR system. Recent trends intend to employ a group of judges, such as outsourcing, to alleviate the potentially biased judgment results stemmed from using only a single expert's judgment. Nevertheless, different judges may have different opinions and may not agree with each other, and the inconsistency in human relevance judgment may affect the IR system evaluation results. Further, previous research focused mainly on the quality of documents, rather on the quality of queries submitted to an IR system. In this research, we introduce Relevance Judgment Convergence Degree (RJCD) to measure the quality of queries in the evaluation datasets. Experimental results reveal a strong correlation coefficient between the proposed RJCD score and the performance differences between two IR systems.

Keywords Relevance judgment · Information retrieval · Information system development

---

D. Zhu (✉) · T. Reiners
School of Management, Curtin University, Perth, WA, Australia
e-mail: d.zhu@curtin.edu.au

T. Reiners
e-mail: t.reiners@curtin.edu.au

S. L. Nimmagadda
Curtin University, Perth, WA, Australia
e-mail: shastri.nimmagadda@curtin.edu.au

K. W. Wong
Murdoch University, Perth, WA, Australia
e-mail: k.wong@murdoch.edu.au

© The Author(s), under exclusive license to Springer Nature Switzerland AG 2023
G. C. Silaghi et al. (eds.), *Advances in Information Systems Development*,
Lecture Notes in Information Systems and Organisation 63,
https://doi.org/10.1007/978-3-031-32418-5_9

1   Introduction

Searching for information from the Web is becoming a ubiquitous activity that is part of our daily life for all sections of society. As highlighted in Saracevic [24], most people seek information according to what they know at hand, and assume that the relevance is based on a "y'know" notion that does not require explanation. The notion of information relevance is also adjudged for the success of search engines, while a formal, complex definition of such relevance is presented in [24]. Furthermore, one of the basic objectives of any IR system is to improve the relevance of search results after a user query (used to express the user's information need) is submitted to an IR system. This basic objective is not limited to IR systems, but also includes recommendation systems, advertising systems, and scientific database systems. Consequently, appropriate measurement criteria of search queries and ground truth test dataset are essential in Information System (IS) development.

The user—IR system interaction pattern implies two sets of relevance. Firstly, the IR "system relevance" is the returned search results that are believed relevant to what the user expressed in the queries that submitted to IR systems. Secondly, the "human relevance" is what an IR system user is looking for. The two sets of relevance may overlap perfectly; and on the other hand, the returned results believed by an IR system that are relevant may not match users' relevance. Therefore, in most cases, the user or social (a group of users) relevance judgment is usually taken as a gold standard for comparison [11, 12, 24].

While different IR systems may return different results for the same query, the relevance judgments made by different users vary as well [3, 6, 10, 14, 29]. Bailey et al. [3] grouped assessors into three categories as "gold", "silver" and "bronze" standards. They found relevant judgment agreements in terms of Jaccard Coefficient among the groups were relatively low, which is only about a third agreed with each other. Consequently, the low level of agreement among assessors negatively impacted the construction of testing datasets used to estimate the performance of different IR systems [3]. In addition, relevance judgment results by "gold standard" group, who were experts in specific information retrieval tasks, usually deliver consistently better outcomes when the performance of an IR system is a concern, rather than just ranking the IR systems [3, 29].

Expert-based relevance judgment and IR system evaluation approach is expensive. As indicated in [1, 24], the evaluation requires a list of resources such as infrastructure, money, time, and organization; and it cannot be scaled up easily. To address the issues, a crowdsourcing approach using Amazon's Mechanical Turk is proposed to answer, "Can we get rid of TREC[1] assessors?". As described in [1], Jaccard Coefficient, Cohen's Kappa and its variants such as Fleiss's Kappa and Krippendorff's Kappa are used to measure the agreement among assessors based on the type of assessments. The researchers found that the agreement degree between crowdsourcing workers and TREC experts could reach about 70% when crowdsourcing

---

[1] Text REtrieval Conference, https://trec.nist.gov/.

results are grouped and averaged. The crowdsourcing results could be considered reliable in the interpretation done in [1].

The aforementioned research assumed that (1) full text documents are available so judges can read the full document before making a relevant decision such as the TREC evaluation. While currently, most of us need to make a relevancy judgment simply based on only Web search results (usually less than 30 words), or Web snippets which are nevertheless more challenging compared to the availability of complete documents. Of course, a user can always click the link in the Web search result to read the full text. Nevertheless, our assumption is that one of the goals of a search engine is to improve search relevance, and the Web snippet itself should present sufficient concise information to facilitate users to make relevant judgments effectively, rather than let users click each link to read the full text to make relevance judgments. (2) experts' relevance judgments are taken as ground truth, even if there were disagreements between TREC experts and other judgement groups [1, 2, 5], and thus judging the quality of the test dataset is questionable. This may result in the evaluation results, either in terms of performance (with regard to precision and recall) or the ranking of the IR systems, were justified on a biased dataset. (3) Almost all the research so far focuses on measuring disagreements among assessors, and few studies on the quality of the queries, especially in Web IR systems evaluation.

To better understand the performance of an IR system, in addition to evaluate the relevance of documents ranked and returned by IR systems, the quality of the query used in evaluation should also be evaluated. If a query is ambiguous and misleading, we hypothesize that the disagreement among relevance assessors would be high; consequently, the query would not be used in the IR evaluation process. However, there are no such criteria to evaluate the quality of queries in the current literature. To fill the research gap, in this research, RJCD, which leverages the measurements of disagreements among relevance judgement assessors', is designed for the query quality evaluation purposed.

The contributions of the research are (1) RJCD is proposed as a novel criterion to measure the quality of a query for Web IR systems, rather than the disagreements among assessors or assessor groups which are what other researchers have conducted by using Kappa and its variants; (2) we verified our hypothesis that low RJCD queries usually result in widely disagreements among relevance assessors; (3) in our experiments, we introduced "no sufficient information to make a decision" item to reduce the coincidental of randomly guesses of assessors, and thus further facilitate to improve the quality of test datasets.

2 Related Work

Relevance can be defined as "the ability (of an information retrieval system) to retrieve material that satisfies the needs of the user" [21]. The concept of relevance has been well known in the area of information retrieval since the late 1950s. According to different assumptions, relevance can be categorized as system-oriented and user-oriented [9, 11, 12, 22, 24, 25], and thus relevance judgment for the two different types of relevance varies on different criteria. A more complex definition of relevance described by Mizzaro [17] was that relevance is a point in a four-dimensional space named as information resources, user information needs representations, time and component such as task and topic, and context. Based on this definition, relevance judgment is somewhat "relevance indetermination on phenomenon" meaning that measuring users' real relevance is difficult. Hjørland [11] reviewed Saracevic's perspective of relevance is fundamentally a "subject based knowledge view" [22], and argued that "the user view" in [22] could be extended to a social point of view, that is, a purely individual view of relevance should not be used as the guideline for designing information systems and services; instead, a consensus view of relevance is more important in practice. Hjørland [11] further found that relevance assessors had difficulty to distinguishing relevant documents from irrelevant ones; Saracevic [23] provided a detailed review of inconsistent relevance judgment issues. The review work however has no clear suggestion on how the issues are resolvable.

Identifying objects or entities, which can take various forms such as documents, images, music, audio, and video, that are of interest and relevance to users' information need is the critical issue in the areas of IR and IS [24]. Among all the challenges in IR and IS, as argued by [11], the notion of relevance is implicated by not only IR itself but also involves cognitive science, logic, philosophy, and domain oriented [11]. As early as 1975, Saracevic [20] discussed five relevance models: system's view, user's view, subject literature view, subject knowledge view, and pragmatic view; however only the first two are widely cited. The system's view implies how relevance is viewed technologically and algorithmically; while the user's view can be described as "the subject knowledge view" which is believed as the most fundamental perspective of relevance [11]. However, Hjørland [11] further pointed out that, biased, individual/idiosyncratic relevance judgment is problematic if used as guidelines for information system development.

Agreement among judges is one of the subjective aspects of relevance in Mizzaro's model [16]. One concern is how the inconsistency of human relevance decision affects the IR evaluation results. Saracevic [24] found that until 2016, there were only seven studies that addressed the issue. Voorhees [29] mentioned that although a consistent conclusion is the inconsistency of assessors seems have only marginal effects on the relative performance of the evaluated IR systems, the averaging policy hides the performance of a given query, thus a limitation yet to be addressed.

To diminish the subject knowledge view of assessors, for TREC evaluation collection, experimental results of [26] revealed that randomly selected "relevant documents" from pooled documents (system's view of relevance) can also exhibit the ability to keep the same performance ranking order of IR systems. This approach has been further developed by [30] where each pooled document is assigned a reference score, and the accumulated scores of different IR systems are compared to decide the rank list of the systems. Spearman and Kendall Tau correlation coefficients are used to compare their ranked list with the official TREC ranked list.

In an interactive IR environment, relevance feedback and automatic query expansion are enabled. In addition, relevance is extended from dichotomous bipolar to highly relevant, fairly relevant, marginally relevant, and irrelevant. Experimental results from 26 participants with the TREC dataset demonstrated users can identify the most highly relevant and half marginal relevant documents [28]. At the same time, users may select off-topic documents for relevance feedback, and thus making the reliability of the relevance feedback results of users questionable. Data topicality judgement, data reliability judgement and data utility judgement patterns are identified which further benefited the designs of cognitive retrieval systems. Various preferences, scores and ties are used to analyze relevance judgements by comparing relevant scales [27].

To address the expensive, time consuming, assessor error, and potential disagreement issues in relevancy judgment, crowdsourcing approaches have been proposed to label the relevance of a test document set [1, 7, 13, 19]. Experiments demonstrated the assessor errors and tasks or domain knowledge of assessors are all factors that can affect the final IR systems performance ranking results [7]. By assigning the same judgment work to five outsourcing assessors, the binary relevance judgment agreement between TREC and the averaged results (three out of five) of outsourcing assessors are 77%. In case of disagreement, outsourcing results are more reliable [1]. However, an individual agreement between the two groups is relatively low, with Fleiss's Kapa only 0.195. To control the quality of outsourcing relevance judgment, the following factors need to be considered: how workers choose the topic of interest; how requesters can find quality workers and their knowledge areas; how to scale up outsourcing and keep quality; and various methods to estimate correlations between TREC experts and outsourcing workers [19].

Our research approaches the issue of disagreements among relevance judgment assessors from different angles. We argue that for Web search engine results evaluation, the disagreements among Web search engine users should be more serious for the following two reasons. First, the quality of queries submitted to Web search engines is another dimension in the IR search result relevance model. The low-quality query is also an import factor that causes high disagreements of relevance judgment results. Second, Web search engine users can only make relevance judgement decision simply based on Web snippets, rather than like TREC evaluation where full text documents are available for relevance judgment decision purpose. The less informative Web snippets is another reason for the wide disagreement among relevance judgment assessors.

3 Issues and Challenges of Information Relevance Judgement

The ambiguous character of natural language and subjective feature of relevance judgment are the sources of the issues. Briefly, they are (1) challenging for search engines to return relevant search results for a given ambiguous search term, and (2) expensive to obtain sufficient labelled training data [1, 19, 24] for supervised learning; and consequently, the readily labelled training datasets are surprisingly scarce [8]. Further, labelling a document involves relevance judgments by human experts. In contrast, the objectiveness of relevance judgment as per categorization is an arguable topic [4, 11, 16, 17, 21, 22] as the relevance judgment itself is a subjective outcome. In addition, both supervised and unsupervised machine learning algorithms are developed and evaluated based on full-length text documents [15, 32]. However, for Web IR, the text to be processed, either manually or automatically by using machine learning algorithms, is the Web snippet, which is less informative than the full-length text and is very sensitive to how the Web snippets are algorithmically extracted and presented by different Web IR systems [32].

The less informative aspects of Web search results have significant implications for relevance judgments which is the core of IR models [17, 21]. Without prior domain knowledge, adaptation of interpreted search results affects the relevance judgement discernment and its inference in user preferences and scores.

Another issue is that we take user relevance judgment results as ground truth to evaluate our IR algorithms. If the relevance judgment is seriously subjective towards only personal preferences biased judgments, the evaluated results can hardly be used as an objective measurement of the performance of the developed algorithms or Web IR systems.

4 Motivation and Research Goal

Motivation and reasoning capacity are vital variables in major social judgment and persuasion models. Literature suggests cognitive performance has high level of motivation that may be detrimental to information judgement performance, mainly when cognitive resources are rare. Test collection is a critical motivation in evaluating the information retrieval systems. Generating relevance judgements involves expensive and time-consuming human assessors. These issues have motivated us to adopt innovative and inexpensive crowdsourcing method for data acquisition. For accuracy and reliability of judgements, the current research is the motivation.

Information systems in the contexts of the interpretation of Web search results construe two focused elements: IR and storage modelling. The current research adds another element "interpretation" to adjudge the information relevance judgement in developing effective retrieval or Web IR systems. The goals of our research are to (1) develop a measuring mechanism of RJCD that can be used to create a less subjective ground truth test dataset for evaluating Web IR systems and algorithms; (2) verify the proposed RJCD has a positive coefficient with the improvement of a Web search results classification and re-rank model; (3) use open-source experimental data, including search queries and the corresponding information needs. Sample questionnaires and all search results with the queries are at https://github.com/simon-oz/relevance-judgement.git.

5 Research Methodology and Web Search Instrument Development

Our research intends to address the above issues which are emerged as a central notion in information science development but have not yet attracted sufficient attention. First, we created a dataset using the search results from a meta search engine. This curated dataset can alleviate the knowledge of relevance judgment inconsistently as discussed in [24]. Since Web snippets may not contain enough information to make a judgment, we introduced a "no sufficient information to make a decision" option to avoid potential random guesses of judges. Second, we introduced the Relevance Judgment Convergence Degree (RJCD) as a measurement to decide if a data item should be included in the testing dataset to maintain the quality of the ground truth dataset. To validate the proposed approach, we have conducted experiments by comparing our re-ranked results with that of a meta-search engine. We test our hypothesis by verifying the positive coefficient between JDC and performance improvement in terms of precision.

The research aims to evaluate how the proposed RJCD can be employed to address the subjectiveness issue of IR system evaluations where disagreements among relevance assessors are potentially caused by the low-quality queries in the IR system. Exploratory and descriptive with empirical research are used to describe and interpret different terminologies with the instances of relevance judgements. In the empirical research, we compare search results improvement between a meta-search engine which uses Yahoo Search Web Service APIs, and a Web search results re-ranking model which classifies the search results into top level topics of the Open Directory Project (ODP).[2] We further re-rank the classified results based on user preference profile [33]. Jansen and Spink [12] found that most users browse only several results in pages, and more than half of the users view only the first page returned by search engines. Therefore, we limit only the top 50 returned items from our meta search engine for each of the 30 queries as discussed in the following sections; and the returned items are then categorized into different ODP categories.

---

[2] http://www.odp.org/homepage.php.

6   Ambiguous Search Term Selection and Relevance Judgment

6.1   Ambiguous Search Term Selection

Search terms used to evaluate IR systems play a critical role because different IR systems usually return different search results for the same information needed when expressed as search terms. Traditionally, the performance of an IR systems is evaluated by a relatively small human-labelled dataset such as TREC with predefined search terms; and an IR system is expected to return as many known relevant documents and as few known irrelevant documents as possible. In the age of information explosion, especially in the area of Web search, search terms submitted to a search engine are different from the well-predefined search terms, as Web users are not limited to only academic staff when TREC was designed; but also include people with various educational backgrounds and knowledge areas.

Therefore, the following principles [33] are employed as a guideline to select search terms which are used in our experiments to evaluate the performances of a baseline IR system and a re-ranking system.

(1)   Real search terms from real users.
(2)   Search terms are short and contain only one or two words.
(3)   Search terms should cover a variety of topics.

Researchers have suggested the minimum number of queries when evaluating an IR system. Zeng et al. [32] used 30 queries with 200 top ranked search results to evaluate the performance of three search engines: Alta Vista, MSN and Google. Manning et al. [15] believe 50 queries is the minimum number for IR evaluation. Buckley and Voorhees [5] suggested that a good experiment needs 25 to 50 queries to produce the desired confidence in experimental results. Xu and Chen [31] found and suggested more search terms would generate more reliable conclusion about the performance of an IR system. Nevertheless, generation of ground truth datasets used to estimate IR systems requires expensive human experts to label the dataset by judging if a document is relevant or not to a given query. Human relevancy judgments per se are inherently subjective which may result in a biased ground truth dataset and scaling up the dataset is empirically difficult [9, 14, 25]. Considering the human cost, scale of the experiments in the research and without losing significance of the experiment results, we selected 30 queries as listed in Table 1. All the search terms are real user search terms submitted to the Microsoft MSN search engine [32] with three categories, "Ambiguous terms", "Entity names" and "General terms" [12].

Table 2 shows the statistical information of the 30 search queries. Among the 30 queries, 84% (25/30) have single work queries, 13% (4/30) have two-word queries, and 3% have three-word queries.

Table 1 Queries used in experiments [33]

Search term		Your information need
Ambiguous terms	Apple	Apple computer company
	Jaguar	Animal jaguar
	Saturn	The planet Saturn
	Jobs	The person Steve Jobes
	Jordan	The Hashemite kingdom Jordan
	Tiger	The animal tiger
	Trec	Text retrieval conference
	Ups	The uninterrupted power supply
	Quotes	How to correctly use quotes in writing
	Matrix	The mathematics concept matrix
Entity names	Susan Dumais	The researcher Susan Dumais
	Clinton	The US ex-president, Bill Clinton
	Iraq	General geographic and demographical information about Iraq
	Dell	The dell computer company
	Disney	The person Walt Disney
	World war 2	History related to world war 2
	Ford	Henry Ford, the founder of the Ford Motor Company
General terms	Health	How to keep healthy
	Yellow pages	The origin of yellow pages
	Maps	How to read maps
	Flower	Wild flower
	Music	Music classification by Genre
	Chat	Computer-mediated chat systems
	Games	History of games
	Radio	History of radio
	Jokes	The most funny jokes
	Graphic design	The art and practice of graphical design
	Resume	How to write a resume
	Time zones	Time zones of the world
	Travel	Travel planning and preparation

Table 2 Features of search terms

Categories	Single term	Two terms	Three terms	Total
Ambiguous terms	10			10
Entity names	5	1	1	7
General terms	10	3		13

6.2 Graded Relevance Judgment Categories

We developed our relevance scales as described below to categorize relevance judgment decisions made by assessors, and accept the perception that the averaged judgment results of users will be taken as the "gold standard for performance evaluation"
[25]. For each of the 30 ambiguous queries in Table 1, we define the corresponding
information needs, which are assumed to be users' true information requirements.
Human assessors are asked to decide, based on the defined information needs, which
of the following four categories a returned Web snippet should belong to:

R: relevant, assessors are sure the link described by the Web snippet is relevant.
P: partial relevant, assessors believes the linked Web page may be relevant.
I: irrelevant, assessors are sure the link described by the Web snippet is irrelevant.
N: the Web snippet doesn't provide sufficient information to make a decision.

Relevance judgment results from five different assessors are collected for each
of the $30 \times 50 = 1500$ returned Web snippets. The assessors are PhD students
from different areas and academic staff from our university. Since the queries are all
commonly used general terms in daily life, thus no domain knowledge is needed to
make a relevance judgment.

Each relevance judgment decision is assigned a numerical score, and a final score
is calculated based on the scores from different assessors. For the four defined judgments categories R, P, N and I, we assign 3, 1, 0, and -3 as the corresponding values.
For each returned result, all assessors' relevance judgment scores will be summed
up to calculate a final score. A binary decision is reached based on the summarized
score: the search results will be classified as relevant if the final score is positive, and
as otherwise irrelevant. If the final score is zero, indicating no decision was made
directly, we follow the link of the website, carefully review the full content of the
linked webpage, and then decide if the website is relevant or irrelevant.

7 Experiments and Evaluation

Precision, recall and P@10 are often employed to measure the performance of IR
systems and prediction models, while the P@n are specially designed to evaluate
the performance of search engines because get all relevant results from the Web for
an arbitrary query is nearly impossible [15]. We define a contingency table for each
class to be evaluated in Table 3, where |TP| denotes the number of relevant items in
the n returned results.

With the contingency table, precision and recall are defined as

$$p_r = precision_i = \frac{TP_i}{TP_i + FP_i}$$

$$r_c = recall_i = \frac{TP_i}{TP_i + FN_i}$$

Table 3 Contingency table for category i

Category i		True judgments	
		Yes	No
Classifier judgments	Yes	TP_i (True Positive)	FP_i (False Positive)
	No	FN_i (False Negative)	TN_i (True Negative)

$$P@N = \frac{|TP|}{n}$$

7.1 Experimental Dataset Generation

There is a total of $50 \times 30 = 1500$ Web snippets collected from the meta-search engine used in the experiments. The dataset is generated by submitting the 30 queries listed in Table 1 to our meta-search engine to obtain the top 50 returned Web snippets. We have uploaded the returned Web snippets onto GitHub for research purpose, refer to our GitHub link in Sect. 4.

7.2 Human Relevant Judgment Results

After data collection, we employed 28 human judges with various skills to conduct relevant judgements. Judges are High Degree by Research students in the field of Accounting, Economics and Finance, Management, Marketing, and Information Systems from our university. The 28 judges are divided into six groups evenly (G1 to G6), with two assigned into two groups to ensure each group have five assessors. Each group is provided with $5 \times 50 = 250$ different Web search results from five different search terms. Assessors spent about 10–40 min finishing the relevancy judgment of the 250 Web snippets. Based on the value of the summarized scores ($R = 3$, $P = 1$, $N = 0$, $I = -3$), we decide if a Web snippet is relevant ($s > 0$) or irrelevant ($s < 0$). If s is zero, an assessor is asked to follow the links provided by the meta search engine to make a final relevant or irrelevant decision.

Following is an example of one relevance judgment result for the search term "resume" as presented in Tables 4 and 5. Table 4 shows Web snippets (*W-S*), four relevant judgment results (*R, P, I* and *N*); a final score (*SC*), true category (*RL*) and assessors' final judgment results (*JG*, a binary judgment as defined previously), new re-ranked results (*NR*), the judgment of the new results (*JG*), number of relevant documents in the new ranked results (*RL'*), recall of the re-ranked results (*Rc'*), and precision of the re-ranked results (*Pr'*). It also provides calculated precision as all the 50 results are reviewed at different recall levels (*Pr* and *Rc*). Table 5 summarizes the precision at ten different recall levels for the baseline search results and the re-ranked results (refer to next session for the re-ranked results).

7.3   Re-ranking Search Results

The returned Web snippets from the meta-search engine are further processed via a re-ranking strategy which involves the following processes [33]:

(1)   Use the ODP data to create a training dataset where the ODP topics are taken as the labels of each item in the training dataset. Categories are Arts, Business, Computers, Games, Health, Home, News, Recreation, Reference, Regional, Science, Shopping, Society, Sports and Kids & Teens.
(2)   Use the generated training dataset to train a Naïve Bayes classifier to organize the 1500 Web snippets into different ODP topics listed above.
(3)   Use KNN to further cluster the Web snippets into different clusters;
(4)   Merge the results from the above two steps.
(5)   Re-rank the results from step 4 based on the user preference profile which is assumed to contain two topics from the ODP topics aforementioned.

The evaluation results are presented in Fig. 1, which contains precision-recall curve of the baseline results from the meta-search engine, and the re-ranked results based on the above process. Note that the curve is drawn based on the averaged results over the 30 search terms. The relevance judgment outcomes are the summed-up results of five judges for each search terms.

Figure 1 illustrates that:

- The re-ranked results outperform the meta-search engine results consistently on all recall levels. The maximum improvement is 12.06% at the recall level of 10%, and the minimum improvement is 5.18% at the recall level of 100%.
- The averaged precisions over all 30 queries of meta-search engine and re-ranked results are 55.55% and 64.29% respectively; this indicates an average 8.74% precision improvement.

The improvements of re-ranked results over baseline meta-search engine results decreases as recall increases; the maximum increase happened at recall level 10%, and it drops down the way to a minimum as recall level increases to 100%. This is a preferable outcome as users usually browse only a few pages of Web search results, and about 50% of them only browse the first page [12].

7.4   Relevance Judgment Convergence Degree (RJCD)

While the average performance of re-ranked search results consistently exhibits superior performance to the baseline meta-search engine results, we also observed that

Table 4 Relevant judgment results of search term "resume" by five assessors [33]. The first column is shortened to save page space

W-S	R(3)	P(1)	I(−3)	N(0)	SC	JG	RL	Rc (%)	Pr (%)	NR	JG	RL'	Rc' (%)	Pr' (%)
1. Resumes	1345			2	12	1	1	3.03	1.00	2	0	0	0.00	0.00
2. Résumé	5	4	13	2	−2	0	0	0.00	0.00	4	1	1	3.03	50.00
3. Get	5	4	13	2	−2	0	0	0.00	0.00	5	1	2	6.06	66.67
4. Resume	345	1		2	10	1	2	6.06	50.00	7	1	3	9.09	75.00
5. Resume	1345			2	12	1	3	9.09	60.00	8	1	4	12.12	80.00
6. Entry	1345			2	12	1	4	12.12	66.67	11	1	5	15.15	83.33
7. Free	345	1		2	10	1	5	15.15	71.43	12	1	6	18.18	85.71
8. Resume	1345			2	12	1	6	18.18	75.00	13	1	7	21.21	87.50
9. JobStar	345	1		2	10	1	7	21.21	77.78	22	1	8	24.24	88.89
10. Free	1345			2	12	1	8	24.24	80.00	29	0	0	0.00	0.00
11. e-resume	5	34	1	2	2	1	9	27.27	81.82	38	0	0	0.00	0.00
12. e-resume	5	34	1	2	2	1	10	30.30	83.33	40	1	9	27.27	75.00
13. Professio	35	4	1	2	4	1	11	33.33	84.62	14	0	0	0.00	0.00
14. Resume		5	134	2	−8	0	0	0.00	0.00	17	0	0	0.00	0.00
15. Resume	145		3	2	6	1	12	36.36	80.00	19	1	10	30.30	66.67
16. e-resume		45	13	2	−4	0	0	0.00	0.00	20	1	11	33.33	68.75
17. FaxRe		5	1234		−11	0	0	0.00	0.00	25	1	12	36.36	70.59
18. Post your			**12,345**		−15	0	0	0.00	0.00	26	1	13	39.39	72.22
19. CV Res	145		3	2	6	1	13	39.39	68.42	27	1	14	42.42	73.68
20. Resume	5	14	3	2	2	1	14	42.42	70.00	42	1	15	45.45	75.00
21. Resume	35	4	1	2	4	1	15	45.45	71.43	49	0	0	0.00	0.00

(continued)

Table 4 (continued)

W-S	R(3)	P(1)	I(−3)	N(0)	SC	JG	RL	Rc (%)	Pr (%)	NR	JG	RL'	Rc' (%)	Pr' (%)
22. Resume	1	345		2	6	1	16	48.48	72.73	1	1	16	48.48	72.73
23. Freshers	345		1	2	6	1	17	51.52	73.91	3	0	0	0.00	00.0
24. eResum	345		1	2	6	1	18	54.55	75.00	6	1	17	51.52	70.83
25. Resumes	5	34	1	2	2	1	19	57.58	76.00	9	1	18	54.55	72.00
26. Sample	135	4		2	10	1	20	60.61	76.92	10	1	19	57.58	73.08
27. Resume	145	3		2	10	1	21	63.64	77.78	15	1	20	60.61	74.07
28. Careers	5	14	3	2	2	1	22	66.67	78.57	16	0	0	0.00	0.00
29. Profes	3		145	2	−6	0	0	0.00	0.00	18	0	0	0.00	0.00
30. Free	1345			2	12	1	23	69.70	76.67	21	1	21	63.64	70.00
31. Resume		35	14	2	−4	0	0	0.00	0.00	23	1	22	66.67	70.97
32. Resume	145	3		2	10	1	24	72.73	75.00	24	1	23	97.0	71.88
33. Resumes	5	34	1	2	2	1	25	75.76	75.76	28	1	24	72.73	72.73
34. Profess		5	134	2	−8	0	0	0.00	0.00	30	1	25	75.76	73.53
35. Basic		45	123		−7	0	0	0.00	0.00	31	0	0	0.00	0.00
36. Best		34	125		−7	0	0	0.00	0.00	32	1	26	78.79	72.22
37.Introduct	15	34		2	8	1	26	78.79	70.27	33	1	27	81.82	72.97
38. ESUME			1345	2	−12	0	0	0.00	0.00	34	0	0	0.00	0.00
39.The write	4		135	2	−6	0	0	0.00	0.00	35	0	0	0.00	0.00
40. What's	135	4		2	10	1	27	81.82	67.50	36	0	0	0.00	0.00
41. Resume	1345		2		9	1	28	84.85	68.29	37	1	28	84.85	68.29
42. How to	14	35		2	8	1	29	87.88	69.05	39	0	0	0.00	0.00

(continued)

Table 4 (continued)

W-S	R(3)	P(1)	I(−3)	N(0)	SC	JG	RL	Rc (%)	Pr (%)	NR	JG	RL'	Rc' (%)	Pr' (%)
43. Resume	1345			2	12	1	30	90.91	69.77	41	1	29	87.88	67.44
44. Professio		3	145	2	−8	0	0	0.00	0.00	43	1	30	90.91	68.18
45. Resume		14	3	25	−1	0	0	0.00	0.00	44	0	0	0.00	0.00
46. Careers		345	1	2	1	1	31	93.94	67.39	45	0	0	0.00	0.00
47. Resume		4	13	25	−5	0	0	0.00	0.00	46	1	31	93.94	65.96
48. Resume	1345			2	12	1	32	96.97	66.67	47	0	0	0.00	0.00
49. Create a		4	13	25	−5	0	0	0.00	0.00	48	1	32	96.97	65.31
50. How to	1345			2	12	1	33	1.00	66.00	50	1	33	1.00	66.00

Table 5 Precision at different recall levels for search term "resume"

Rc-Lv	10	20	30	40	50	60	70	80	90	100
Pr meta	83.3	83.3	83.3	76.9	76.9	76.9	76.7	69.8	69.8	66
Pr Re-Ranked	87.5	87.5	74.1	74.1	74.1	74.1	73	73	68.2	66

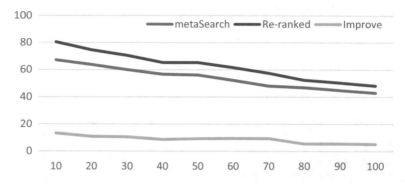

Fig. 1 Precision-recall curve of meta-search results and re-ranked results

there are nine search terms (namely maps, music, jokes, games, Disney, resume, Susan Dumais, graphic design, and Saturn) for which the baseline results outperform the re-ranked results marginally. To further investigate the situation, the concept of RJCD is introduced to depict for a given search term, to what degree the relevancy assessors agree with each other; and thus propose to use RJCD as a criteria to measure the quality of a query.

Let h be the number of human assessors, and k be the number of relevance judgment options an assessor can select from, here $k = 4$ corresponding to the four options R, P, N and I. If n is the total number of Web snippets returned by an IR system for a given query, we define *Agreement Number AN* = the total number the sort of judgments for that all h judges to make the same relevance judgment decision; and *Judgment Number JN* = the total number of choices made by the h judges over all $n \times k$ possible choices. Formally, we denote $\Omega = \{R, P, N, I\}$, $k = |\Omega|$, a relevance judgment by assessor j for the ith returned result as $R_j(i) \in \Omega$, $j \in [1, \dots h]$, $i \in [1, \dots n]$, further, let

$$\gamma(i) = \left[\left[\bigcup_{j=1}^{h} R_j(i) \right] \right] = |\Omega'| \qquad (1)$$

be the size of $\Omega' \subseteq \Omega$ which contains distinct relevance judgment results from Ω. We specially define $\gamma(i)|_1 \equiv 1$, which indicates that all assessors reach the same relevant judgment decision, no matter what the relevant category it is; for example, all h judges give the R decision. RJCD for a given query can then be defined in the following equation as ρ where $\gamma(i)$ is calculated based on Eq. (1)

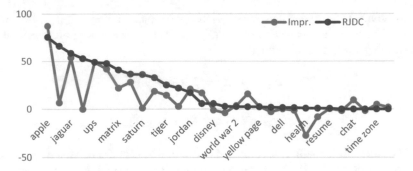

Fig. 2 Precision improvement of the re-ranked results and RJDC values over the 30 queries

$$\rho = \frac{\sum_{i=1}^{n} \gamma(i)|_1}{\sum_{i=1}^{n} r(i)} \triangleq \frac{AN}{JN} \tag{2}$$

Use data in Table 4 as an example, for search term "resume", we need first calculate $\gamma(1), \gamma(2), \ldots \gamma(50)$. By definition, $\gamma(1) = |\{R, N\}|=2$, $\gamma(2) = |\{R, P, I, N\}| = 4,\ldots,$ $\gamma(18) = |\{I\}| = 1,\ldots$, so we can get JN by summing up $\gamma(i)$, and from Eq. (2), we have AN = 1 and JN = 145. Note also that we have only $\gamma(18) = 1$, that is, $AN =$ 1, so our final score of RJCD is 1/145 = 0.006897.

Figure 2 illustrates the relationship between RJCD and the precision improvement of the re-ranked results over the baseline meta-search engine results; it demonstrates that there are positive relations between precision improvement and the values of the RJCD. When RJCD scores are high (left side), the improvements are all positive and relatively high; whereas as when RJCD scores are low (right side), the improvements are relatively small, or even negative. We will analyze its correlation in the following session.

7.5 Correlation Analysis Between RJCD and the Re-Ranked Results

Figure 2 demonstrates an improvement of precision attribute with a corresponding increasement in RJCD. When RJCD is small, the corresponding precision improvements are either very small or even negative; indicating the re-ranked results are worse than the baseline meta search engine results. The average RJCD score is only 5.5% for the nine negative search terms; while for the positive queries, the average RJCD score is about 20%.

Let us estimate the correlation coefficient of precision improvement and RJCD. The correlation coefficient is defined for two random variables X and Y [18]:

$$\beta = \frac{cov(X, Y)}{\sqrt{V(X)V(Y)}} = \frac{\sigma_{XY}}{\sigma_X \sigma_Y} = \frac{E[(X - \mu_X)(Y - \mu_Y)]}{\sigma_X \sigma_Y}$$

where cov(X,Y), also denoted as σ_{XY}, is the covariance of X and Y, μ_X is the mean value of X, μ_Y is the mean value of Y, V(X), V(Y) are the variance of X and Y, which are denoted as σ_X^2 and σ_Y^2 defined as

$$\sigma_X^2 = V(X) = E[(X - \mu)^2]$$

$$\sigma_Y^2 = V(Y) = E[(Y - \mu)^2]$$

The correlation coefficient computed between RJCD and precision improvement is 0.725, with p-value 0.000006, which strongly indicates that the two variables are positively related. It can also be observed by the trends of RJCD in Fig. 2, where when RJCD is high (on the left of Fig. 2), the precision improvements are also high; and as the RJCD reduces to zero in the right part of Fig. 2, the improvements are marginal or negative. Therefore, RJCD is a reliable measurement to evaluate if a search term is a good representation of users' real information needs or not. If RJCD is less than 5%, we recommend it is reasonable to use an alternative search term to represent the users' information needs, and the search term with low RJCD should not be included in a labelled training dataset to be used to evaluate the performance of IR and related systems.

8 Conclusion and Future Work

Relevancy judgment is an essential part of evaluating IR systems. Previous research focuses more on the agreement among different assessors or assessor groups, where full length documents are available. For Web IR systems, users need to make a relevance judgment decision based on the returned search results, or Web snippets which are usually much less informative than normal documents. When a dataset is created to evaluate the performance of a Web IR system, we suggested the quality of queries should also be measured by the proposed RJCD to exclude those that are too ambiguous to make relevance judgments of assessors largely diverge. Relevance Judgment Convergence Degree was employed in the research as a criterion to measure the quality of ambiguous queries in Web IR evaluation and test datasets construction. We evaluated the performance of a baseline IR system based on a meta-search engine with 30 ambiguous search terms and top 50 Web snippets for each of the queries. We then improved the ranking of the baseline results by combining classification and clustering techniques. Experimental results revealed positive correlation exists between RJCD and performance improvements. We recommended that if the RJCD of a query is less than 5%, the query and the returned search results should not be included in the test dataset.

In future, we will extend our experiments with more queries and more Web IR systems to verify the effectiveness of RJCD as a criterion to measure the quality of ambiguous search terms. Meanwhile, we will validate RJCD effectiveness by examining correlation coefficient among RJCD and the performance improvements among Web IR systems.

References

1. Alonso, O., & Mizzaro, S. (2012). Using crowdsourcing for TREC relevance assessment. *Information Processing & Management, 48*, 1053–1066.
2. Baeza-Yates, R., & Ribeiro-Neto, B. (1999). *Modern Information Retrieval* (p. 544). Harlow: Addison Wesley.
3. Bailey, P., et al. (2008). Relevance assessment: Are judges exchangeable and does it matter? In *Proceedings of the 31st Annual International ACM SIGIR Conference on Research and Development in Information Retrieval*. Singapore: ACM.
4. Borlund, P. (2003). The concept of relevance in IR. *Journal of the American Society for Information Science and Technology, 54*(10), 913–925.
5. Buckley, C., & Voorhees, E. M. (2000). Evaluating evaluation measure stability. In *Proceedings of the 23rd Annual International ACM SIGIR Conference on Research and Development in Information Retrieval*. Athens Grace: ACM Press.
6. Burgin, R. (1992). Variations in relevance judgments and the evaluation of retrieval performance. *Information Processing and Management, 28*(5), 619–627.
7. Carterette, B., & Soboroff, I. (2010). The effect of assessor errors on IR system evaluation. In *The 33rd International ACM SIGIR Conference on Research and Development in Information Retrieval*. Geneva, Switzerland: ACM.
8. Davidov, D., Gabrilovich, E., & Markovitch, S. (2004). Parameterized generation of labeled datasets for text categorization based on a hierarchical directory. In *Proceedings of the 27th Annual International ACM SIGIR Conference on Research and Development in Information Retrieval*. Sheffield, UK: ACM Press.
9. Harter, S. P. (1992). Psychological relevance and information science. *Journal of the American Society for Information Science, 43*(9), 602–615.
10. Harter, S. P. (1996). Variations in relevance assessments and the measurement of retrieval effectiveness. *Journal of the American Society for Information Science, 47*(1), 37–49.
11. Hjørland, B. (2010). The foundation of the concept of relevance. *Journal of the American Society for Information Science and Technology, 61*(2), 217–223.
12. Jansen, B. J., & Spink, A. (2006). How are we searching the world wide web? A comparison of nine search engine transaction logs. *Information Processing and Management, 42*(1), 248–263.
13. Kazai, G., Milic-Frayling, N., & Costello, J. (2009). Towards methods for the collective gathering and quality control of relevance assessments. In *The 32nd International ACM SIGIR Conference on Research and Development in Information Retrieval*. Boston, Massachusetts: ACM.
14. Lesk, M. E., & Salton, G. (1969). Measuring the agreement among relevance judges. *Information Storage and Retrieval, 4*, 343–359.
15. Manning, C. D., Raghavan, P., & Schütze, H. (2008). *Introduction to Information Retrieval*. Cambridge University Press.
16. Mizzaro, S. (1997). Relevance: The whole history. *Journal of the American Society for Information Science, 48*(9), 810–832.
17. Mizzaro, S. (1998). How many relevances in information retrieval. *Interacting with Computers, 10*(3), 303–320.
18. Montgomery, D. C., & Runger, G. C. (2018). *Applied Statistics and Probability for Engineers* (7th ed., p. 710). Wiley.
19. Samimi, P., & Devi, R. (2014). Creation of reliable relevance judgments in information retrieval systems evaluation experimentation through crowdsourcing: A review. *The Scientific World Journal, 2014*, 13.

20. Saracevic, T. (1975). Relevance: A review of and a framework for the thinking on the notion of information science. *Journal of the American Society for Information Science, 26*(6), 321–343.
21. Saracevic, T. (2007). Relevance: A review of the literature and a framework for the thinking on the notion of information science. Part II: Nature and manifestations of relevance. *Journal of the American Society for Information Science and Technology, 58*(13), 1915–1933
22. Saracevic, T. (2007). Relevance: A review of the literature and a framework for the thinking on the notion of information science. Part III: Behavior and effects of relevance. *Journal of the American Society for Information Science and Technology, 58*(13), 2126–2144.
23. Saracevic, T. (2008). Effects of inconsistent relevance judgments on information retrieval test results: A historical perspective. *Library Trends, 56*(4), 763–783.
24. Saracevic, T. (2016). The notion of relevance in information science—Everybody knows what relevance is. But what is it really? In G. Marchionini (Ed.), *Synthesis Lectures on Information Concepts, Retrieval, and Services* (p. 130). Morgan & Claypool.
25. Smyth, B. (2007). A community-based approach to personalizing web search. *Computer, 40*(8), 42–50.
26. Soboroff, I., Nicholas, C., & Cahan, P. (2001). Ranking retrieval systems without relevance judgments. In *The 24th annual international ACM SIGIR conference on Research and development in information retrieval (SIGIR'01)*. New Orleans, Louisiana: ACM.
27. Spink, A., & Greisdorf, H. (2001). Regions and levels: Measuring and mapping users' relevance judgments. *Journal of the American Society for Information Science and Technology, 52*(2), 161–173.
28. Vakkari, P., & Sormunen, E. (2004). The influence of relevance levels on the effectiveness of interactive information retrieval. *Journal of the American Society for Information Science and Technology, 55*(11), 963–969.
29. Voorhees, E. M. (2000). Variations in relevance judgments and the measurement of retrieval effectiveness. *Information Processing and Management, 36*, 697–716.
30. Wu, S., & Crestani. F. (2003). Methods for ranking information retrieval systems without relevance judgments. In *The 2003 ACM symposium on Applied Computing*. Melbourne, Florida: ACM.
31. Xu, Y., & Chen, Z. (2006). Relevance judgment: What do information users consider beyond topicality? *Journal of the American Society for Information Science and Technology, 57*(7), 961–973.
32. Zeng, H.-J., et al. (2004). Learning to cluster web search results. In *Proceedings of the 27th Annual International ACM SIGIR Conference on Research and Development in Information Retrieval*. Sheffield, UK: ACM Press.
33. Zhu, D. (2010). Improving the relevance of web search results by combining web snippet categorization, clustering and personalization. In *School of Information Systems* (p. 264). Curtin University of Technology: Curtin University of Technology.

Studies on Neural Networks as a Fusion Method for Dispersed Data with Noise

Małgorzata Przybyła-Kasperek⊙ and **Kwabena Frimpong Marfo**⊙

Abstract In this paper, the issues of classification based on dispersed data are considered. For this purpose, an approach is used in which prediction vectors are generated locally using the k-nearest neighbors classifier. However, in central server, the final fusion of prediction vectors is made with the use of a neural network. The main aim of the study is to check the influence of noise intensity, various data characteristics (the number of conditional attributes, the number of objects, the number of decision classes) and the degree of dispersion on the quality of classification of the considered approach. For this purpose, 270 data sets were generated that differed by the above factors. It was found that each of the examined factors has a statistically significant impact on the quality of classification. The main conclusions are as follows. For dispersed data, multidimensionality is very good. The greater the dispersion in data, the worse the quality of classification. Only when the noise intensity significantly increased, we can observe a significant increase in the classification error in comparison with the lower noise level. This means that the classification method for dispersed data with neural network is immune to noise to some extent.

1 Introduction

Many different classification methods have been proposed in machine learning so far. These methods have found applications in numerous information systems used in banking, stock exchange, electronic markets, medicine, among others. Most of the traditional classification methods are dedicated to data stored in one decision table, yet, this approach is increasingly seen as insufficient. In today's global society, federated learning is a critical issue [24]. This approach responds to the widespread

M. Przybyła-Kasperek (✉) · K. F. Marfo
University of Silesia in Katowice, Institute of Computer Science, Będzińska 39, 41-200
Sosnowiec, Poland
e-mail: malgorzata.przybyla-kasperek@us.edu.pl

K. F. Marfo
e-mail: kwabena.marfo@us.edu.pl

© The Author(s), under exclusive license to Springer Nature Switzerland AG 2023   169
G. C. Silaghi et al. (eds.), *Advances in Information Systems Development*,
Lecture Notes in Information Systems and Organisation 63,
https://doi.org/10.1007/978-3-031-32418-5_10

occurrence of dispersed data provided by various units that wish to keep their data private. In all of the applications mentioned above, examples of dispersed data can be found [14]. Currently, we are dealing with data collected in a dispersed manner by various units, institutions, websites, and mobile devices [1]. When local data is used together, better quality of classification can be obtained than when we rely on one fragment of data. Even so, using dispersed data is not a simple task. First and foremost, there is a great possibility of the presence of inconsistencies in the data—independently collected data may have different set of attributes as well as different set of objects, but the possibility of having common elements among dispersed data is not excluded. In this case, it is not possible to merge such data into one table. Secondly, the difficulty of using dispersed data stems from the fear of freely sharing data. Often, data-owners want to preserve data privacy, thus, we cannot construct a method that accesses all data from various sources.

Scientists wonder if it is necessary to propose many methods for solving real problems [5]. On the other hand, we have a no-free lunch theorem [1] which justifies proposing new methods dedicated to specific problems. In the context of such considerations, it is important to characterize methods in terms of the problem and data characteristics for which the method is dedicated to. To do this, the method should be tested in terms of both varying data and different contexts. The differences in data can be considered in terms of the following characteristics: the number of objects, the number of conditional attributes, the number of decision classes, informativeness and redundancy of attributes. Other important concepts to consider are presence of imbalance decision classes and the presence of noise in the data.

As an instance, suppose we want to build an automated diagnostic system using records of patients across multiple hospitals. Depending on the above mentioned data characteristics, the performance of the learning algorithm could be greatly affected and one would not have a clear approach to address this issue. However, with the use of an information system, we could drill down to the factors that truly cause the deterioration in the learning algorithm. In the paper [18], a method for classification with the use of dispersed data was proposed. This method uses the k-nearest neighbors and the neural networks classifiers. The k-nearest neighbors classifier is used for local data—a prediction vector is generated, which is then transferred to a central server. Then the neural network makes the final decision based on all prediction vectors. In this way, we maintain data privacy as only the prediction vectors are shared. The paper [18] presents that this approach gives unambiguous results, which cannot be said about other fusion methods such as the Majority Voting, the Borda Count method, the Sum Rule, the method based on decision templates and the method based on theory of evidence. Moreover, it was shown that the approach with neural networks achieves better quality of classification than the above-mentioned fusion methods.

However, there are still many questions to be answered. Does the number of conditional attributes/the number of objects/the number of decision classes in local data affect the quality of classification? Does information noise disturb the classification of dispersed data with the use of neural networks, and if so, to what extent? If the informative attributes are dispersed among local data, are we able to make a good classification based on fragmented data? How does high data dispersion affect the quality of classification? The aim of this paper is to answer these questions. In this way, the scope of applications of the classification method for dispersed data using the k-nearest neighbors and the neural network classifiers will be determined.

The article focuses on the extent to which data characteristics mentioned above, as well as noise in data affects the classification accuracy of method proposed in this paper. This issue is very important in the case of dispersed data with noise, for example, data from social media. For this purpose, 18 data sets were generated with varying number of objects, attributes and decision classes. To each of them, noise was added in three different degrees of intensity. The data was divided into five different versions of dispersion (with different number of local data) in such a way as to guarantee different, but not necessarily disjoint sets of attributes in each of the local sets. Thus, 270 dispersed data was obtained. Experiments using these data and different number of neurons in the hidden layer were performed. The obtained results were compared and conclusions were drawn.

The main contribution of the study is to justify the following conclusions:

- The classification method for dispersed data with neural network is immune to noise to some extent. Only when the noise intensity significantly increased (twice or more than the lowest investigated noise level), we can observe a significant increase in the classification error in comparison with the lower noise level.
- The variety of attributes occurring in local tables and a greater number of them has a positive effect on the quality of classification.
- The more training objects, the better results we obtain. But the total number of conditional attributes in dispersed data is much more important for the quality of classification.
- The greater the dispersion, the worse the quality of classification.

The article is an expanded version of the paper presented at the conference Information Systems Development 2022 [17].

The article is organized in the following way. Section 2 provides a literature overview. The next section describes the classification approach of the dispersed data and the method of data generation. In Sect. 4, the results of the experiments are presented and analyzed. The article ends with conclusion.

2 Literature Review

The issues of data stored in local sets are considered mainly in two contexts; an ensemble of classifiers [2, 3, 15, 19]—where local data is created based on a single data set in order to improve the quality of classification. In this approach we have control over the form of local data created. Local data meets certain conditions, for example, independence and variety. The most common approach in distributed learning is the model in which local classifiers are built independently, and the final decision is simply generated by applying fusion methods. Various models have been proposed, both parallel [12] and hierarchical [4, 16]. Agent collaboration is also key concept here [6]. In this paper, a completely different approach is considered because dispersed data do not have to fulfill any of these constraints.

Dispersed data is also considered in federated learning topics [7, 21]. Similar to the data considered in this paper, the local data are collected independently and we have no influence on their form. Federated learning involves applying machine learning methods locally to each local device separately, without sharing the training objects with a central server [14]. This approach makes it possible to learn a common model while maintaining data privacy. Federated learning issues are widely used in applications such as smart healthcare, smart transportation, Unmanned Aerial Vehicles, smart cities, and smart industry [13].

Neural networks in the context of federated learning are considered in many papers. In [23], neural networks are built locally, and their weights are sent to a central server in order to build the final model. The paper [8] also analyzes the use of neural networks in the context of federated learning, but the main focus is on passing the weights to the central server more efficiently. In [11] a model with a deep graph neural network is proposed to classify the nodes based on their structures and features. In this paper, however, the combination of the k-nearest neighbors classifier, which will be used locally, with a neural network, which will be built on a central server, is considered. Such an approach was investigated in [18] although the influence of various data characteristics, degree of dispersion and noise intensity on the quality of classification of this method was not analyzed there. Such studies are performed in this work. In the paper [10] the Radial Basis Function Network was used for dispersed data but only in its basic version.

3 Methods and Data

In this section, we first briefly introduce the dispersed data classification approach that uses the k-nearest neighbors and the neural network classifiers. Next, the method of generating and preprocessing data sets used in the experimental analysis is described.

3.1 Dispersed Classification Method with k-Nearest Neighbors and the Neural Network Classifiers

The approach used in this paper to classify based on dispersed data consists of two steps. We assume that each local data is stored in the form of a local decision table. In the first stage, the calculations are performed independently in local des-tinations. A modified k-nearest neighbors algorithm is used and predictions from the measurement level are designated. We assume that a set of decision tables $D_{ag} = (U_{ag}, A_{ag}, d)$, $ag \in Ag$ from one discipline is available, where U_{ag} is the universe, a set of objects; A_{ag} is a set of conditional attributes; d is a decision attribute. Based on each of the local tables, a classifier is built. Ag is a set of classifiers, and ag is a single classifier. For each local table and for each test object x, a probability vector over decision classes (denoted by $\mu_{ag}(x)$) is designated. The dimension of vectors $\mu_{ag}(x) = [\mu_{ag,1}(x), \ldots, \mu_{ag,c}(x)]$ is equal to the number of decision classes $c = card\{V^d\}$, where V^d is a set of values of decision attributes from all decision tables and $card\{V^d\}$ is the cardinality of this set. Each coefficient $\mu_{ag,j}(x)$ is determined using the k-nearest neighbors of the test object x belonging to a given decision class j and decision table D_{ag}. The gower similarity measure is used in this approach. For numerical data used in this paper, the gower measure is equivalent to the Manhattan distance.

Only the prediction vectors are made available for centralized computation. A global decision for a test object is generated with the use of a neural network. The structure of the network consists of three layers. The hidden layer has a varying number of neurons that will be studied experimentally. The number of neurons in the input layer is equal to the product of the number of prediction vectors and the dimension of the vector, i.e. $card\{Ag\} \times card\{V^d\}$. The output layer has the number of neurons equal to the number of decision classes. For the hidden layer, the ReLU (Rectified Linear Unit) activation function is used. For the output layer, the SoftMax activation function is used, which is recommended when we deal with a multi-class problem [9]. The back-propagation method, the Adam optimizer and the categorical cross-entropy loss function are used in the study.

Of course, a neural network must be trained using a certain set of objects. Since the training objects were used to generate the prediction vectors with the k-nearest neighbors classifier, they cannot be reused to train the neural network. Thus, a 10-fold cross-validation method was used for the test set. Each time, the neural network was trained using 9 folds, while the last independent fold was classified using the neural network constructed based on the 9 folds. This procedure was repeated ten times for each of the folds, and the final quality of classification was assigned using the results obtained from these ten performances. For a more detailed description, please refer to [18].

The big advantage of the approach described above is that it generates unambiguous decisions, which cannot be said about many other fusion methods [1]. Moreover, in comparison with fusion methods such as the Majority Voting, the Borda Count method, the Sum Rule, the method based on decision templates and the method based on theory of evidence; the approach described above gives in most cases a better quality of classification. But it is obvious that the proposed approach is not appropriate in every case or for every data set. Therefore, the question remains—with which data does the dispersed classification method with neural network handles best. To answer this question, data sets were generated that differ in many factors. A total of 270 dispersed data sets were tested, which is described below.

3.2 Data

The data was generated artificially as the aim was to systematically compare the results obtained from data with specific characteristics. The aim was to compare results obtained with the use of dispersed classification method with neural network in relation to the following issues with respect to the impact on the performance of the proposed algorithm:

- the impact that the number of conditional attributes in data has on the quality of classification (multidimensionality of data),
- the impact that the number of objects in data has on the quality of classification,
- the impact that the number of decision classes in data has on the quality of classification,
- the impact that the degree of dispersion has on the quality of classification,
- the impact that the noise intensity in data has on the quality of classification.

The generation of artificial data sets was carried out in several stages:

1. In the first stage, data sets were generated using the Weka [20] software. For this purpose, the RandomRBF was used. This function, at first, randomly generates centers for each decision class. Then to each center, a weight is randomly assigned as well as a central point per attribute, and a standard deviation. A new object is generated as follows; a center is selected according to the weights. Then attribute values are randomly generated and offset from the center. After, the vector is scaled so that its length is equal to a value sampled randomly from the Gaussian distribution of the center. In this way, 18 data sets were generated with different number of conditional attributes, decision classes, objects and centroids. The number of objects in decision classes is imbalanced. The characteristics are presented in Table 1.

There are two main reasons why the training and testing methods used in this paper are the best methods to evaluate the quality of classification for dispersed data. To begin, when we deal with dispersed data, it significantly increases computational complexity. Also, there are different sets of conditional attributes in different local tables, and the test object must have specific values on all of these attributes. Thus, at first, each of the data sets was randomly but in a stratified way divided into training set (70% of the data) and testing set (30% of the data).

One of the study goals was to check the influence of noise intensity on the quality of classification. For this purpose, three different levels of noise intensity were applied to the training set (70% of the data), thus, the density of the noise was 100% of the training set. After dividing each data into training and testing set, 3 training data sets with Gaussian noise intensity were further constructed. For each set, mean value equal to 0 and different values of standard deviation (std) were used: $\{mean = 0, std = 0.01\}$, $\{mean = 0, std = 0.1\}$ and $\{mean = 0, std = 0.2\}$ respectively. In this way, based on 18 training sets, 54 data sets with different noise intensities were created.

Table 1 Data set characteristics

Data Set	No. of objects	No. of conditional attributes	No. of decision classes	No. of centroids
1	650	30	10	100
2	650	50	10	100
3	650	70	10	100
4	1300	30	10	100
5	1300	50	10	100
6	1300	70	10	100
7	650	30	5	50
8	650	50	5	50
9	650	70	5	50
10	1300	30	5	50
11	1300	50	5	50
12	1300	70	5	50
13	650	30	5	100
14	650	50	5	100
15	650	70	5	100
16	1300	30	5	100
17	1300	50	5	100
18	1300	70	5	100

Another research goal was to check the influence of the degree of dispersion on the quality of classification. Each of the 54 data sets prepared in the previous step was divided into five versions of dispersion—3, 5, 7, 9, 11 local tables were constructed from each training data set with different number of conditional attributes. Local decision tables were constructed in a way such that each local table has a unique set of conditional attributes and also some conditional attributes that are present in other local tables. The number of attributes in local tables varied from 3 to 35. For a finer dispersion, a greater number of local tables contain a smaller number of conditional attributes.

The above described approach is used to generate 270 dispersed data. Thus, for each of the original training set (70% of the data), we have dispersed data with 3, 5, 7, 9, 11 local tables for $mean = 0$, $std \in \{0.01, 0.1, 0.2\}$ Gaussian noise intensities.

The code of the function that defines the Gaussian noise intensities for each training data set is given below.

Gaussian Noise Intensity for Training Data Sets

```
# df: Original training data set read into a Dataframe
# col: A list of conditional attributes
# mu: mean value for Gaussian noise
# sigma: standard deviation value for Gaussian noise

def get_noise(df, col:list, mu:float,sigma:float):
noise = np.random.normal(mu, sigma, size(df))
return pandas.DataFrame(noise, columns=col)
```

The quality of classification was evaluated based on the test set using the estimator of classification error e. It is defined as a fraction of the total number of objects in the test set that were classified incorrectly. With the use of the analyzed approach, the decisions generated are always unambiguous—thus, one decision class is always generated by the system.

4 Results

For each dispersed set (one of the 270 analyzed) the experiments were carried out according to the following scheme:

- Generating vectors of predictions based on local tables using the k-nearest neighbors classifier. For each data set, three different values of the k parameter were tested, namely $k \in \{1, 5, 10\}$. One parameter value was selected for each dispersed data set that produced the best overall results. For the majority of data—$k = 1$ were selected. Only for data set 4 and the dispersion with 9 and 11 local tables, $k = 5$ was selected.
- Generating a global decision using a neural network with one hidden layer and different number of neurons in the hidden layer. For each data set, the following number of neurons in the hidden layer were tested: $\{1, 3, 4, 4.25, 4.5, 4.75, 5\} \times$ the number of neurons in the input layer. Different number of neurons in the hidden layer was also checked. However, it was noticed that the accuracy of the respective models improves as the number of neurons in the hidden layer increases, but significant improvement declines around $5\times$ the number of neurons in the input layer. The number of neurons in the input layer depends on the number of local tables. Thus, the more dispersed data we have, the more complex the structure of the neural network is.

It should be noted once again that to use the neural network, a 10-fold cross-validation was used on the test set, i.e., the neural network was trained 10 times with

9 folds and tested on one remaining fold. In addition, each test was performed three times to ensure that the results were reliable and not distorted by the influence of randomness. The results for the neural network approach that are given below are the average of the obtained results.

The results obtained for the optimal number of neurons in the hidden layer are presented in Table 2. We do not present the individual results obtained for a different number of neurons in the hidden layer ($\{1, 3, 4, 4.25, 4.5, 4.75, 5\} \times$ the number of neurons in the input layer) due to the limited space. However, for many data sets, the optimal number was around $4\times$ the number of neurons in the input layer. In Table 2, 18 data sets are listed in the rows, the columns distinguish between three different noise levels and five different versions of dispersion.

As can be seen, some data sets were trivial for the analyzed approach. These are data sets 6, 8, 9, 15, 17 and 18 for which the classification error was almost always equal to 0 regardless of the version of dispersion and noise intensity. As can be seen from data characteristics—Table 1, the main factor affecting data simplicity is the number of conditional attributes occurring in the data. The data sets 6, 9, 15 and 18 have 70 attributes (which were split into local tables). However, the approach of using dispersed data perfectly copes with the information stored in local tables and makes correct decisions. For the two remaining data sets 8 and 17, the number of conditional attributes was equal to 50—so it is also a large number, while here the factor influencing the simplicity of the data was a small number of centroids (for set 8) and a large number of objects (for set 17).

The general hypotheses that can be made based on the results in Table 2 in relation to the effect each data set had on the performance of the algorithm proposed in this paper are as follows:

- The more conditional attributes occurred in the data, the better the quality of classification. Multidimensionality is beneficial for dispersed data.
- The greater the number of training objects, the better the quality of classification.
- The greater the number of decision classes, the worse the quality of classification.
- For greater dispersion (number of local tables 3, 5, 7, 9, 11) the quality of classification deteriorates.
- The analyzed method is not immune to noise; high noise and significant dispersion (a large number of local tables) gives poorer quality of classification.

The tests of statistical significance for all of the above hypotheses are presented below.

4.1 Comparison of Experimental Results for Different Numbers of Conditional Attributes

In order to investigate how the number of conditional attributes affects the quality of classification for dispersed data and the approach using neural network, all

Table 2 Results of classification error e for the dispersed system with neural network

Data set	Noise std = 0.01					Noise std = 0.1					Noise std = 0.2				
	No. of local tables														
	3	5	7	9	11	3	5	7	9	11	3	5	7	9	11
1	0.039	0.049	0.059	0.09	0.138	0.049	0.065	0.085	0.133	0.247	0.179	0.241	0.324	0.483	0.636
2	0.029	0.034	0.026	0.032	0.031	0.026	0.029	0.013	0.036	0.031	0.041	0.056	0.076	0.092	0.142
3	0.003	0	0	0.001	0	0.005	0	0	0.001	0.003	0.006	0.013	0.022	0.016	0.016
4	0.017	0.035	0.04	0.058	0.094	0.028	0.065	0.058	0.088	0.203	0.069	0.138	0.383	0.584	0.699
5	0.001	0.002	0.003	0.005	0.006	0.001	0.003	0.005	0.006	0.012	0.002	0.018	0.036	0.084	0.152
6	0	0	0	0	0	0	0	0	0	0	0	0.002	0.006	0.005	0.035
7	0.017	0.022	0.029	0.029	0.041	0.01	0.025	0.03	0.035	0.071	0.018	0.041	0.063	0.102	0.193
8	0	0	0	0	0	0	0	0	0	0	0	0	0	0	0
9	0	0	0	0.003	0.001	0	0	0.004	0.002	0.008	0.007	0.005	0.01	0.007	0.007
10	0.01	0.017	0.019	0.028	0.031	0.01	0.021	0.017	0.029	0.042	0.017	0.024	0.035	0.072	0.123
11	0.002	0.002	0.001	0.002	0.005	0.002	0.002	0.002	0.002	0.005	0.002	0.004	0.003	0.003	0.005
12	0.001	0.003	0.002	0.003	0.003	0.003	0	0.002	0.003	0.003	0.002	0.003	0.003	0.003	0.003
13	0.048	0.058	0.068	0.077	0.115	0.056	0.058	0.061	0.09	0.145	0.073	0.131	0.211	0.366	0.591
14	0.005	0.006	0.011	0.008	0.013	0.01	0.008	0.015	0.01	0.016	0.008	0.025	0.027	0.041	0.051
15	0	0	0.005	0	0.003	0	0	0	0	0	0.003	0.008	0.011	0.005	0.023
16	0.007	0.017	0.026	0.047	0.064	0.016	0.023	0.031	0.055	0.078	0.024	0.047	0.11	0.347	0.636
17	0	0	0	0.001	0.001	0	0	0	0.001	0.003	0	0.001	0.01	0.021	0.028
18	0	0	0	0	0.005	0.001	0.001	0	0.001	0.003	0.002	0	0.002	0.003	0.01

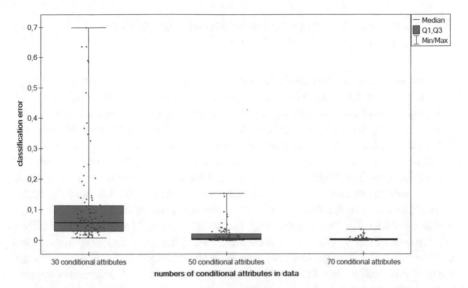

Fig. 1 Box-plot chart with (Median, the first quartile—Q1, the third quartile—Q3) the value of classification error *e* for the neural network with different numbers of conditional attributes in data

results from Table 2 were used—each number of conditional attributes as a separate group. Thus, we have three independent samples for data with 30 conditional attributes, 50 conditional attributes, 70 conditional attributes. Each sample containing 90 observations—results obtained for different versions of dispersion and noise intensity with a constant number of conditional attributes. The Kruskal-Wallis test confirmed that differences among the classification error in these three groups are significant, with a level of $p = 0.000001$, $\chi^2(2) = 151.257$. Then, to determine the pairs of groups between which statistically significant differences occur, the Mann-Whitney test were performed. The test showed that there is a significant difference with $p < 0.0005$ between each pair.

Additionally, comparative box-plot chart for the values of the classification error was created (Fig. 1)—the classification error values obtained for the data with different numbers of conditional attributes are presented. Three different groups of data sets were created: with 30 conditional attributes, with 50 conditional attributes and with 70 conditional attributes. For each group, the quartiles, median, maximum and minimum values of classification error are presented in the chart. As can be observed, distributions of the classification error values in groups are very different. For dispersed data, multidimensionality is very good. The total number of conditional attributes occurring in local tables above 30 already gives a very good quality of classification when using neural network as a fusion method. Anyway, it also reflects the real situation when various units participate in making joint decision. The variety of attributes occurring in local tables has a positive effect on the quality of decisions made.

4.2 Comparison of Experimental Results for Different Numbers of Training Objects

In order to investigate how the numbers of training objects affects the quality of classification for dispersed data and the approach using neural network, all results from Table 2 were used—each number of training objects in data as a separate group. Thus, we have two independent samples for data with 455 training objects and 910 training objects. Each sample containing 135 observations—results obtained for different versions of dispersion and noise intensity with a constant number of training objects. The Mann-Whitney test for independent groups were performed. The test showed that there is significant difference with $p < 0.03$ between groups.

Additionally, comparative box-plot chart for the values of the classification error was created (Fig. 2)—the classification error values obtained for the data with different numbers of training object are presented. Two different groups of data sets were created: with 455 training objects and with 910 training objects. For each group, the quartiles, median, maximum and minimum values of classification error are presented in the chart. As can be observed, distributions of the classification error values in groups are not so different as at the previous graph. This means that the number of objects in dispersed data does not affect the quality of classification as much as the number of conditional attributes. Of course, the difference in results is statistically significant, so the more training objects, the better, but the total number of conditional attributes in dispersed data is much more important.

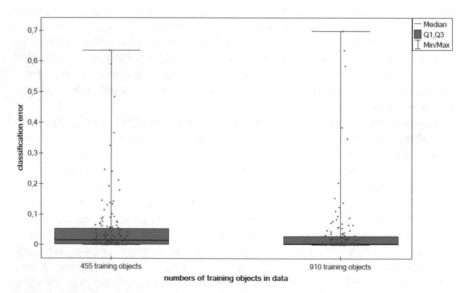

Fig. 2 Box-plot chart with (Median, the first quartile—Q1, the third quartile—Q3) the value of classification error e for the neural network with different numbers of training objects in data

4.3 Comparison of Experimental Results for Different Numbers of Decision Classes

In order to investigate how the numbers of decision classes affects the quality of classification for dispersed data and the approach using neural network, all results from Table 2 were used—each number of decision classes in data as a separate group. Thus, we have two independent samples for data with 5 decision classes and 10 decision classes. The first sample contains 180 observations and the second sample contains 90 observations—results obtained for different versions of dispersion and noise intensity with a constant number of decision classes. The Mann-Whitney test for independent groups confirmed that there is significant difference with $p < 0.0005$ between groups.

Additionally, comparative box-plot chart for the values of the classification error was created (Fig. 3)—the classification error values obtained for the data with different numbers of decision classes are presented. Two different groups of data sets were created: with 5 decision classes and with 10 decision classes. For each group, the quartiles, median, maximum and minimum values of classification error are presented in the chart. As can be observed, the difference between distributions of the classification error values in groups is less noticeable than for the number of conditional attributes, but more visible than for the number of training objects. It is more or less obvious that the more decision classes we have, the more difficult it is to make a correct decision. However, it can be concluded that the number of decision classes

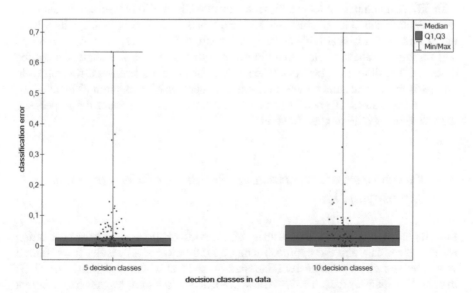

Fig. 3 Box-plot chart with (Median, the first quartile—Q1, the third quartile—Q3) the value of classification error e for the neural network with different number of decision classes in data

in the dispersed data set is less significant in terms of data difficulty than the number
of conditional attributes.

4.4 Comparison of Experimental Results for Different Degree of Dispersion

As the degree of dispersion, we understand the number of local tables occurring in
the dispersed data. In order to investigate how the numbers of local tables affects the
quality of classification for dispersed data and the approach using neural network,
all results from Table 2 were used—each number of local tables in data as a separate
group. Thus, we have five dependent samples (as one data set was divided into a
different number of local tables) for data with 3, 5, 7, 9 and 11 local tables. Each
sample contain 55 observations—results obtained for different data sets and noise
intensity with a constant number of local tables. The Friedman's test confirmed
that differences among the classification error in these five groups are significant,
with a level of $p = 0.000001$. Then, to determine the pairs of groups between which
statistically significant differences occur, the Wilcoxon pair test for dependent groups
were performed. The test showed that there is significant difference with $p < 0.00004$
between each pair.

Additionally, comparative box-plot chart for the values of the classification error
was created (Fig. 4)—the classification error values obtained for the dispersed data
with different numbers of local tables are presented. Five different groups of data sets
were created: with 3 local tables, with 5 local tables, with 7 local tables, with 9 local
tables and with 11 local tables. For each group, the quartiles, median, maximum
and minimum values of classification error are presented in the chart. As can be
observed, the difference between distributions of the classification error values in
groups is most noticeable between the extreme degrees of dispersion (3 local tables
and 11 local tables). The results can be summarized that the greater the dispersion,
the worse the quality of classification.

4.5 Comparison of Experimental Results for Different Noise Intensity in Data

In order to investigate how the intensity of noise affects the quality of classification
for dispersed data and the approach using neural network all results from Table 2
were used—each noise intensity (Gaussian noise level with $std \in \{0.01, 0.1, 0.2\}$)
in data as a separate group. Thus, we have three dependent samples (as three different
noise levels were generated based on one data set) for data with noise $std = 0.01$,
$std = 0.1$ and $std = 0.02$. Each sample contain 90 observations—results obtained
for different data sets and number of local tables with a constant noise intensity.

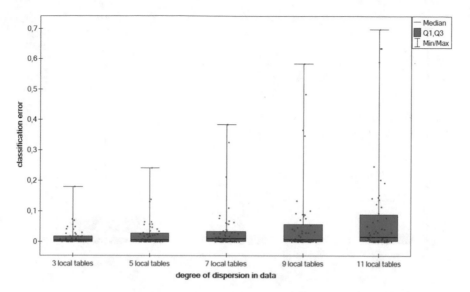

Fig. 4 Box-plot chart with (Median, the first quartile—Q1, the third quartile—Q3) the value of classification error e for the neural network with different degree of dispersion in data

The Friedman's test confirmed that differences among the classification error in these three groups are significant, with a level of $p = 0.000001$. Then, to determine the pairs of groups between which statistically significant differences occur, the Wilcoxon pair test for dependent groups were performed. The test showed that there is significant difference with $p < 0.00002$ between each pair.

Additionally, comparative box-plot chart for the values of the classification error was created (Fig. 5)—the classification error values obtained for the data with different noise intensity $std \in \{0.01, 0.1, 0.2\}$ are presented. Three different groups of data sets were created: with Gaussian noise level $std = 0.01$, with Gaussian noise level $std = 0.1$, and with Gaussian noise level $std = 0.2$. For each group, the quartiles, median, maximum and minimum values of classification error are presented in the chart. For noise intensities equal to $std = 0.01$ and $std = 0.1$, the difference in the distributions is not so noticeable. Only when the noise intensity significantly increased to the level of $std = 0.2$, we can observe a significant increase in the classification error in comparison with the lower noise level. This means that although the classification method for dispersed data with neural network is immune to noise to some extent, it does not cope well with information noise at the $std = 0.2$ level.

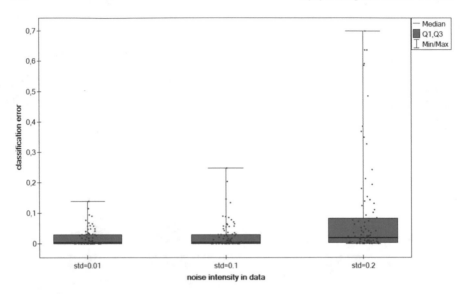

Fig. 5 Box-plot chart with (Median, the first quartile—Q1, the third quartile—Q3) the value of classification error e for the neural network with different noise intensity in data

5 Conclusion

In the paper, the approach to classification based on dispersed data was analyzed, in which the k-nearest neighbors algorithm was used as a local classifier and the neural network as a fusion method. The analyzed approach takes into account the assumptions of data protection and privacy like in federated learning domain and does not interfere with the form of local data. The main aim of the study was to examine the impact of different data characteristics, the degree of dispersion and noise intensity on the classification quality of the above-mentioned approach. For this purpose, 270 different data sets were generated and experiments were performed. Analysis of obtained results and statistical tests were made.

The main conclusions are as follows. Regarding the data sets characteristics, in the case of dispersed data, the number of conditional attributes has the greatest impact on the quality of classification. Multidimensional dispersed data guarantees better quality of classification. The second most important factor is the number of decision classes. The fewer decision classes, the easier the set for classification. The number of training objects has the least influence on the quality of classification. The more objects in the data set, the better the quality of classification we get. The degree of dispersion has a significant impact on the quality of classification. With significant dispersion (11 local tables), the quality of classification significantly decreases in comparison with the results obtained for data with low dispersion (3 local tables). In the case of small dispersion (3, 5, 7 local tables) the impact on the results is not that significant. Noise occurrence also negatively affects the quality of classification. To some extent it can be said that the method is immune to noise. For Gaussian noise level with an average value 0 and standard deviation not exceeding 0.1, the method generates results in which the difference is not that drastic. Nevertheless, for the Gaussian noise level with the standard deviation equal to 0.2, large decrease in the quality of classification has been noted. The method does not cope well with a high noise level.

In future study, it is planned to propose a classification method for dispersed data, which enables conflict analysis and coalitions creation in order to eliminate the negative impact of high degree of dispersion on the quality of classification. In addition, it is planned to apply the proposed approach to dispersed business data, more specifically stock exchange data.

References

1. Adam, S. P., Alexandropoulos, S. A. N., Pardalos, P. M., & Vrahatis, M. N. (2019). No free lunch theorem: A review. *Approximation and Optimization*, 57–82.
2. Blachnik, M. (2019). Ensembles of instance selection methods: A comparative study. *International Journal of Applied Mathematics and Computer Science, 29*(1).
3. Bolon-Canedo, V., & Alonso-Betanzos, A. (2019). Ensembles for feature selection: A review and future trends. *Information Fusion, 52*, 1–12.
4. Czarnowski, I. (2022). Weighted Ensemble with one-class Classification and Over-sampling and Instance selection (WECOI): An approach for learning from imbalanced data streams. *Journal of Computer Science, 61*, 101614.
5. Fernández-Delgado, M., Cernadas, E., Barro, S., & Amorim, D. (2014). Do we need hundreds of classifiers to solve real world classification problems? *The Journal of Machine Learning Research, 15*(1), 3133–3181.
6. Gupta, O., & Raskar, R. (2018). Distributed learning of deep neural network over multiple agents. *Journal of Network and Computer Applications, 116*, 1–8.
7. Kołodziej, T., & Rościszewski, P. (2021) Towards Scalable Simulation of Federated Learning. In *International Conference on Neural Information Processing* (pp. 248–256). Springer, Cham.
8. Konecny, J. H., McMahan, B., Yu, X., Richtarik, P., Suresh, A.T., & Bacon, D. (2016). Federated learning: Strategies for improving communication efficiency. In *NIPS Workshop on Private Multi-Party Machine Learning*.
9. Li, X., Li, X., Pan, D., & Zhu, D. (2020). On the learning property of logistic and softmax losses for deep neural networks. In *Proceedings of the AAAI Conference on Artificial Intelligence* (vol. 34, pp. 4739–4746).
10. Marfo, K. F., & Przybyła-Kasperek, M. (2022). Radial basis function network for aggregating predictions of k-nearest neighbors local models generated based on independent data sets. *Procedia Computer Science, 207*, 3234–3243.
11. Mei, G., Guo, Z., Liu, S., & Pan, L. (2019). SGNN: A graph neural network based federated learning approach by hiding structure. In *2019 IEEE International Conference on Big Data (Big Data)* (pp. 2560–2568).
12. Ng, W. W., Zhang, J., Lai, C. S., Pedrycz, W., Lai, L. L., & Wang, X. (2018). Cost-sensitive weighting and imbalance-reversed bagging for streaming imbalanced and concept drifting in electricity pricing classification. *IEEE Transactions on Industrial Informatics, 15*, 1588–1597.
13. Nguyen, D. C., Ding, M., Pathirana, P. N., Seneviratne, A., Li, J., & Poor, H. V. (2021). Federated learning for internet of things: A comprehensive survey. *IEEE Communications Surveys and Tutorials*.

14. Pfitzner, B., Steckhan, N., & Arnrich, B. (2021). Federated learning in a medical context: A systematic literature review. *ACM Transactions on Internet Technology (TOIT), 21*(2), 1–31.
15. Pławiak, P. (2018). Novel genetic ensembles of classifiers applied to myocardium dysfunction recognition based on ECG signals. *Swarm and Evolutionary Computation, 39*, 192–208.
16. Pławiak, P., Abdar, M., Pławiak, J., Makarenkov, V., & Acharya, U. R. (2020). DGHNL: A new deep genetic hierarchical network of learners for prediction of credit scoring. *Information Sciences, 516*, 401–418.
17. Przybyła-Kasperek, M., & Marfo, K. F. (2022). Influence of noise and data characteristics on classification quality of dispersed data using neural networks on the fusion of predictions. In R. A. Buchmann, G. C. Silaghi, D. Bufnea, V. Niculescu, G. Czibula, C. Barry, M. Lang, H. Linger, & C. Schneider (Eds.), *Information Systems Development: Artificial Intelligence for Information Systems Development and Operations (ISD2022 Proceedings).* Cluj-Napoca, Romania: Babeş-Bolyai University.
18. Przybyła-Kasperek M., & Marfo K. F. (2021). Neural network used for the fusion of predictions obtained by the k-nearest neighbors algorithm based on independent data sources. *Entropy 23*(12), 1568. https://doi.org/10.3390/e23121568
19. Przybyła-Kasperek, M. (2019). Three conflict methods in multiple classifiers that use dispersed knowledge. *International Journal of Information Technology & Decision Making, 18*(02), 555–599.
20. Russell, I.; & Markov, Z. (2017). An introduction to the Weka data mining system. In *Proceedings of the 2017 ACM SIGCSE Technical Symposium on Computer Science Education*, Seattle, WA, USA, 8–11 Mar 2017 (pp. 742–742).
21. Yang, Q., Liu, Y., Cheng, Y., Kang, Y., Chen, T., & Yu, H. (2019). Federated learning, synthesis lectures on artificial intelligence and machine. *Learning, 13*(3), 1–207.
22. Yang, Q., Liu, Y., Chen, T., & Tong, Y. (2019). Federated machine learning: Concept and applications. *ACM Transactions on Intelligent Systems and Technology (TIST), 10*(2), 1–19.
23. Yurochkin, M., Agarwal, M., Ghosh, S., Greenewald, K., Hoang, N., & Khazaeni, Y. (2019). Bayesian nonparametric federated learning of neural networks. In *International Conference on Machine Learning* (pp. 7252–7261). PMLR.
24. Zimmermann, A., Schmidt, R., & Sandkuhl, K. (2019). Multiple perspectives of digital enterprise architecture. In *ENASE* (pp. 547–554)

Temporal VIKOR—A New MCDA Method Supporting Sustainability Assessment

Jarosław Wątróbski⬤, Aleksandra Bączkiewicz⬤, Ewa Ziemba⬤, and Wojciech Sałabun⬤

Abstract Sustainability is a widely incorporated trend into national policies. It implies developing metrics and indicators to measure sustainability. It is evidenced by the development of Sustainable Development Goals (SDG), included in the 2030 Agenda for Sustainable Development proposed by the United Nations (UN). A framework with a complete set of indicators requires a tool including all objectives simultaneously, such as Multi-Criteria Decision Analysis (MCDA) methods. Due to the dynamic nature of sustainable development, a static MCDA approach to evaluating current performance is insufficient. Therefore, this paper proposes a framework with a newly developed method called the Temporal VIKOR and measurement of data variability that allows aggregation of alternatives' efficiency over investigated time. The practical application of this framework is presented in the temporal assessment of sustainable cities and communities concerning the UN's SDG 11 frame. The SDG 11 framework includes goals essential for cities and communities to achieve sustainable development with a focus on achieving equality of access to basic needs meeting for all inhabitants, providing safe, green living space, and reducing harmful environmental impacts. The results prove the proposed framework's potential usefulness for sustainability assessment information systems.

Keywords Temporal MCDA assessment · Sustainability assessment · Temporal VIKOR · Data variability

J. Wątróbski (✉) · A. Bączkiewicz
Institute of Management, University of Szczecin, ul. Cukrowa 8,71-004 Szczecin, Poland
e-mail: jaroslaw.watrobski@usz.edu.pl

E. Ziemba
Department of Business Informatics and International Accounting, Faculty of Finance, University of Economics in Katowice, ul. 1 Maja 50, 40-287 Katowice, Poland

W. Sałabun
National Institute of Telecommunications, ul. Szachowa 1, 04-894 Warsaw, Poland

© The Author(s), under exclusive license to Springer Nature Switzerland AG 2023
G. C. Silaghi et al. (eds.), *Advances in Information Systems Development*,
Lecture Notes in Information Systems and Organisation 63,
https://doi.org/10.1007/978-3-031-32418-5_11

1 Introduction

Effective implementation of sustainability principles and priorities requires regular evaluation and measurement of progress. Furthermore, the concept of sustainable development requires tools suitable for its relevance measurement [13]. Therefore, information systems for evaluating alternatives against the sustainability framework should be designed and implemented to simultaneously and efficiently incorporate multiple evaluation metrics, allow for comparisons with other options, and identify progress over the examined periods of time [5]. The reliability of results provided by information systems for sustainability assessment depends mainly on carefully selected and integrated scientific methods. Thus, for sustainability assessments with multiple objectives and dynamics over time, Multi-Criteria Decision Analysis (MCDA) methods and methods that are useful in measuring performance variability over time are recommended. MCDA methods have become very popular in sustainability assessment because of their ability to simultaneously consider multiple attributes with opposing objectives characteristic of a complex sustainability assessment process [29]. However, sustainable development is not a static or finite process [30]. Still, it is changeable and complex, so the basic MCDA approach of considering a static evaluation of alternatives against criteria is insufficient for sustainability assessment [24]. Thus, there is a need to develop MCDA methods to allow simultaneous assessment of alternatives against criteria at different periods.

This paper aims to present a framework for sustainability assessment based on a newly developed, own method called Temporal VIKOR that enables temporal sustainability assessment in any domain. The implemented framework can be employed as an information system backend engine to evaluate sustainable development involving multiple sustainable development goal indexes and their variability in investigated time. The proposed approach is based on the multi-criteria decision-making method VIKOR (Vise Kriterijumska Optimizacija I Kompromisno Resenje) [28], including data variability measurement over time. The practical application of the developed framework is illustrated in the problem of evaluating sustainable cities and communities regarding the SDG 11 frame proposed by the United Nations (UN) Agenda 2030 for Sustainable Development, based on data provided in the Eurostat database.

The SDG 11 framework incorporates goals related to sustainable urban and community development, such as the renovation and organization of cities and human settlements in a way that ensures more equal opportunities for all inhabitants regarding access to basic services, energy, transportation, housing, and green public spaces, while reducing resource consumption and harmful environmental impacts [4, 18, 27]. It implies organizing inclusive, resilient, safe urban settlements, increasing involvement in urban management with a focus on aspects of waste management and pollution reduction and ensuring access to safe public spaces for everybody [25]. Indicators developed by the UN provided in SDG 11 support cities in assessing their efforts to achieve sustainable development [7].

The rest of the paper is organized as follows. In Sect. 2 literature review is provided. Section 3 gives methodology of performed research. Results are presented in discussed in Sect. 4. Finally, in the last Sect. 5 conclusions and a summary of the research are included, and future work directions are drawn.

2 Literature Review

The 17 Sustainable Development Goals (SDGs) and 169 related targets are at the heart of the UN's 2030 Agenda for Sustainable Development. They provide a new policy framework worldwide for ending all forms of poverty, fighting inequalities, and tackling climate change while ensuring that no one is left behind [30]. However, the priority of sustainable development proposed in the UN's Agenda 2030 raises many challenges for countries. Among them is a reliable assessment of achieving Sustainable Development Goals, considering the diversity of objectives required to be addressed and the need to grasp the dynamics of change over time. Indeed, sustainable development is not static but is characterized by variability in achieving the goals over time, representing the progress demonstrated by a country [8]. The sustainability challenges discussed can be overcome by intelligent use of relevant data collected in databases and technology that incorporates the appropriate integration of scientific methods with proven effectiveness [10]. Many methodological approaches for reliable, temporal sustainability assessment can be found in the literature. Among the methods used are statistical machine learning methods for time series data [10], statistical analysis methods [6], and MCDA methods [11]. It can be observed that MCDA methods are widely popular for assessing sustainable development because of their ability to address multiple assessment dimensions and indicators simultaneously.

Due to the dynamic nature of sustainability, the classical MCDA approach of considering assessment at a single point in time is insufficient [24]. It implies the need to develop extensions to MCDA methods that allow for evaluating alternatives with performance variability regarding the time factor. The literature review shows that some attempts toward adapting MCDA methods for temporal assessment have been made. A paper in which the authors adapted the TOPSIS method for the temporal evaluation of sustainable forest management is worth mentioning [5]. The proposed method is based on a re-evaluation of the TOPSIS decision matrix containing utility function values given by TOPSIS for particular periods of investigated time in the previous stage. However, the presented method requires assigning significant values, namely weights, for particular periods. Therefore, the authors suggest setting the highest significance to the most recent period. However, this procedure needs to assign weights representing the relevance of each period, which requires expert knowledge. Besides, there needs to be a more detailed procedure to determine the values of the weights for each period, called confidence levels. Among the proposed temporal assessment multi-criteria approaches, there are also methods using forgetting function involving aggregation of utility function values received for particular periods [12]. These approaches require assigning weight values for examined periods based on the decision maker's knowledge. The literature review demonstrated that PROMETHEE II is also an adapted method for temporal assessment for sustainable forest management assessment [24] and road safety assessment [19]. The method proposed by the authors requires conducting pairwise comparisons between criteria for each period examined and aggregating the results received. In the next step, obtained rank relations are transformed into preference relations for each pair of alternatives and each period [24]. The complexity of the presented procedure makes it problematic for hierarchical models, considering a large number of evaluation criteria. The limitations in available research papers identified during the literature review inspired the authors to further research in adapting MCDA methods for reliable but uncomplicated and automatized temporal evaluation, not requiring the participation of the decision-maker in determining periods significance.

To develop a framework for temporal sustainability assessment, the authors chose the multi-criteria VIKOR method and integrated standard deviation to measure the variability of results over time. The performance of this method is to evaluate each alternative concerning each criterion considered by measuring the distance of each solution to the ideal solution. Therefore, this procedure requires significance values, namely weights for the criteria, which the decision-maker can determine subjectively or using objective weighting methods. The results of the VIKOR method are utility function values for each alternative representing proximity to the ideal solution. The alternative closest to the ideal solution is the ranking leader [23]. Standard deviation, chosen by the authors as a measure of variability, is one of the best indicators to assess the level of data variability [16]. This measure establishes the temporal evaluation data variability for each period without requiring decision-makers to assign period significance. Since the authors' goal was to develop a fully autonomous, analyst-independent framework that does not require the involvement of experts to determine the importance of criteria, the objective Entropy weighting method was used as the weighting technique. This method determines the criteria weights based on the measurement of information in the decision matrix with performance data [17]. The basic assumptions and mathematical formulas of all the methods integrated into the proposed framework are given in Sect. 3.

3   Methodology

Since this paper aims to introduce the Temporal VIKOR method, the primary assumption of the VIKOR method is to rank alternatives by measuring the closeness of the evaluated variants to the ideal solution in the presence of conflicting criteria. Furthermore, VIKOR has been applied to the sustainability assessment of the energy sector [20], healthcare system [9], and logistics [26]. However, mentioned works involve a static approach that considers evaluating the current performance of alternatives. Therefore, the authors' main contribution is to propose the extension of VIKOR with aggregating results from different periods to generate a ranking considering the variability of results over time.

3.1   The Temporal VIKOR Method

The proposed method is based on alternatives' utility function values determined by VIKOR for each period and the standard deviation measuring results' variability over time without involving an expert to assign appropriate significance for each period. The flowchart of the proposed framework of Temporal VIKOR is displayed in Fig. 1.

In the Temporal VIKOR method, after conducting the VIKOR evaluation for each decision matrix containing performance values from each year, a matrix $X = [x_{pi}]_{t \times m}$ including the utility function values calculated for the alternatives in subsequent years is created. Criteria significance values (weights) are determined for each year by the objective Entropy weighting method based on data included in decision matrices for each investigated year. The entropy weighting method is detailed in Sect. 3.2.

The result of applying the VIKOR method for a single period p is a vector with utility function values S_i^p for m alternatives ($i = 1, 2, \ldots, m$). In the next step, the direction and value of the utility function values' variability over the analyzed time are determined for each alternative by standard deviation. Then the variability value is added to alternatives' utility function values received by VIKOR for the recent year, which is the most significant for a decision-maker, with the sign consistent with the direction of variability. The final value of the utility function considers the strength and direction of the results' variability. The steps of Temporal VIKOR are presented in the following steps.

Step 1. Create a matrix with vectors of utility function values calculated using the VIKOR method for subsequent analyzed periods: $S = [s_{pi}]_{t \times m}$ where m denotes the number of alternatives ($i = 1, 2, \ldots, m$) and t denotes the number of evaluated periods ($p = 1, 2, \ldots, t$).

The subsequent steps of the VIKOR method are given below, based on [2].

Step 1.1 Determination of the best f_j^* and the worst f_j^- values for each criteria functions. For profit criteria Eq. (1) is applied and for cost criteria Eq. (2) is employed.

$$f_j^* = \max_i f_{ij}, \quad f_j^- = \min_i f_{ij} \tag{1}$$

$$f_j^* = \min_i f_{ij}, \quad f_j^- = \max_i f_{ij} \tag{2}$$

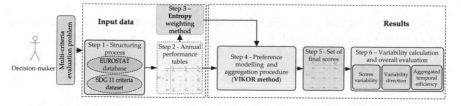

Fig. 1 Flowchart presenting the framework of the Temporal VIKOR Method.

Step 1.2 Computation of the S_i and R_i values according to Eqs. (3) and (4).

$$S_i = \sum_{j=1}^{n} w_j (f_j^* - f_{ij})/(f_j^* - f_j^-) \tag{3}$$

$$R_i = \max_j [w_j (f_j^* - f_{ij})/(f_j^* - f_j^-)] \tag{4}$$

Step 1.3 Calculation of the Q_i values as Eq. (5) presents

$$Q_i = v(S_i - S^*)/(S^- - S^*) + (1 - v)(R_i - R^*)/(R^- - R^*) \tag{5}$$

where $S^* = min_i S_i$, $\quad S^- = max_i S_i$, $\quad R^* = min_i R_i$, $\quad R^- = max_i R_i$,
v represents the weight assigned for the strategy of "most criteria". For calculations performed in this research $v = 0.5$ was selected.

Step 1.4 The rankings of alternatives are constructed by sorting S, R, and Q values in ascending order. The result is three ranked lists.

Step 1.5 A compromise solution is proposed considering the conditions of good advantage and acceptable stability within the three vectors obtained in the previous step [3]. The best alternative is the one with the lowest value and the leading position in the ranking Q [14]. The final matrix S, including vectors with VIKOR utility function values (scores) for each $p - th$ year y_p in rows for alternatives a_i in columns, is demonstrated by Eq. (6).

$$
S = \begin{array}{c|ccccc}
 & a_1 & \dots & a_i & \dots & a_m \\
\hline
y_1 & s_{11} & \dots & s_{1i} & \dots & s_{1m} \\
\vdots & \vdots & \dots & \vdots & \dots & \vdots \\
y_p & s_{p1} & \dots & s_{pi} & \dots & s_{pm} \\
\vdots & \vdots & \dots & \vdots & \dots & \vdots \\
y_t & s_{t1} & \dots & s_{ti} & \dots & s_{tm}
\end{array}
\tag{6}
$$

Step 2. For each alternative, determine the standard deviation as Eq. (7) shows.

$$\sigma_i = \sqrt{\frac{\sum_{p=1}^{t}(s_{pi} - \bar{s}_i)^2}{t}} \tag{7}$$

Step 3. Determine the direction of variability dir_i for each alternative applying Eqs. (8) and (9).

$$b_i = \sum_{p=2}^{t} s_p - s_{p-1} \tag{8}$$

$$dir_i = \begin{cases} -1 & b_i < 0 \\ 1 & b_i > 0 \\ 0 & b_i = 0 \end{cases} \tag{9}$$

Step 4. Update the most recent utility function value S_i^t obtained for the last evaluated year t for each alternative by the variability value σ_i according to its direction dir_i, as Eq. (10) presents.

$$S_i = S_i^t + dir_i \cdot \sigma_i \tag{10}$$

Step 5. Rank the alternatives in ascending order of S_i value. The alternative with the lowest S_i value is the best-ranked alternative.

3.2 The Entropy Weighting Method

The subsequent steps of the Entropy weighting method are presented below, based on [17].

Step 1. Normalize decision matrix using sum normalization method to get normalized decision matrix $P = [p_{ij}]_{m \times n}$, where $i = 1, 2, \ldots, m$ and $j = 1, 2, \ldots, n$, m denotes alternatives number, and n represents criteria number.

Step 2. Calculate the entropy values E_j for each jth criterion as Eq. (11) demonstrates.

$$E_j = -\frac{\sum_{i=1}^{m} p_{ij} ln(p_{ij})}{ln(m)} \tag{11}$$

Step 3. Calculate d_j as Eq. (12) shows.

$$d_j = 1 - E_j \tag{12}$$

Step 4. Calculate the entropy weights for each jth criterion following Eq. (13).

$$w_j = \frac{d_j}{\sum_{j=1}^{n} d_j} \tag{13}$$

3.3 Spearman Rank Correlation Coefficient—r_s

The Spearman Rank Correlation Coefficient is calculated as Eq. (14) demonstrates, where N means size of vector x and y [21]. This coefficient is computed to compare two rankings x and y, and determine their correlation. High values of r_s, which are close to 1, denote high correlation.

$$r_s = 1 - \frac{6 \cdot \sum_{i=1}^{N}(x_i - y_i)^2}{N \cdot (N^2 - 1)} \tag{14}$$

3.4 Weighted Spearman's Rank Correlation Coefficient—r_w

The r_w correlation coefficient is calculated to compare two rankings x, and y as Eq. (15) demonstrates. N represents a number of rank values x_i and y_i. High values of r_w, close to 1, indicate a high correlation of compared rankings [22].

$$r_w = 1 - \frac{6 \sum_{i=1}^{N}(x_i - y_i)^2((N - x_i + 1) + (N - y_i + 1))}{N^4 + N^3 - N^2 - N} \tag{15}$$

3.5 Other Measures of Data Variability

3.5.1 The Gini Coefficient

The Gini coefficient is a quantitative index employed to determine data variability and illustrate differences appearing in investigated data sets [15]. In following Equations i means index of particular alternative $i = 1, 2, \ldots, m$, p denotes each period examined $p = 1, 2, \ldots, t$ and s_{pi} defines the i-th alternative efficiency score related to p-th period explored. $\bar{s}_i$ means the expected value for efficiency scores from all periods addressed for the i-th alternative. It is computed as its mean value. If $\bar{s}_i$ is not equal to 0, the Gini coefficient of the particular criterion is computed using Eq. (16). Otherwise, Eq. (17) is employed.

$$G_i = \sum_{p=1}^{t} \sum_{k=1}^{t} \frac{|s_{pi} - s_{ki}|}{2t^2 \bar{s}_i} \tag{16}$$

$$G_i = \sum_{p=1}^{t} \sum_{k=1}^{t} \frac{|s_{pi} - s_{ki}|}{t^2 - t} \tag{17}$$

3.5.2 Statistical Variance

The statistical variance is explained based on [1]. Statistical variance determines the dispersion of values regarding their mean value. Unlike statistical analyses that primarily analyze outliers, statistical variance explores all data points and establishes their distribution. Thus, statistical variance delivers helpful information about data distribution. Compute the statistical variance following Eq. (18) where $X = [x_{ij}]_{m \times n}$

represents the decision matrix containing m alternatives and n criteria. N defines the number of criteria in columns of the decision matrix X.

$$v_j = \frac{\sum_{j=1}^{N}(x_{ij} - \overline{x}_j)^2}{N} \tag{18}$$

3.6 The Dataset

This research covers applying the proposed method to assess sustainable development in selected European countries concerning the Sustainable development indicator SDG 11 (Sustainable cities and communities). SDG 11 is one of the seventeen Sustainable Development Goals, which are the basis of the United Nations (UN) 2030 Agenda for Sustainable Development 2030, a new policy framework worldwide toward ending all forms of poverty, fighting inequalities, and tackling climate change. The temporal assessment of selected countries was performed concerning ten criteria included in the SDG 11 indicator listed in Table 1.

The country assessment was based on data provided by the Eurostat website (accessed on 10 April 2022). Data on the performance values of the examined coun-

Table 1 Evaluation criteria of the SDG 11 framework

C_j	Name	Unit	Target
C_1	Overcrowding rate	% of population	↓
C_2	Suffering from noise	% of population	↓
C_3	Settlement area	m^2 per capita	↑
C_4	Road traffic deaths	Rate (number per 100 000 persons)	↓
C_5	Exposure to air pollution by particulate matter (particulates $< 10\,\mu m$)	$\mu g/m^3$	↓
C_6	Recycling of municipal waste	% of total waste generated	↑
C_7	Poor dwelling conditions	% of population	↓
C_8	Connection to at least secondary wastewater treatment	% of population	↑
C_9	Collective passenger transport (Share of buses and trains)	% of total inland passenger-km	↑
C_{10}	The reported occurrence of crime	% of population	↓

Table 2 Performance data for examined countries collected for 2019

A_i	Country	C_1	C_2	C_3	C_4	C_5	C_6	C_7	C_8	C_9	C_{10}
A_1	Belgium	5.7	16	583.5	5.6	18.9	54.7	16.7	84.25	18.7	13.3
A_2	Bulgaria	41.1	8.9	623.4	9	30.4	31.5	11.6	64.51	15.3	20.2
A_3	Czechia	15.4	14	634.4	5.8	20.3	33.3	7.3	82.6	26.2	7.8
A_4	Denmark	10	20.1	1053.8	3.4	16.5	51.5	14.9	97.5	17.3	7.5
A_5	Germany	7.8	26.1	586.7	3.7	16.1	66.7	12	95.97	15.2	13.1
A_6	Estonia	13.9	8.2	1484.4	3.9	10.8	30.8	13.8	83.45	19.9	7.4
A_7	Ireland	3.2	8.2	972.7	2.8	12.7	37.4	12.5	61.86	18.2	8.8
A_8	Greece	28.7	19.7	710.2	6.4	27.5	21	12.5	94.8	17	16.9
A_9	Spain	5.9	14.1	577.5	3.7	19.4	39.3	14.7	86.62	15.4	11.6
A_{10}	France	7.7	17.3	845.1	4.8	17.4	43.9	11.5	79.3	16.8	14.7
A_{11}	Croatia	38.5	8.2	722.5	7.3	30.9	30.2	10.2	36.9	15.8	2.7
A_{12}	Italy	28.3	11.9	484.3	5.3	25.5	51.4	14	59.6	17.9	9.4
A_{13}	Cyprus	2.2	15.4	939	5.9	26	16.3	31.1	29.8	18.5	12.7
A_{14}	Latvia	42.2	13.1	1276.1	6.9	20.2	41	19.3	80.1	17.2	6.1
A_{15}	Lithuania	22.9	13.3	1090.5	6.7	21.9	49.7	14	76.45	9.4	3.2
A_{16}	Luxembourg	7.1	20.2	565.2	3.5	20.3	48.9	15.4	98.1	17.4	11.2
A_{17}	Hungary	20.3	9.7	811.5	6.2	24.4	35.9	22.3	80.26	28.4	5.3
A_{18}	Netherlands	4.8	26.6	456.9	3.4	19.1	56.9	14.7	99.5	14.4	16.3
A_{19}	Austria	15.1	19.5	740.1	4.7	17.4	58.2	9.4	99.78	23	8.4
A_{20}	Poland	37.6	12.6	633.7	7.7	27	34.1	10.8	74.44	19.3	4.4
A_{21}	Portugal	9.5	22.7	689.1	6.7	18.6	28.9	24.4	84.64	11.7	6.7
A_{22}	Romania	45.8	18.2	528.4	9.6	25.6	11.5	9.4	49.4	21.1	9.6
A_{23}	Slovenia	11.6	14.5	625.1	4.9	20.4	58.9	20.6	69	13.4	8
A_{24}	Slovakia	34.1	10.5	631.8	5	21	38.5	5.7	68.1	26.2	5.6
A_{25}	Finland	7.7	12.8	2447.6	3.8	10.2	43.5	4.1	85	16.1	6.4
A_{26}	Sweden	15.6	17	2223	2.2	12.3	46.6	7	95	17.7	13
A_{27}	United Kingdom	4.8	19.8	426.9	2.8	15.3	44.1	17.6	100	12.6	24.2

tries for the last analyzed year, 2019 is provided in Table 2. Detailed data sources in the form of links to the data for each criterion for each investigated year are provided in the GitHub repository. Additionally, ready-to-use datasets in the form of CSV files containing decision matrices with performance values for each evaluated year are also available in the GitHub repository at https://github.com/energyinpython/ ISD-2022-Temporal-VIKOR. Based on the requirement for completeness of data, the authors selected a set of 27 countries for the assessment covering the eight most recent years available in the Eurostat database (2012–2019). Evaluated countries are displayed in Fig. 3 in Sect. 4.

Table 3 Entropy criteria weights determined for 2012–2019

Years	C_1	C_2	C_3	C_4	C_5	C_6	C_7	C_8	C_9	C_{10}
2012	0.346	0.045	0.139	0.064	0.057	0.116	0.075	0.043	0.038	0.078
2013	0.343	0.047	0.144	0.067	0.050	0.109	0.090	0.044	0.036	0.072
2014	0.346	0.041	0.147	0.070	0.041	0.096	0.102	0.043	0.032	0.081
2015	0.349	0.047	0.159	0.068	0.048	0.083	0.088	0.041	0.032	0.086
2016	0.342	0.046	0.167	0.061	0.050	0.076	0.090	0.041	0.032	0.094
2017	0.342	0.051	0.162	0.070	0.058	0.068	0.088	0.036	0.035	0.090
2018	0.328	0.060	0.141	0.059	0.044	0.072	0.094	0.036	0.034	0.130
2019	0.316	0.062	0.143	0.072	0.043	0.064	0.096	0.036	0.032	0.137

4 Results

This section presents the results of European countries' sustainability assessment obtained using the Temporal VIKOR method. Table 3 provides vectors with values of particular criteria determined with the objective Entropy weighting method for each year considered in this research.

Figure 2 visualizes the weights by displaying their values for each criterion and year in a column graph. It can be observed that the highest values of weights in all explored years occurred for criterion C_1 (Overcrowding rate). It implies that criterion C_1 is highly significant in sustainability assessment with the SDG 11 framework. Table 4 presents a matrix with the utility function values calculated by the VIKOR method for each explored year for all investigated alternatives. Vectors with utility function values are located in particular columns of the presented matrix for each year. For the VIKOR method, the best-evaluated alternatives have the lowest utility function value. Table 5 shows the annual rankings of all analyzed alternatives for 2012–2019. Rankings are generated based on utility function values sorted in

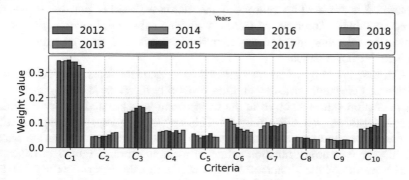

Fig. 2 Entropy criteria weights determined for each investigated year.

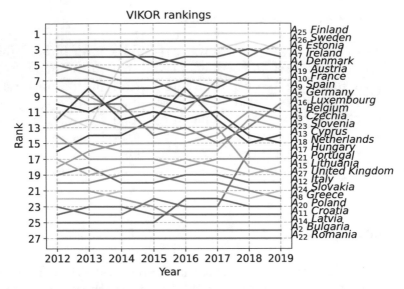

Fig. 3 Rankings of classical VIKOR for examined periods.

ascending order according to the VIKOR method rule. It can be observed that option A_{25} (Finland) is the stable leader in the rankings in all years examined.

On the other hand, option A_6 (Estonia) shows an excellent progression, as it was promoted from the thirteenth place taken in 2013 to second place in 2018. In the case of such different results, the classical multi-criteria evaluation conducted individually for each year is insufficient. Outcome annual rankings of classical VIKOR for 2012–2019 are displayed in Fig. 3. Rank 1 denotes the best-scored leader country. There is a clear need for a temporal approach that considers the dynamics and direction of results variability over the years under investigation. This gap is addressed by the Temporal VIKOR approach proposed in this work. The input for Temporal VIKOR is the S matrix prepared as presented in Table 6.

Matrix S is prepared by transposing the matrix with utility function values displayed in Table 4. The rows of matrix S include subsequent years, and columns contain the following alternatives (countries). Matrix S is then evaluated by the Temporal VIKOR method.

First, the variability of scores obtained in subsequent years is calculated with the standard deviation measure, and the variability direction is determined. Then, utility function values received in the most recent year are updated by variability values according to variability direction. This way, new, aggregated, temporal utility function values for alternatives are obtained. Finally, evaluated options are ranked according to new utility function values in ascending order. Table 7 provides the research results of the Temporal VIKOR method in the form of utility function values (TMP Util.), ranking (TMP Rank), variability of utility function values (Var.), and directions (Dir.) of scores' variability considering improvement or worsening for

Table 4 The matrix with VIKOR utility function values for each investigated year

A_i	2012	2013	2014	2015	2016	2017	2018	2019	A_i	2012	2013	2014	2015	2016	2017	2018	2019
A_{25}	0.000	0.000	0.000	0.000	0.000	0.000	0.000	0.000	A_{18}	0.230	0.242	0.280	0.337	0.376	0.367	0.378	0.400
A_{26}	0.037	0.035	0.061	0.117	0.151	0.146	0.201	0.200	A_{17}	0.775	0.781	0.795	0.776	0.779	0.800	0.394	0.412
A_6	0.228	0.320	0.205	0.205	0.211	0.197	0.190	0.205	A_{21}	0.320	0.374	0.392	0.424	0.444	0.423	0.398	0.414
A_7	0.104	0.131	0.159	0.217	0.238	0.227	0.201	0.210	A_{15}	0.332	0.505	0.534	0.500	0.439	0.469	0.415	0.434
A_4	0.121	0.135	0.163	0.217	0.248	0.248	0.230	0.253	A_{27}	0.255	0.266	0.297	0.349	0.396	0.382	0.409	0.440
A_{19}	0.211	0.232	0.261	0.327	0.348	0.353	0.303	0.325	A_{12}	0.469	0.502	0.553	0.602	0.589	0.575	0.569	0.590
A_{10}	0.203	0.209	0.232	0.293	0.330	0.320	0.313	0.327	A_{24}	0.674	0.694	0.708	0.691	0.694	0.691	0.644	0.631
A_9	0.219	0.248	0.278	0.327	0.354	0.338	0.332	0.348	A_8	0.519	0.540	0.546	0.579	0.609	0.630	0.639	0.669
A_5	0.197	0.222	0.249	0.315	0.349	0.354	0.339	0.355	A_{20}	0.830	0.805	0.813	0.797	0.771	0.799	0.778	0.756
A_{16}	0.217	0.248	0.276	0.356	0.393	0.391	0.365	0.357	A_{11}	0.798	0.779	0.782	0.791	0.797	0.806	0.784	0.773
A_1	0.219	0.252	0.270	0.327	0.353	0.353	0.340	0.362	A_{14}	0.672	0.678	0.776	0.780	0.812	0.810	0.874	0.817
A_3	0.349	0.350	0.358	0.392	0.403	0.386	0.358	0.363	A_2	0.852	0.847	0.893	0.849	0.894	0.911	0.926	0.927
A_{23}	0.327	0.344	0.378	0.398	0.410	0.397	0.364	0.376	A_{22}	1.000	1.000	1.000	1.000	1.000	1.000	1.000	1.000
A_{13}	0.329	0.333	0.318	0.347	0.348	0.375	0.384	0.387									

Table 5 The matrix with VIKOR rankings for each investigated year

A_i	2012	2013	2014	2015	2016	2017	2018	2019	A_i	2012	2013	2014	2015	2016	2017	2018	2019
A_{25}	1	1	1	1	1	1	1	1	A_{18}	12	8	12	11	12	11	14	15
A_{26}	2	2	2	2	2	2	4	2	A_{17}	23	24	24	22	23	23	16	16
A_6	11	13	5	3	3	3	2	3	A_{21}	14	17	17	17	18	17	17	17
A_7	3	3	3	5	4	4	3	4	A_{15}	17	19	18	18	17	18	19	18
A_4	4	4	4	4	5	5	5	5	A_{27}	13	12	13	13	14	13	18	19
A_{19}	7	7	8	8	7	8	6	6	A_{12}	19	18	20	20	19	19	20	20
A_{10}	6	5	6	6	6	6	7	7	A_{24}	22	22	21	21	21	21	22	21
A_9	9	9	11	10	11	7	8	8	A_8	20	20	19	19	20	20	21	22
A_5	5	6	7	7	9	10	9	9	A_{20}	25	25	25	25	22	22	23	23
A_{16}	8	10	10	14	13	15	13	10	A_{11}	24	23	23	24	24	24	24	24
A_1	10	11	9	9	10	9	10	11	A_{14}	21	21	22	23	25	25	25	25
A_3	18	16	15	15	15	14	11	12	A_2	26	26	26	26	26	26	26	26
A_{23}	15	15	16	16	16	16	12	13	A_{22}	27	27	27	27	27	27	27	27
A_{13}	16	14	14	12	8	12	15	14									

Table 6 Fragment of the S matrix with the VIKOR utility function values for each examined year

A_i	A_1	A_2	A_3	A_4	A_5	A_6	A_7	A_8	A_9	A_{10}	…
2012	0.2193	0.8521	0.3495	0.1210	0.1973	0.2279	0.1044	0.5191	0.2192	0.2035	…
2013	0.2519	0.8469	0.3499	0.1352	0.2218	0.3196	0.1308	0.5398	0.2481	0.2094	…
2014	0.2698	0.8931	0.3585	0.1629	0.2486	0.2053	0.1589	0.5462	0.2778	0.2321	…
2015	0.3266	0.8491	0.3916	0.2165	0.3153	0.2055	0.2169	0.5789	0.3266	0.2933	…
2016	0.3530	0.8938	0.4026	0.2477	0.3489	0.2114	0.2377	0.6089	0.3537	0.3299	…
2017	0.3534	0.9110	0.3858	0.2477	0.3544	0.1972	0.2272	0.6304	0.3381	0.3197	…
2018	0.3398	0.9261	0.3576	0.2297	0.3390	0.1903	0.2008	0.6392	0.3319	0.3128	…
2019	0.3617	0.9271	0.3627	0.2528	0.3553	0.2053	0.2098	0.6694	0.3479	0.3266	…

evaluated countries. Additionally, the ranking obtained using the Temporal VIKOR method was compared with two benchmarking rankings. One of the benchmarking rankings was received using the VIKOR for average performance values for the analyzed years (AVG). The second one was determined for the most recent year evaluated (2019). An explanation of the abbreviations used in Table 7 is provided as follows: 2019 Util.—Utility function values for 2019, AVG Util.—Utility function values for averaged (AVG) performance values for 2012–2019, TMP Util.—Utility function values for Temporal (TMP) VIKOR for 2012–2019, Var.—variability of obtained scores.

The complete results and the datasets are available on GitHub at the previous link. The most significant improvement was observed for Hungary (A_{17}) and Estonia (A_6). Contrarily, the most significant regression was noted for Latvia (A_{14}), the United Kingdom (A_{27}), and Luxembourg (A_{16}). The two countries with different performances demonstrated the highest stability. The first of them is Finland (A_{25}), which was consistently the leader in the rankings throughout the observation period. The second country with stable performance is Romania (A_{22}), which was rated the worst in all years. Significant progress was observed for Estonia (A_6), which climbed from 13th place in 2013 to fifth place in 2014, third place in 2015, and second place in 2018. It is definitely better reflected by the Temporal VIKOR ranking. Estonia was ranked second in Temporal VIKOR ranking because of the development progress achieved. It reveals Estonia's progress better than the ranking gained for averaged performances, in which it is ranked fifth. For Hungary (A_{17}), a significant promotion by eight positions appeared in 2018 from 24th place, in 2013, to 16th place in 2018. Hungary retained 16th rank in 2019. The ranking derived from performance averages, in which Hungary ranked 22nd, does not consider progress in recent years. The significant improvement in performance taken into account by the Temporal VIKOR method resulted in Hungary's final ranking of third. Latvia (A_{14}) ranked 21st in 2012–2013, dropped steadily in subsequent years and ranked 25th in 2016.

The average ranking, which classified Latvia at 23rd place, does not reflect this phenomenon. In contrast, the Temporal VIKOR ranking of 25th better reflects both the trend of decline in recent years and the 25th place in the most recent year most

Table 7 Comparison of Temporal VIKOR results with benchmarking approaches

A_i	2019 Util.	2019 Rank	AVG Util.	AVG Rank	TMP Util.	TMP Rank	Var.	Dir.
A_1	0.3617	11	0.3247	10	0.4127	13	0.0510	↓
A_2	0.9271	26	0.8857	26	0.9589	26	0.0317	↓
A_3	0.3627	12	0.3804	15	0.3819	9	0.0192	↓
A_4	0.2528	5	0.2166	4	0.3032	6	0.0504	↓
A_5	0.3553	9	0.3115	7	0.4159	14	0.0606	↓
A_6	0.2053	3	0.2280	5	0.1664	2	0.0389	↑
A_7	0.2098	4	0.2015	3	0.2552	4	0.0455	↓
A_8	0.6694	22	0.5929	20	0.7197	22	0.0504	↓
A_9	0.3479	8	0.3182	9	0.3951	10	0.0472	↓
A_{10}	0.3266	7	0.2903	6	0.3773	8	0.0508	↓
A_{11}	0.7728	24	0.7918	24	0.7623	24	0.0104	↑
A_{12}	0.5902	20	0.5638	19	0.6342	21	0.0440	↓
A_{13}	0.3867	14	0.3629	14	0.4113	12	0.0246	↓
A_{14}	0.8172	25	0.7809	23	0.8828	25	0.0655	↓
A_{15}	0.4343	18	0.4608	18	0.4937	18	0.0594	↓
A_{16}	0.3574	10	0.3399	12	0.4214	15	0.0640	↓
A_{17}	0.4116	16	0.7009	22	0.2461	3	0.1655	↑
A_{18}	0.3995	15	0.3375	11	0.4616	17	0.0620	↓
A_{19}	0.3254	6	0.3117	8	0.3757	7	0.0503	↓
A_{20}	0.7557	23	0.7959	25	0.7334	23	0.0223	↑
A_{21}	0.4141	17	0.4138	17	0.4501	16	0.0360	↓
A_{22}	1.0000	27	1.0000	27	1.0000	27	0.0000	=
A_{23}	0.3755	13	0.3899	16	0.4019	11	0.0263	↓
A_{24}	0.6310	21	0.6824	21	0.6058	20	0.0252	↑
A_{25}	0.0000	1	0.0000	1	0.0000	1	0.0000	=
A_{26}	0.2005	2	0.1244	2	0.2640	5	0.0635	↓
A_{27}	0.4396	19	0.3577	13	0.5044	19	0.0648	↓

relevant to the assessment. United Kingdom (A_{27}) dropped to 19th from its 12th place ranking in 2013, a drop of seven positions represents a significant deterioration reflected in Temporal VIKOR ranking the United Kingdom at 19th place. Results analysis also allows observing an interesting occurrence when some countries such as A_3, A_{13}, A_{21}, and A_{23} registered a promotion despite the variability toward worsening determined by the Temporal VIKOR method. This phenomenon appears because, at that time, other countries experienced higher variability with a decreasing trend, which allowed countries with less worsening performance to advance. Finally, it is worth noting that the proposed method, during variability determination, considers utility function values instead of places in the ranking.

This strategy enables obtaining more precise results and allows catching and accurately reflecting subtle differences. Table 8 displays the values of the two rank-

Table 8 Correlation of Temporal VIKOR ranking with benchmarking approaches

r_s	2019	Average	r_w	2019	Average
Temporal	0.9194	0.8132	Temporal	0.8968	0.7938

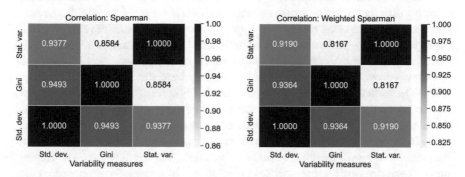

Fig. 4 Correlations between rankings provided with different variability measures used in Temporal VIKOR

ing correlation coefficients, namely Spearman (r_s) and Weighted Spearman (r_w) rank correlation coefficients representing the degree of convergence of the ranking obtained using the Temporal VIKOR method compared to the VIKOR rankings for 2019 and the averaged data from 2012–2019. High values of r_s and r_w coefficients imply high convergence of the compared rankings, which in the case of the problem solved in this paper implies a good result. The presented results confirm that the Temporal VIKOR method mainly incorporates more recent results than results from earlier years, consistently assuming the greatest significance of the most recent year.

Besides standard deviation, there are other measures of data variability, for example, the Gini coefficient and statistical variance. Additional measures are useful in the comparative analysis conducted to confirm the reliability of the proposed method. In this case, to confirm the reliability of Temporal VIKOR, a correlation test was performed on the results obtained using standard deviation as a measure of variability and Gini coefficient and statistical variance. Correlations between rankings were determined using two coefficients: Spearman and Weighted Spearman. Correlation values are displayed in Fig. 4.

The results show high correlations of the Temporal VIKOR ranking using the standard deviation measure of variation with the reference ranking obtained using the Gini coefficient and statistical variance. It is reflected in high correlation values exceeding 0.9. The results confirm the reliability of Temporal VIKOR because it gives consistent results even when changing the type of variability measure.

5   Conclusion

A proper and complete assessment of sustainable development, in addition to simultaneous consideration of multiple criteria belonging to various dimensions and representing different objectives, also requires consideration of the variability of results over time. Such a strategy provides an opportunity to assess the achievement of long-term goals, determine the potential of individual alternatives, and identify trends for development or regression. The multi-criteria method of temporal sustainability assessment proposed in this paper fulfills these requirements. In addition, the Temporal VIKOR method allows considering the variability of results over time measured by standard deviation, eliminating the involvement of experts. The presented approach provides an opportunity to grasp the variability and direction simultaneously in the utility function values and utilize them in creating a single final ranking that evaluates the overall progress of the alternatives at a given time. The result obtained is simple to interpret and does not require complex calculations. Moreover, the proposed method can also be useful in analyzing the variability of evaluation criteria performance, which seems helpful for broader analyses, including managerial implications.

Since the limitations of this research paper are the use of only one MCDA method (VIKOR) and one measure of variability (standard deviation), among the directions for further work is a broader exploration of the framework for temporal sustainability assessment incorporating the employment of other MCDA methods. It also seems interesting to extend the research by using other measures of data variability such as entropy, statistical variance, and Gini coefficient and comparing the results with the standard deviation measure. Directions for future work also include testing the developed framework for datasets representing other multi-criteria, temporal sustainability problems and testing the effectiveness of the proposed method for larger datasets.

Acknowledgements This research was funded in part by National Science Centre, Poland 2022/45/B/HS4/02960. For the purpose of Open Access, the author has applied a CC-BY public copyright licence to any Author Accepted Manuscript (AAM) version arising from this submission

References

1. Bączkiewicz, A., & Wątróbski, J. (2022). A multi-criteria approach to sustainable energy management evaluation focusing on renewable energy sources. *Procedia Computer Science, 207*, 4640–4650.
2. Bera, B., Shit, P.K., Sengupta, N., Saha, S., & Bhattacharjee, S. (2021). Susceptibility of deforestation hotspots in terai-dooars belt of Himalayan foothills: a comparative analysis of VIKOR and TOPSIS models. *Journal of King Saud University-Computer and Information Sciences* .
3. Cao, Z., Zou, Y., Zhao, X., Hong, K., & Zhang, Y. (2021). Multidimensional fairness equilibrium evaluation of urban housing expropriation compensation based on VIKOR. *Mathematics, 9*(4), 430.

4. Delanka-Pedige, H., Munasinghe-Arachchige, S., Abeysiriwardana-Arachchige, I., & Nirmalakhandan, N. (2021). Wastewater infrastructure for sustainable cities: assessment based on UN sustainable development goals (SDGs). *International Journal of Sustainable Development & World Ecology, 28*(3), 203–209.
5. Frini, A., & Benamor, S. (2018). Making decisions in a sustainable development context: A state-of-the-art survey and proposal of a multi-period single synthesizing criterion approach. *Computational Economics, 52*(2), 341–385.
6. Fritz, S., See, L., Carlson, T., Haklay, M. M., Oliver, J. L., Fraisl, D., et al. (2019). Citizen science and the United Nations sustainable development goals. *Nature Sustainability, 2*(10), 922–930.
7. Giles-Corti, B., Lowe, M., & Arundel, J. (2020). Achieving the SDGs: Evaluating indicators to be used to benchmark and monitor progress towards creating healthy and sustainable cities. *Health Policy, 124*(6), 581–590.
8. Giupponi, C., & Gain, A. K. (2017). Integrated spatial assessment of the water, energy and food dimensions of the sustainable development goals. *Regional Environmental Change, 17*(7), 1881–1893.
9. Hariz, H. A., Dönmez, C. Ç., & Sennaroglu, B. (2017). Siting of a central healthcare waste incinerator using GIS-based Multi-Criteria Decision Analysis. *Journal of Cleaner Production, 166*, 1031–1042.
10. Holloway, J., & Mengersen, K. (2018). Statistical machine learning methods and remote sensing for sustainable development goals: A review. *Remote Sensing, 10*(9), 1365.
11. Kandakoglu, A., Frini, A., & Ben Amor, S. (2019). Multicriteria decision making for sustainable development: A systematic review. *Journal of Multi-Criteria Decision Analysis, 26*(5–6), 202–251.
12. Karczmarczyk, A., Wątróbski, J., & Jankowski, J.: Comparative study of different MCDA-based approaches in sustainable supplier selection problem. In *Information Technology for Management: Emerging Research and Applications* (pp 176–193). Springer (2018)
13. Klopp, J. M., & Petretta, D. L. (2017). The urban sustainable development goal: Indicators, complexity and the politics of measuring cities. *Cities, 63*, 92–97.
14. Kumar, M., & Samuel, C. (2017). Selection of best renewable energy source by using VIKOR method. *Technology and Economics of Smart Grids and Sustainable Energy, 2*(1), 8.
15. Lai, H., Liao, H., Šaparauskas, J., Banaitis, A., Ferreira, F. A., & Al-Barakati, A. (2020). Sustainable cloud service provider development by a z-number-based dnma method with gini-coefficient-based weight determination. *Sustainability, 12*(8), 3410.
16. Li, H., Wang, W., Fan, L., Li, Q., & Chen, X. (2020). A novel hybrid MCDM model for machine tool selection using fuzzy DEMATEL, entropy weighting and later defuzzification VIKOR. *Applied Soft Computing, 91*, 106207.
17. Lotfi, F. H., & Fallahnejad, R. (2010). Imprecise Shannon's entropy and multi attribute decision making. *Entropy, 12*(1), 53–62.
18. MacDonald, A., Clarke, A., Ordonez-Ponce, E., Chai, Z., & Andreasen, J. (2020). Sustainability managers: The job roles and competencies of building sustainable cities and communities. *Public Performance & Management Review, 43*(6), 1413–1444.
19. Martins, M. A., & Garcez, T. V. (2021). A multidimensional and multi-period analysis of safety on roads. *Accident Analysis & Prevention, 162*, 106401.
20. Sahabuddin, M., & Khan, I. (2021). Multi-criteria decision analysis methods for energy sector's sustainability assessment: Robustness analysis through criteria weight change. *Sustainable Energy Technologies and Assessments, 47*, 101380.
21. Sajjad, M., Sałabun, W., Faizi, S., Ismail, M., & Wątróbski, J. (2022). Statistical and analytical approach of multi-criteria group decision-making based on the correlation coefficient under intuitionistic 2-tuple fuzzy linguistic environment. *Expert Systems with Applications, 193*, 116341.
22. Sałabun, W., Wątróbski, J., & Shekhovtsov, A. (2020). Are MCDA Methods Benchmarkable? A Comparative Study of TOPSIS, VIKOR, COPRAS, and PROMETHEE II Methods. *Symmetry, 12*(9), 1549.

23. Sari, F. (2021). Forest fire susceptibility mapping via multi-criteria decision analysis techniques for Mugla, Turkey: A comparative analysis of VIKOR and TOPSIS. *Forest Ecology and Management, 480,* 118644.

24. Urli, B., Frini, A., & Amor, S. B. (2019). PROMETHEE-MP: a generalisation of PROMETHEE for multi-period evaluations under uncertainty. *International Journal of Multicriteria Decision Making, 8*(1), 13–37.

25. Wallis, A.K., Westerveld, M.F., & Burton, P. (2022). Ensuring communication-friendly green and public spaces for sustainable cities: Sustainable Development Goal 11. *International Journal of Speech-Language Pathology, 1,* 1–5.

26. Wang, C. N., Nguyen, N. A. T., Dang, T. T., Lu, C. M., et al. (2021). A compromised decision-making approach to third-party logistics selection in sustainable supply chain using fuzzy AHP and fuzzy VIKOR methods. *Mathematics, 9*(8), 886.

27. Wątróbski, J., Bączkiewicz, A., Król, R., & Sałabun, W. (2022). Green electricity generation assessment using the CODAS-COMET method. *Ecological Indicators, 143,* 109391.

28. Wątróbski, J., Bączkiewicz, A., & Sałabun, W. (2022). New multi-criteria method for evaluation of sustainable RES management. *Applied Energy, 324,* 119695.

29. Wątróbski, J., Bączkiewicz, A., Ziemba, E., & Sałabun, W. (2022). Sustainable cities and communities assessment using the DARIA-TOPSIS method. *Sustainable Cities and Society,* 103926.

30. Xu, Z., Chau, S. N., Chen, X., Zhang, J., Li, Y., Dietz, T., et al. (2020). Assessing progress towards sustainable development over space and time. *Nature, 577*(7788), 74–78.

Topic Classification for Short Texts

Dan Claudiu Neagu⃝, Andrei Bogdan Rus⃝, Mihai Grec⃝,
Mihai Boroianu⃝, and Gheorghe Cosmin Silaghi⃝

Abstract In the context of TV and social media surveillance, constructing models
to automate topic identification of short texts is a key task. This paper constructs
worth-to-consider models for practical usage, employing Top-K multinomial classification methodology. We describe the full data processing pipeline, discussing
about dataset selection, text preprocessing, feature extraction, model selection and
learning, including hyperparameter optimization. We will test and compare popular
methods including: standard machine learning, deep learning, and a fine-tuned BERT
for topic classification.

1 Introduction

Part of Natural Language Processing (NLP), document classification assigns a document to one or more classes or categories. When the input is text, we speak about text
classification, which is a popular technique applied to automate various processes
like spam filtering [20], humor detection [15], sentiment analysis [26] and many more

D. C. Neagu · A. B. Rus · M. Grec · M. Boroianu
Cicada Technologies, Bd. Nicolae Titulescu 18 apt. 82, 400420 Cluj-Napoca, Romania
e-mail: dan.neagu@ubbcluj.ro

A. B. Rus
e-mail: bogdanr@cicadatech.eu

M. Grec
e-mail: mihaig@cicadatech.eu

M. Boroianu
e-mail: mihaib@cicadatech.eu

D. C. Neagu · G. C. Silaghi (✉)
Babes-Bolyai University, Str. Theodor Mihali 58-60, 400591 Cluj-Napoca, Romania
e-mail: gheorghe.silaghi@ubbcluj.ro

A. B. Rus
Technical University, Str. Memorandumului 28, 400114 Cluj-Napoca, Romania

© The Author(s), under exclusive license to Springer Nature Switzerland AG 2023   207
G. C. Silaghi et al. (eds.), *Advances in Information Systems Development*,
Lecture Notes in Information Systems and Organisation 63,
https://doi.org/10.1007/978-3-031-32418-5_12

including topic classification. This last term refers to identifying abstract topics that occur in a collection of texts or documents, with the motivation of discovering the interests discusses or described within the textual data.

Opposed to sentiment analysis where the overall target is to determine the polarity of a text (i.e. positive, neutral or negative), in topic classification the number of classes could be extremely high and in many cases, overlapping, thus the problem becoming much more difficult [17, 26].

Rather than considering topic classification as a standard classification problem, we employ a *Top-K* multinomial classification methodology [19, 24], with the goal of inferring the k highest probable classes for each text, from a set of predefined topics.

Special focus is towards social media, as its texts are of great informative value. In general, social media platforms disseminate short unstructured texts, generated by their authors from mobile devices in short time intervals, with plenty of bad language [14]. These characteristics of social media inputs bring in additional challenges, because such a short text does not provide sufficient word occurrences for a traditional text classification based on "Bag-Of-Words" document representations [21].

The work presented here is done under the umbrella of a media surveillance project [12], aiming to investigate specific habits of people interacting with TV and social media. Several restrictions and limitations are imposed on the project like: frequent model retraining and deployment due to the volatile nature of the environment, the need to processed immense volumes of data in short time intervals, and the need to adhere to data privacy laws and security standards. Given that, this paper describes our efforts for building a worth-to-consider classifier for short texts which can be applied on social media data. Besides searching for a good topic prediction accuracy of the various classifiers, the processing time is also highly important.

We present in detail the steps involved in the full NLP pipeline, from raw texts to topic prediction, and the Top-1, Top-2, and Top-3 accuracies achieved by various classifiers. The pipeline contains the following processes: dataset selection, data cleaning and preprocessing, feature extraction, training and testing various classical machine learning and deep learning models, and the hyper-parameter optimization methodology used for identifying the best parameters for each trained ML model.

The rest of the paper is structured as following: in Sect. 2 we present related work competing or influencing our research. Section 3 introduces the data under study and the steps followed to construct the topic classification models. Section 4 present the achieved results and Sect. 5 concludes our work.

2   Related Work

Discovering abstract topics that occur in a collection of texts or documents could be done with either *Topic Classification* or *Topic Modeling*.

Topic modeling is a popular unsupervised technique for extracting latent variables from large datasets, being well suited for textual data [7, 44]. Among the most used methods for topic modeling we mention Probabilistic Latent Semantic Analysis (PSLA) and Latent Dirichlet Allocation (LDA). In essence, conventional topic models reveal topics within a text corpus by implicitly capturing the document-level word co-occurrence patterns [8, 46]. Directly applying these models on short texts will suffer from the severe data sparsity problem, i.e. the sparse word co-occurrence patterns in individual document [21]. Some workarounds try to alleviate the sparsity problem. Albanese & Feuerstein aggregate a number of short texts to create a lengthy pseudo-document [2], its effectiveness being heavily data-dependent. The Biterm Topic Model [10] extracts unordered word pairs (i.e. biterms) co-occuring in short texts and the latent topic components being modeled using these biterms. This method seems to perform better for short texts compared to other traditional approaches.

The main advantage of topic modeling methods is that they do not require labeled data, thus data collection becomes more accessible and could be done in a fully or partially automated manner. Despite its popularity, topic modeling is prone to serious issues with optimization, noise sensitivity, and instability, which could occur if training data is unreliable [1].

If labeled training data is available, the supervised learning approach could be used for *topic classification*, to alleviate majority of the issues related to topic modeling. Having a set of training records $D = \{X_1, X_2, \ldots, X_N\}$ where each record X_i refers to a data point (i.e. document, paragraph, sentence, word) and each record is labeled with a topic value from a set of k different discrete values, the purpose is to build ML models which are able to generalize text patterns based on the training records in order to predict with reliable accuracy rates the topic of texts never seen before.

Learning models on a small dataset with around 770 tweets distributed over 18 classes, Lee et al. [25] achieved an accuracy of $\approx 65\%$ with the multinomial Naive Bayes classifier and $\approx 62\%$ with the standard SVM classifier. Rahman & Akter [40] worked with 6000 texts extracted from *Amazon's product review corpus*[1] distributed over only 6 very specific topics and achieved a very high classification rate of $\approx 92\%$ with NB, $\approx 82\%$ with k-NN and $\approx 79\%$ with decision trees. Zeng et al. [47] proposes a hybrid approach, extracting the most relevant latent features with topic modeling and then, feeding them to supervised ML algorithms like SVM, CNN and LSTM. For the experiments they used the Twitter dataset released by TREC2011[2] with around 15000 tweets, semi-automatically labeled into 50 topic classes. The best obtained accuracy is with CNN and is poor: only $\approx 39.5\%$, and the topic modeling seems not to significantly improve the learning.

Difficulty of topic classification resides also in the big number of target classes. To overcome this, some authors [19, 33] use the Top-K accuracy instead of the standard one. Rather than classifying a text to just one class and matching it to the a-priori label, the model will produce the most K probable classes and if the label is among

---

[1] https://jmcauley.ucsd.edu/data/amazon/.

[2] http://trec.nist.gov/data/tweets.

them, we consider the text as being correctly classified. In our work we will report the standard accuracy (i.e. Top-1), the Top-2 and Top-3 accuracies.

3   Data Processing Methodology

In the following subsections we present dataset and the whole pipeline methodology for topic classification.

All processing modules were implemented in Python 3.9 and experiments were run on a powerful machine with the following specifications: 2 × Intel Xeon Gold 6230 CPUs (20 Core at 2.1 GHz), 128 GB DDR4 internal RAM, 8 × NVIDIA Tesla V100 32 GB.

3.1   Dataset Description

The dataset selected for our topic classification experiments is the *News Category dataset* available on Kaggle[3] [30]. This dataset contains 202372 news headlines collected between 2012 up to 2018 from HuffPost[4] The site offers news, satire, blogs, original content, and covers a variety of topics like politics, business, entertainment, technology, popular media, and more.

There are a number of reasons why we selected this dataset as the benchmark for our experiments: (i) it contains short texts similar to those found on social media platforms, (ii) the topics are fairly general and the number of topics is large enough, (iii) the category of each article was manually labeled, (iv) high data volume, and (v) it was relatively recently collected. Each record of the dataset contains the following attributes: *category* (41 categories), *headline*, *short_description*, *authors*, *date* (of the publication), and *link* (URL link of the article).

For our classification problem we will focus only on the headline and short description attributes of the dataset, ignoring the authors and date of publication. Therefore, we merged the headline and the short description attributes and created a novel attribute named *text_merged*.

The vast majority of merged texts contain between 94 and 254 characters, with the mean being ≈ 174 and the standard deviation almost 80 characters. This proves that the generated texts have the characteristics of short texts similar to those present in social media platforms (a Twitter tweet is limited to 280 characters, a Youtube comment is limited to 300 characters).

Figure 1a shows the distribution of the records among the 41 categories. The top-3 most popular classes are: "POLITICS" which contains ≈ 16% of the records,

---

[3] https://www.kaggle.com/datasets/rmisra/news-category-dataset.

[4] https://www.huffpost.com/, formerly The Huffington Post until 2017, is an American news aggregator and blog with localized and international editions.

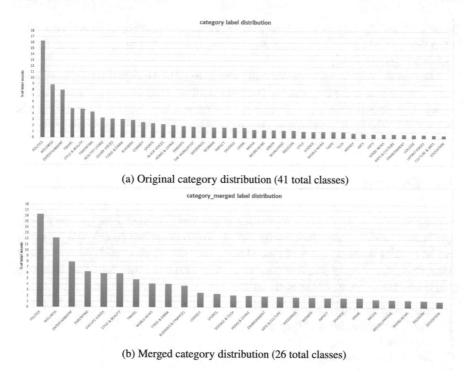

(a) Original category distribution (41 total classes)

(b) Merged category distribution (26 total classes)

Fig. 1 Class distributions for the News Category dataset

"WELLNESS" which contains ≈ 9% of the records, and "ENTERTAINMENT" which contains ≈ 8% of the records. The least most popular 4 classes are: "COLLEGE", "LATINO VOICES", "CULTURE & ARTS", and "EDUCATION" each containing around 0.5% of the records.

Some classes have different labels but denote the same topic, for example the classes "ARTS & CULTURE" and "CULTURE & ARTS". Other classes are highly granular, like "SCIENCE" and "TECH" but can be naturally grouped together in a common class. In order to improve the quality of the data, we decided to cluster together a number of classes. Therefore, we transformed the following classes as follows: "HEALTHY LIVING" was relabeled as the existing "WELLNESS" class; "PARENTS" was relabeled as the existing "PARENTING" class; "STYLE" was relabeled as the existing "STYLE & BEAUTY" class; "GREEN" was relabeled as the existing "ENVIRONMENT" class; "TASTE" was relabeled as the existing "FOOD & DRINK" class; "COLLEGE" was relabeled as the existing "EDUCATION" class; "THE WORLDPOST" and "WORDPOST" were relabeled as the existing "WORLD NEWS" class; "ARTS" and "CULTURE & ARTS" were relabeled as the existing "ARTS & CULTURE" class; "BUSINESS" and "MONEY" were relabeled as a new class named "BUSINESS & FINANCES"; "SCIENCE" and "TECH" were relabeled as a new class named "SCIENCE & TECH"; "QUEER VOICES", "BLACK

VOICES", and "LATINO VOICES" were relabeled as a new class named "GROUPS VOICES"; "FIFTY" and "GOOD NEWS" were relabeled as a new class named "MISCELLANEOUS".

The new class feature was named *category_merged* and it contains only 26 distinct topics, compared to the original 41. The full distribution of the merged topics can be seen in Fig. 1b. After the topic clustering, no class has less than 1% of record labels, meaning that the least popular class has more than 2000 records in the dataset.

3.2   Text Preprocessing

In order to remove the natural noise which is existent in textual data, we developed a specialized module for preprocessing (PP). It contains various functionalities which can be applied on many types of textual data, not only on short texts. Some of them relies on SpaCy[5] library [22]. For the News Category dataset we applied the following preprocessing steps, in this specific order:

(1) extra white space removal,
(2) word lemmatisation and tokenization,
(3) stop-word removal,
(4) lower case capitalization and
(5) punctuation mark removal

In step 1, all consecutive white spaces which appear more than two times are removed from the texts, i.e. "Foo   bar!" becomes "Foo bar!". In step 2, we performed word lemmatisation and tokenization, as advised by [32]. The input for this step are strings of the *text_merged* attribute and the generated output is the list of tokens, where each token is either a number, lemmatised word, or symbol. In step 3, stop-word tokens are identified and removed using the stop-word dictionary offered by SpaCy. Stop-word removal is a common task in text preprocessing, as indicated by [26]. In step 4, all tokens are transformed in lower case capitalization in order to reduce the number of tokens which are written in different capitalizations but refer to the same concept. The final step 5 removes all extra punctuation marks within tokens.

Table 1 presents the preprocessing output for three random records of the dataset.

For the BERT classifier, a single preprocessing step consisting of sentence tokenization was applied.

After the preprocessing step, the dataset was split into training and testing sets. The training set contains 75% of the data while the testing test contains the remaining 25%. The split was made such that the class distribution between the train and test set is similar.

---

[5] https://spacy.io/.

Table 1 Text preprocessing example

Text_merged	Preprocessed text_merged
"There Were 2 Mass Shootings In Texas Last Week, But Only 1 On TV. She left her husband. He killed their children. Just another day in America"	["2", "mass", "shootings", "texas", "last", "week", "1", "tv", "leave", "husband", "kill", "child", "day", "america"]
"Jim Carrey Blasts 'Castrato' Adam Schiff And Democrats In New Artwork. The actor gives Dems an ass-kicking for not fighting hard enough against Donald Trump"	["jim", "carrey", "blasts", "castrato", "adam", "schiff", "democrats", "new", "artwork", "actor", "dems", "ass", "kicking", "fight", "hard", "donald", "trump"]
"Edward Snowden: There's No One Trump Loves More Than Vladimir Putin. But don't count on Robert Mueller to nail him, the NSA whistleblower warns."	["edward", "snowden", "one", "trump", "love", "more", "vladimir", "putin", "count", "robert", "mueller", "nail", "nsa", "whistleblower", "warn"]

3.3 Feature Extraction

Feature extraction is a key process of every NLP task. It starts from an initial set of text data and builds derived values (features) intended to be informative and non-redundant, facilitating the subsequent learning and generalization steps [17, 28]. Here, we considered *Term Frequency-Inverse Document Frequency (TFIDF or TF-IDF)* [42] and *Word2Vec* [29]. TFIDF is still widely used today [4] together with classical ML methods, although it can not account for the similarity between the words in the document and in general, Word2Vec is seen as facilitating deep learning.

We trained a TFIDF vectorizer on the training set. The TFIDF was applied on the preprocessed token lists and the vocabulary was set to contain the tokens which appear at least 5 times. This was done in order to remove a large number of tokens which are very rarely used or tokens which may have been erroneously built in the preprocessing step. The trained TFIDF vocabulary contains around 25000 tokens. Due to the sparse nature of TFIDF, the large number of training instances, and the vocabulary size, the trained vectors are stored and used in the *Compressed Sparse Row (CRS)* format.

Word2Vec[29] uses a neural network model to learn word associations from a large corpus of texts, being able to better capture the language semantics. We used the Gensim[6] library [41] for learning the word vectors from our training data and we finally kept only the tokens which appear at least 5 times. The Word2Vec algorithm was applied using the Continuous Bag-Of-Words (CBOW) architecture model. The vector embedding size for each token was set to 300. The model was trained with the following parameters: learning rate *alpha* of 0.025, *window* of 5, over 5 *epochs*. After this step, each token from the vocabulary is represented by a feature vector of size 300.

---

[6] https://radimrehurek.com/gensim/.

In order to fine-tune the BERT classifier, the pre-trained BertTokenizer[7] was applied on the tokenized sentences. This process generated the specific BERT encodings consisting of word mappings and an attention masks.

3.4 Classifier Selection

Many supervised classifiers have been applied for text classification tasks [17, 26]. For our experiments we selected the following methods for classification:

- Classic ML: Bernoulli Naive Bayes (Bernoulli NB), Random Forest, Support Vector Machine (SVM)
- Deep Learning: Long Short-Term Memory (LSTM), Convolutional Neural Network (CNN)
- BERT plus a classification layer

Bernoulli NB[27] is a probabilistic classifier designed to use an implicit mixture model for generation of the underlying documents. It can handle irrelevant or missing features which are very common in text classification and in some NLP tasks this is the reference model [28]. Due to its simplistic nature, model training times are usually very low. Random forest [9] is a popular choice for classification tasks over a large features set, including text classification [17]. SVMs [24] are reported to achieve state of the art prediction performances for text classification compared to other classic ML algorithms. Thus, we selected SVM among our classifiers and we trained the models with a linear kernel in order to better scale to large number of samples and to reduce the training time.

Deep Learning (DL) with the help of artificial neural networks has achieved state of the art results across many domains, including a wide variety of NLP applications. Thus, we selected two variations of DL for our task: the Long short-term memory (LSTM) network [35] as a type of recurrent neural networks (RNNs) and the Convolutional Neural Network (CNN) [23].

The BERT model available on the Hugging Face transformers[8], was used with the standard English uncased variant. On top of BERT we added a simple neural network with one hidden dense layer with 128 nodes and ReLU activation function, followed by the standard classification layer with 26 nodes which will generate the topic. We selected Adam as the optimization function, with a learning rate of 2×10^{-5} and $\epsilon = 10^{-8}$. The loss function was set to Categorical Cross-Entropy. The BERT classifier was fine-tuned on the specific BERT encodings generated in Sect. 3.3.

Compared to the standard ML algorithms presented above, LSTMs and CNNs are able to process sequences of data as is the case with the multidimensional representation of Word2Vec. Due to this, the LSTM and CNN algorithms were applied

---

[7] https://huggingface.co/docs/transformers/main_classes/tokenizer.

[8] https://huggingface.co/docs/transformers/model_doc/bert.

on the Word2Vec features while the classic learning algorithms (Bernoulli NB, Random Forest, and SVM) were applied only on the TFIDF features. In order to apply LSTM and CNN on the sequenced data, we introduced an embedding layer between the input layer and the hidden layers. The embedding layer maps each token from an instance to its corresponding Word2Vec representation, being equipped with the word embeddings generated during feature extraction (see Sect. 3.3).

The classic learning algorithms were implemented with the help of *Scikit-Learn* library [37], the deep learning algorithms with *Keras* [11], and the BERT classifier with PyTorch [36].

3.5   Hyperparameter Optimization

Hyperparameter optimization or tuning is the step of choosing the optimal parameters for a classifier such as to minimize the generalization error [6]. Among various alternatives that could be considered, like exhaustive grid search, random search [5] or Bayesian optimization [43], we opted for evolutionary optimization (EO).

Evolutionary optimization using population-based probabilistic search algorithms [38] could drastically speed up the hyperparameter optimization while producing a good-enough combination of parameter values. Noticing the vast literature accompanying the metaheuristic design of DNNs [34] or recent applications of DL where parameters were selected with the help of genetic algorithms [18, 45] or suggestions that EO could outperform Bayesian optimization [31], we decided to employ a classical genetic algorithm for hyperparameter search.

We used Sklearn-genetic-opt library[9][3] for implementing the GA-based EO. Sklearn-genetic-opt makes usage of the Deap framework[10] [16], which supplies many evolutionary algorithms needed for solving optimization problems.

The GA was designed as following: given a number n of parameters to optimize for some specific classifier, a chromosome is a vector $(P_1, P_2, ..., P_n)$ of values selected for each parameter. A population consisting of 10 individuals which are evolved over 20 generations, with a crossover probability of 0.8 and mutation probability to 0.1. Individuals are selected for the next generation with a standard elitist tournament of size 3. Internally, each individual is evaluated using the accuracy as fitness function, computed with 3-folds cross-validation.

In the case of the classic ML algorithms all the parameters described in the official Sklearn documentation were optimized. In the case of the LSTM and CNN, we considered among the parameters the following: the network capacity (the number of hidden layers and the number of units per layer), the activation function, the regularization function, drop-out rate. Because both CNN and LSTM need the embedding weight parameter which is 2D tensor, we modified the source code of Sklearn-genetic-opt in order to transmit the multi-dimmensional parameters directly

---

[9] https://sklearn-genetic-opt.readthedocs.io/.

[10] https://github.com/deap/deap.

Table 2 Optimal parameters identified with EO hyperparameter search

Classifier	Optimal parameters (parameter_name=parameter_value)
Bernoulli NB	alpha=0.222, binarize=0.07, fit_prior=True
Random Forest	n_estimators=23, criterion=entropy, max_depth=None, min_sample_split=18, min_sample_leaf=8, max_features=None, max_leaf_nodes=None, min_impurity_decrease=0.01, bootstrap=True, oob_score=True, warm_start=False, class_weight=None, ccp_alpha=0.005
Linear SVM	dual=False, C=0.233, penalty=l2, fit_intercept=True, intercept_scaling=2.575, class_weight=None, tol=0.0001, loss=squared_hinge, multiclass=ovr, max_iter=431
LSTM	batch_size=559, epochs=16, activation=tanh, recurrent_activation=sigmoid, kernel_initializer=lecun_normal, recurrent_initializer=he_uniform, bias_initializer=zeros, unroll=False, kernel_regularizer=None, bias_regularizer=None, activity_regularizer=None, use_bias=True, recurrent_regularizer=l1, mask_zero=False, optimizer=rmsprop, loss=sparse_categorical_crossentropy, dropout_rate=0.484, embedding_layer_size=300, n_hidden_layers=2, first_hidden_layer_size=89, second_hidden_layer_size=63
CNN	batch_size=880, epochs=17, activation=softsign, kernel_initializer=orthogonal, use_bias=True, bias_initializer=glorot_normal, kernel_regularizer=None, bias_regularizer=l1, activity_regularizer=l2, optimizer=adamax, mask_zero=True, kernel_size=3, padding=same, pool_size=2, pool_strides=1, loss=sparse_categorical_crossentropy, dropout_rate=0.264, embedding_layer_size=300, n_hidden_layers=1, hidden_layer_size=112

to Deap. Other additional parameters important for DL were optimized: batch size, number of epochs, initializer functions.

In general, convergence can be seen after 10–15 generations, thus evolving the populations over 20 generations is enough to guarantee a good parameter selection. In Table 2 we present the parameters and their optimum values for each classifier used in our experiments.

In the case of BERT classifier, training and testing just one model is extremely time consuming therefore we decided not to perform evolutionary optimization. Instead of cross-validation, 10% of the training data was used for validation. The model was trained for 4 epochs because after this number the accuracy on the validation set started to decrease.

Figure 2 summarizes all steps presented in this section.

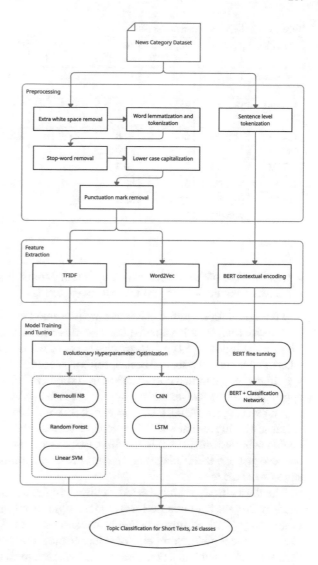

Fig. 2 Architecture of the topic classification system

4 Experiments and Results

As mentioned in Sect. 3.1, we worked with the *News Category* dataset. We applied all the processing steps presented in Fig. 2, while considering three encodings of the dataset. The optimization and training was done on $\approx$ 151000 instances (75% of the dataset) while the testing on $\approx$ 51000 (25% of the dataset). We collected the following performance metrics for each model:

- Top-1, Top-2 and Top-3 accuracy on the test set (%),
- execution time of the hyperparameter optimization process $\rightarrow$ opt (s),

Table 3 Classification performances

Classifier	Feature extraction	Top-1 Acc. (%)	Top-2 Acc. (%)	Top-3 Acc. (%)	Opt (s)	Train (s)	Test (s)
Bernoulli NB	TFIDF	64.2	78.9	85.2	443	0.66	0.04
Random Forest	TFIDF	31.0	40.7	50.2	2992	14.5	0.1
Linear SVM	TFIDF	68.0	81.8	87.1	8005	25.8	0.03
LSTM	Word2vec	67.6	80.5	85.6	286062	130.2	9.5
CNN	Word2Vec	66.2	80.1	85.3	37317	46.5	1.5
BERT	BERT encoder	75.52	88.13	92.3		11189	357

- training time of the classifier with optimum parameters → train (s), and
- classifier prediction time on the test set → test (s).

The results for all tested classifiers are presented in Table 3.

As expected, BERT achieved the best classification accuracy in all three cases. The Top-1, Top-2, and Top-3 accuracies are approximately 7.5%, 6%, and 5% higher when compared to the second best algorithm, Linear SVM. But all of this came with a very high computational cost. Fine tuning a single BERT classifier over 4 epochs was approx. 430 times slower when compared to Linear SVM. The difference on the test data is even bigger, BERT taking around 350 s while Linear SVM taking less than 1 s. Because training a single BERT model took around 3 h, hyperparameter optimization could not be performed on this classifier. But, as we noticed, this process is not needed because just one BERT classifier trained with the recommended parameters supplies state-of-the-art results.

The third best algorithm, LSTM, achived similar accuracies to SVM in the Top-1 and Top-2 cases but underperformed more significantly in the Top-3 case. In terms of accuracy CNN performed slightly worse than LSTM but the difference can be considered negligible. Bernoulli NB achieved the second worse Top-1 accuracy score, of around 64%, but had a comparable performance to CNN and LSTM in the Top-2 and Top-3 cases. The Random Forest classifier had by far the worst accuracy, even the Top-3 accuracy being considerably lower than the Top-1 accuracy of the Bernoulli NB.

We took advantage of a very powerful machine to run all experiments. Even so, time spent for hyperparameter optimization and model training, with the exception of Bernoulli NB, are not negligible (especially for BERT and the deep learning algorithms). The optimization time for Bernoulli was around 7 min while for linear SVM was almost 50 min. Searching for the best structure and parameters for CNN took ≈ 10 h and for LSTM ≈ 79 h.

Regarding the training time, Bernoulli NB was by far the faster with a training time of under 1 s. This was excepted due to the simplistic nature of the algorithm. Random

Forest and Linear SVM had the second and third best training times of around 15 s and 25 s, respectively. Compared to Linear SVM, CNN took about double the time to train while LSTM was 5 times slower. Regarding the testing times, all the classic algorithms performed extremely well, having execution times of under 0.2 s. CNN had a testing time of around 1.5 s while LSTM of around 9.5. Although considerably slower than the classic algorithms, these times are very good considering that the testing was made on over 50000 records. BERT classifier had by far the slowest training and testing times.

If no a-priori English language knowledge in the form of pre-trained Word2Vec embeddings like Glove [39] or the deployment of a BERT [13] model is infeasible due to hardware limitations, we shall note that SVM remains the best option. Probably better results could be achieved with LSTM or CNN with pre-trained embeddings, but with an additional computational cost: number of weights to learn being increased due to the size of the pre-trained language models.

5 Conclusions

Within the larger scope of a media surveillance project [12] we constructed a system capable of inferring the topic discussed within short texts, which are common within social media platforms. Due to the lack of a publicly available social media dataset with manually labeled topic classes, we identified an appropriate candidate which can be used for training machine learning models. After augmenting the quality of the selected public dataset we inspected the average text lengths and conclude that these are similar with those usually found in microblogging.

After processing the data following the standard recommended methodology found in the literature, we built and evaluated various models constructed using standard machine leaning, deep learning, and fine-tuned the state-of-the-art BERT model for the topic classification task. We consider that the 26 topic classes used in our work should be enough for any general topic analysis task. Given the big number of parameters to optimize for the classic and deep learning models, we opted to perform hyperparameter search using the evolutionary optimization approach.

Considering the limitations imposed on our project, we found that the SVM with a linear kernel is the most robust one, and TF-IDF encoding is sufficient if no additional linguistic resources are available. Using LSTM with Word2Vec embeddings achieves a similar accuracy to linear SVM but with a significantly increased computational cost. As indicated by the literature, Bernoulli Naive Bayes gives robust results, but Random Forest does not perform well, having a Top-1 accuracy of 31% which is only around 3-4% above what ZeroR classification would achieve.

If one disposes plenty of available resources, and processing times are not a barrier, then a fine-tuned BERT classifier will deliver the best classification performance.

Acknowledgements This paper was financed by the project with the title "*Platformă inovativă pentru măsurarea audienței TV, identificarea automată a telespectatorilor și corelarea cu date analitice* *din platforme de socializare online*" (Innovative platform for measuring TV audience, automatic identification of viewers and correlating it with analytic data from social media). The project was cofinanced by "Fondul European de Dezvoltare Regională prin Programul Operațional Competitivitate (POC) 2014–2020, Axa prioritară: 2-Tehnologia Informației și Comunicațiilor (TIC) pentru o economie digitală competitivă". (the European Regional Development Fund (ERDF) through the Competitiveness Operational Program 2014–2020, Priority Axis 2 - Information and Communication Technology (ICT) for a competitive digital economy), project code SMIS 2014+:128960, beneficiary: CICADA TECHNOLOGIES S.R.L. The project is part of the call: POC/524/2/2/ "Sprijinirea creșterii valorii adăugate generate de sectorul TIC și a inovării în domeniu prin dezvoltarea de clustere" (Supporting the added value generated by the ICT sector and innovation in the field through cluster development). The content of this material does not necessarily represent the official position of the European Union or the Romanian Government.

References

1. Agrawal, A., Fu, W., & Menzies, T. (2018). What is wrong with topic modeling? and how to fix it using search-based software engineering. *Information and Software Technology, 98*, 74–88.
2. Albanese, F., & Feuerstein, E. (2021) Improved topic modeling in twitter through community pooling. In *String Processing and Information Retrieval—28th International Symposium, SPIRE 2021*, LNCS (vol. 12944, pp. 209–216). Springer.
3. Arenas Gomez, R. (2021). GASearchCV—sklearn genetic opt 0.4.0 documentation. https://sklearn-genetic-opt.readthedocs.io/en/0.4.0/api/gasearchcv.html
4. Beel, J., Gipp, B., Langer, S., & Breitinger, C. (2016). Research-paper recommender systems: A literature survey. *International Journal on Digital Libraries, 17*(4), 305–338.
5. Bergstra, J., & Bengio, Y. (2012). Random search for hyper-parameter optimization. *Journal of Machine Learning Research, 13*, 281–305.
6. Bergstra, J., Bardenet, R., Bengio, Y., & Kégl, B. (2011). Algorithms for hyper-parameter optimization. In *Proceedings of the 25th Annual Conference on NIPS Advances in Neural Information Processing Systems* (vol. 24, pp. 2546–2554).
7. Blei, D. M. (2012). Probabilistic topic models. *Communications of the ACM, 55*(4), 77–84.
8. Boyd-Graber, J.L., & Blei, D.M. (2008). Syntactic topic models. In *Proceedings of the 22nd Annual Conference on Neural Information Processing Systems* (pp. 185–192)
9. Breiman, L. (2001). Random forests. *Machine Learning, 45*(1), 5–32.
10. Cheng, X., Yan, X., Lan, Y., & Guo, J. (2014). Btm: Topic modeling over short texts. *IEEE Transactions on Knowledge and Data Engineering, 26*(12), 2928–2941.
11. Chollet, F. et al. (2015). Keras. https://keras.io
12. Cicada Technologies. (2020). Innovative platform for measuring tv audience, automatic identification of viewers and correlating it with analytic data from social media. https://www.cicadatech.eu/projects/
13. Devlin, J., Chang, M., Lee, K., & Toutanova, K. (2019). BERT: Pre-training of deep bidirectional transformers for language understanding. In *Proceedings of the 2019 Conference of the North American Chapter of the Association for Computational Linguistics: Human Language Technologies, NAACL-HLT 2019* (Long and Short Papers), ACL (vol. 1, pp. 4171–4186)
14. Eisenstein, J. (2013). What to do about bad language on the Internet. In *Human Language Technologies: Conference of the North American Chapter of the Association of Computational Linguistics, ACL*(pp. 359–369).
15. Fan, X., Lin, H., Yang, L., Diao, Y., Shen, C., Chu, Y., & Zou, Y. (2020). Humor detection via an internal and external neural network. *Neurocomputing, 394*, 105–111.
16. Fortin, F. A., De Rainville, F. M., Gardner, M. A., Parizeau, M., & Gagné, C. (2012). DEAP: Evolutionary algorithms made easy. *Journal of Machine Learning Research, 13*, 2171–2175.

17. Gentzkow, M., Kelly, B., & Taddy, M. (2019). Text as data. *Journal of Economic Literature, 57*(3), 535–74.
18. Gorgolis, N., Hatzilygeroudis, I., Istenes, Z., & Gyenne, L. (2019). Hyperparameter optimization of LSTM network models through genetic algorithm. In *10th International Conference on Information, Intelligence, Systems and Applications, IISA 2019, IEEE* (pp. 1–4).
19. Gupta, M. R., Bengio, S., & Weston, J. (2014). Training highly multiclass classifiers. *Journal of Machine Learning Research, 15*(1), 1461–1492.
20. Guzella, T. S., & Caminhas, W. M. (2009). A review of machine learning approaches to spam filtering. *Expert Systems with Applications, 36*(7), 10206–10222.
21. Hong, L., & Davison, B. D. (2010). Empirical study of topic modeling in Twitter. In *3rd Workshop on Social Network Mining and Analysis, SNAKDD 2009, ACM* (pp. 80–88).
22. Honnibal, M., & Johnson, M. (2015). An improved non-monotonic transition system for dependency parsing. In *2015 Conference on Empirical Methods in Natural Language Processing, EMNLP 2015, ACL* (pp. 1373–1378)
23. Jaderberg, M., Simonyan, K., Vedaldi, A., & Zisserman, A. (2016). Reading text in the wild with convolutional neural networks. *International journal of computer vision,116*(1), 1–20.
24. Joachims, T. (1998). Text categorization with support vector machines: learning with many relevant features. In *10th European Conference on Machine Learning, ECML-98, Springer, LNCS* (vol. 1398, pp. 137–142)
25. Lee, K., Palsetia, D., Narayanan, R., Patwary, M. M. A., Agrawal, A., & Choudhary, A. N. (2011). Twitter trending topic classification. In *2011 IEEE 11th International Conference on Data Mining Workshops (ICDMW), IEEE* (pp. 251–258)
26. Liu, B. (2020). *Sentiment analysis: Mining opinions, sentiments, and emotions.* Cambridge University Press.
27. McCallum, A., & Nigam, K. (1998). A comparison of event models for naive bayes text classification. In *Learning for Text Categorization: Papers from the 1998 AAAI Workshop* (pp. 41–48)
28. Medhat, W., Hassan, A., & Korashy, H. (2014). Sentiment analysis algorithms and applications: A survey. *Ain Shams Engineering Journal, 5*(4), 1093–1113.
29. Mikolov, T., Sutskever, I., Chen, K., Corrado, G. S., & Dean, J. (2013). Distributed representations of words and phrases and their compositionality. In *27th Annual Conference on Neural Information Processing Systems 2013* (pp. 3111–3119)
30. Misra, R. (2018). News Category Dataset—Sculpturing Data for ML. http://doi.org/10.13140/RG.2.2.20331.18729
31. Mori, N., Takeda, M., & Matsumoto, K. (2005) A comparison study between genetic algorithms and bayesian optimize algorithms by novel indices. In *7th Annual Conference on Genetic and Evolutionary Computation, ACM* (pp. 1485–1492)
32. Müller, T., Cotterell, R., Fraser, A. M., & Schütze, H. (2015). Joint lemmatization and morphological tagging with lemming. In *2015 Conference on Empirical Methods in Natural Language Processing, EMNLP 2015, ACL* (pp. 2268–2274)
33. Oh, S. (2017). Top-k hierarchical classification. In: *31st AAAI Conference on Artificial Intelligence* (pp. 2450–2456). AAAI Press
34. Ojha, V. K., Abraham, A., & Snásel, V. (2017). Metaheuristic design of feedforward neural networks: A review of two decades of research. *Engineering Applications of Artificial Intelligence, 60*, 97–116.
35. Pascanu, R., Mikolov, T., & Bengio, Y. (2013). On the difficulty of training recurrent neural networks. In *30th International Conference on Machine Learning, ICML 2013, JMLR.org, JMLR Workshop and Conference Proc.* (vol. 28, pp. 1310–1318)
36. Paszke, A., Gross, S., Massa, F., Lerer, A., Bradbury, J., Chanan, G., Killeen, T., Lin, Z., Gimelshein, N., Antiga, L., Desmaison, A., Kopf, A., Yang, E., DeVito, Z., Raison, M., Tejani, A., Chilamkurthy, S., Steiner, B., Fang, L., Bai, J., Chintala, S. (2019). Pytorch: An imperative style, high-performance deep learning library. *Advances in Neural Information Processing Systems,32*, 8024–8035.

37. Pedregosa, F., Varoquaux, G., Gramfort, A., Michel, V., Thirion, B., Grisel, O., Blondel, M., Prettenhofer, P., Weiss, R., Dubourg, V., Vanderplas, J., Passos, A., Cournapeau, D., Brucher, M., Perrot, M., & Duchesnay, E. (2011). Scikit-learn: Machine learning in Python. *Journal of Machine Learning Research, 12*, 2825–2830.
38. Pelikan, M., Goldberg, D. E., & Lobo, F. G. (2002). A survey of optimization by building and using probabilistic models. *Computational Optimizations and Applications, 21*(1), 5–20.
39. Pennington, J., Socher, R., & Manning, C. D. (2014). Glove: Global vectors for word representation. In *2014 Conference on Empirical Methods in Natural Language Processing, EMNLP 2014, ACL* (pp. 1532–1543).
40. Rahman, M. A., & Akter, Y. A. (2019). Topic classification from text using decision tree, K-NN and Multinomial Naïve Bayes. In *2019 1st International Conference on Advances in Science Engineering and Robotics Technology (ICASERT), IEEE* (pp. 1–4).
41. Řehůřek, R., & Sojka, P. (2010) Software framework for topic modelling with large corpora. In *LREC 2010 Workshop on New Challenges for NLP Frameworks, ELRA* (pp. 45–50)
42. Salton, G., & Buckley, C. (1988). Term-weighting approaches in automatic text retrieval. *Information Processing and Management, 24*(5), 513–523.
43. Snoek, J., Larochelle, H., & Adams, R. P. (2012). Practical bayesian optimization of machine learning algorithms. In *26th Annual Conference on Neural Information Processing Systems 2012* (pp. 2960–2968)
44. Vayansky, I., & Kumar, S. A. (2020). A review of topic modeling methods. *Information Systems, 94*, 101582.
45. Violos, J., Tsanakas, S., Androutsopoulou, M., Palaiokrassas, G., & Varvarigou, T. (2020). Next position prediction using lstm neural networks. In *11th Hellenic Conference on Artificial Intelligence, ACM* (pp. 232–240).
46. Wang, X., & McCallum, A. (2006). Topics over time: A non-Markov continuous-time model of topical trends. In *12th ACM SIGKDD International Conference on Knowledge Discovery and Data Mining, ACM* (pp. 424–433).
47. Zeng, J., Li, J., Song, Y., Gao, C., Lyu, M. R., & King, I. (2018). Topic memory networks for short text classification. In *2018 Conference on Empirical Methods in Natural Language Processing, ACL* (pp. 3120–3131).

What Do They Study?: A Survey on Factors Influencing the Selection of Information Systems as a Major

Joni Matias Rajala, Netta Iivari, Marianne Kinnula, Dorina Rajanen, and Tonja Molin-Juustila

Abstract There is a shortage of employees in the Information and Communication Technology (ICT) field, including Information Systems (IS). Student recruitment is a challenge in IS in many countries despite different student marketing efforts and extensive research on the topic. We conducted a survey with first year students in a Finnish university to understand what factors seem to affect their career choice. Our findings indicate that ICT students mostly share their view of ICT with other students, with the exception that they seemed to see the field as more creative, and people oriented. We highlight the creative aspects of the work in IS to potentially attract new students, including more women, to study in IS.

Keywords Student recruitment · ICT · Choice of major · IS enrollment · Creativity

1 Introduction

Information and Communications Technology (ICT) industry is prospering due to the ongoing digital transformation. However, there is a shortage of employees. For example, the International Labour Organization (ILO) [19] forecasts in their latest

J. M. Rajala (✉) · N. Iivari · M. Kinnula · D. Rajanen · T. Molin-Juustila
University of Oulu, Oulu, Finland
e-mail: joni.rajala@oulu.fi

N. Iivari
e-mail: netta.iivari@oulu.fi

M. Kinnula
e-mail: marianne.kinnula@oulu.fi

D. Rajanen
e-mail: dorina.rajanen@oulu.fi

T. Molin-Juustila
e-mail: tonja.molin-juustila@oulu.fi

© The Author(s), under exclusive license to Springer Nature Switzerland AG 2023
G. C. Silaghi et al. (eds.), *Advances in Information Systems Development*,
Lecture Notes in Information Systems and Organisation 63,
https://doi.org/10.1007/978-3-031-32418-5_13

report an acute shortage of labor force in the ICT field Skills mismatch and gaps, and shortages in skills needed are seen in many countries (see e.g. [19]). In the European Union (EU) area, 55% of companies recruiting ICT professionals had difficulties in 2019 [18]. Talented professionals will be critical in reaching the EU ambitious goal of "a human centered, sustainable and more prosperous digital future", and the global competition of these talents will be fierce [12].

Increasing the intake of students can be an effective way to educate more professionals, but there might not be enough applicants interested in ICT as their career choice. There already is a huge literature base on why students choose or do not choose ICT[1] majors [1, 9, 32]. The reasons for choosing an ICT major include previous experiences, personal interests, influence from family and friends, and students' perception of career possibilities [1, 9, 23]. A range of techniques has been used to attract new students, for example marketing campaigns [16], campus visits [23], company visits [14], and workshops [22]. The aim for most of these programs is to change how potential applicants view higher education institutes or the study programs involved. However, the problem of student recruitment still persists with the number of jobs having raised during the last decade [13] and but universities have not managed to keep up with their intake [25].

The problem of student recruitment and factors affecting major choice have been examined also in the Information Systems (IS) field [1, 21, 30]. Interestingly, studies have found that one of the biggest downfalls of IS marketing comes from its assumed technical and mathematical nature, and from the subject seen as a male dominated nerdy field [21, 28]; hence, the same aspects that are seen to characterize ICT are associated with IS as well [21, 30, 31]. These problems are pronounced in relation to girls' major choice and girls not showing interest to apply to the field [4, 29–31]. Important to note is that there are differences in the positioning of the IS in universities globally. In Europe, IS is variably located in business schools or in ICT or natural sciences faculties. In our Finnish university, IS was previously located in the faculty of science, while it is now in the ICT faculty. We have a degree program with a curriculum that combines IS and software engineering (SE), equivalent to Swedish 'informatik' or German 'informatics'. When located within ICT faculty, the technical and mathematical nature of IS may become underscored rather than the business, organization, design or human oriented nature. However, studies have shown that students have had problems perceiving the difference between ICT and IS also elsewhere [28], including business schools in the US [4, 21].

One way to market IS to potential applicants is to change the perception they have of the field and thus fix the potential image problems. However, the relationship between image problems and applying is complicated. If we consider there is an image problem in IS, i.e., that such an image exists that prevents some students from applying, it suggests that students either believe in an untrue image of the field, they

---

[1] We use ICT major as an umbrella term to cover various computing related majors: software, hardware and telecommunications related ones, including Computer Science (CS), several Science, Technology, Engineering, Mathematics (STEM) majors as well as Information Systems and Software Engineering majors, of which the former represents a heavily business, organization, management and user oriented major.

have a narrow view of the field in general, or they are not interested in IS and related fields despite any kind of image. However, at the same time there are also students applying to IS, so those students either see the "problematic" image of the ICT field as a positive, or they might have a different view of the field. In any case, the image of the IS field is an effect when students select their major.

In the current study, our aim is to understand which views are prevalent in the Finnish academic enrolment, and how those views shape students' enrolment. To gather data on this topic, we created a survey for all the first-year students at the University of Oulu in Finland in October 2021, regardless of their major, asking about their perception of work in the ICT field and their reasons for choosing their own major. We compared those results to what they are currently studying as their current major. As for the ICT field, we focused on work relevant from the viewpoint of our degree program (IS and SE), i.e., work in software industry, excluding work on hardware and telecommunications that are more relevant for other degree programs of our ICT faculty. The data is used to answer the following research questions: 1. *Does new students' perception of work in ICT affect their choice of major?* 1.1. *Does new ICT students' perception of the work in software industry differ from the perception of new students of other majors?* 1.2. *Does new ICT students value the prevalent perceptions of the work in software industry more than new students of other majors?*

The paper is structured as follows. Section 2 introduces related research. Section 3 presents the research design, including the participants and procedures for data collection and analysis. Section 4 presents the results while Sect. 5 discusses the implications of those results. Section 6 concludes the paper.

2   Related Research

There is plenty of literature on factors affecting students' major choice, trying to figure out how to attract students to majors. Such literature is extensively produced also within the ICT field [6, 15, 26, 32], including in IS [1, 4, 11, 20, 21, 29, 33]. The literature shows different kinds of historical, social and discursive factors as affecting the major choice in IS: different kinds of stakeholders have strong impact but also personal interests, attitudes and experiences in ICT derived through education as well as through everyday life overall, not to mention the influence of societal level images, stereotypes, norms and discourses [9, 28, 29, 31]. One problem when making the career choice is students' unfamiliarity with what work in the IS field entails in practice [1, 2, 14] and unclarity of how different ICT majors differ from each other [8, 17, 29]. However, one study found that job expectations between ICT majors and non-ICT majors did not markedly differ [3].

Several prior studies have indicated the impact of existing beliefs or perceptions of the field or of the professionals working in the field on students' major choice [4, 11, 21, 33]. A general interest in, even fascination on the work in ICT field has been found—not surprisingly—to be a huge motivation to choose an IS/ICT career

[9]. A belief that one's own work values match with IS careers as well as positive encouragement towards that specific career particularly from someone close to the person have been found to have a positive effect [20]. High demand of workforce in the ICT field has also been found as a motivating factor [9]. Self-efficacy, that is, high confidence in ICT abilities, has also been found to increase the likelihood in choosing an IS/ICT career [2, 20]. Particularly perception of abilities to learn programming can have an effect [20] but also technical capital in general [9]. On the other hand, unfortunately, even extensive ICT use does not necessarily lead into an increased interest in an IS career [29].

Following these studies, we will inquire the perceptions new students have about the work in the software industry. First year students in universities (ages 18–25) are typically at the development phase of 'emerging adults' [5], i.e. between adolescence and adulthood. In this phase, adult roles and preferred occupations are emerging and social norms within a particular society have a great influence. For example, gender is an important factor, and if something is considered as a way of being a (wo)man, it affects one's behaviour [5]. In this study, we build on the study by Downey and colleagues [11] who have examined factors affecting students' major choice in IS and CS. However, we complement their study by examining some additional stereotypes of the work in software industry that have already been reported in the literature.

The significance of stereotypes has been acknowledged to affect the students' major choice in the ICT field [6, 33], including IS [28], although differing findings also exist [20]. Positive and negative stereotypes have been studied a lot, often from the perspective on how stereotypes negatively affect girls applying to the ICT field [6], with very similar results to the IS field [28, 29, 31]. According to these stereotypes, these fields are male dominated, technology focused and solitary pursuits. There are also similar stereotypes on how these fields are math intensive, and only geniuses or nerds can succeed in them. The stereotypes often are negative and self-enforcing, in that if people do not see any visible contradictions to these stereotypes, only students who value those stereotypes pursue a career in these fields. Furthermore, the male dominated nature can make girls feel unwelcome and student councillors not suggest ICT for girls. These stereotypes and views are often formed through engagement with media, peers, teachers, and family, especially for IS [6, 28, 29, 31, 33].

3   Research Design

This research was conducted as a survey for the first-year students at the University of Oulu in Finland in October 2021. As the aim of the survey was to find out how students' perception of software industry related to their major selection when applying to study in the university, it was important to send the survey to students from all majors, to be able to compare the answers between student groups. To ensure that the study respondents' perceptions of the field actually presented their views during enrolment and application process, the survey was only sent to the first-year students, who had only been students for less than two months when the survey was conducted. If the participants had been students for longer, there is a risk that their perception of the work in software industry might have changed [21], or they might not remember the reasons for why they applied to their selected major. Compared to countries where higher education students can choose their major after few years of studying, university students in Finland must choose their major when applying to university. This means that the survey was conducted on students who already had made the choice of major about 4 months before the survey, when they decided whether they take the offered study place or not.

The questionnaire was sent to a common mailing list for all university students, with clear instructions that the survey was meant for the first-year students of all majors, and it measured their perception of software industry and factors that affected their selection of the major. All questions were in Finnish. In addition to the student mailing list, the survey was sent by email to all students taking an introductory course on IS and SE to obtain large enough sample of students from our IS/SE degree program to which other students could be compared.

The survey questions were created to map the participants' perception of the work in software industry. Questions were assembled from previous survey questions aimed to map reasons why students applied to the IS field as a major [10]. Additional questions were identified to map other possible views found in the literature. Negative views, such as the view of the ICT field as a solitary field had not been measured in any previous survey, so they were included from sources that discussed IS stereotypes in general [7]. The survey had three major parts, in which participants assessed their agreement with various statements using five-point Likert scale. The first part asked all respondents how they saw statements to fit the work in software industry. The second part asked students who were not studying software industry related field how those same statements matched their current selection of major. This part contained instruction to not answer these questions, if they were studying in software industry related field, as they already had given their perceptions in the first part. For analysis, if they did not answer this set of questions, the respondents' answers were copied from their views on software industry. Also, if ICT students answered these questions, they were removed from the data set. This was done because ICT faculty in the University of Oulu includes electrical engineering and other hardware related subjects that are not part of software industry. Removing students that did perceive themselves as software engineers from ICT enabled this study to focus on the perception of software engineering students against students from other faculties. In total, answers of 13 students were removed this way, and their removal had very little impact on the results.

The last part asked all students to assess to what extent those views were the reason they applied to their major. In addition to these major parts, background information was gathered to categorize students and make sure the data came from first-year students. The questionnaire contained questions on age, year of admission, current and applied majors, and whether their current major was their first major. In addition, there were questions on students' previous experience in ICT (previous work experience in software industry and if they knew anyone who worked in software industry).

The survey was sent to the mailing list twice, with one week interval between the initial posting and the reminder. After the reminder, the students were given two weeks to submit their answers. After the data was collected, it was prepared for data analysis. The Likert scale answers were mapped for analysis to values between -2 and $+2$, where $+2$ was "I agree" and -2 was "I disagree". Because the questionnaire was sent to a student mailing list, we had to filter out students who had studied for more than a year. Only data from students who had begun their studies in 2021 was analyzed. The number of respondents per major typically varied between 5 and 15, but three majors had more respondents, namely IS/SE (our own study program) (49), CS (24) and medicine (34). Because of the small number of answers per major and to focus on the ICT related majors, students were grouped by faculty, and the analysis was done by comparing faculties. This grouping was possible because the University of Oulu has an ICT faculty. Thus, for the data analysis, all ICT students were in one group and there were no ICT students in the other groups.

For the data analysis, we have calculated descriptive statistics (frequencies and means) to characterize each faculty or how different gender responded to the survey's questions. We used the Mann–Whitney U test to compare students' perceptions and reasons by faculty and gender, as the data was not normally distributed. Each survey question was analyzed separately from each other. Each faculty was compared against the ICT faculty separately and as a group to find the differences of perception between them. The majors in the ICT faculty include electrical engineering, telecommunications, CS and IS/SE. As many studies on students' perception of IS as well as on ICT in general focus on women and girls, and their enrolment is important, special attention was paid on women's perceptions.

4 Findings

4.1 Frequencies

The survey gathered 360 responses in total, though 64 of them were from students who were not first year students, and two had not answered all necessary questions, so they were removed from the data set. In addition, to answer the research questions, we removed all ICT students from the data set who did not view software industry as their field. This was done by looking at the responses given to the second set of questions, that asked students to not answer if their field was in software industry. If the student had answered that question, then that student was removed from the data. For example, electrical engineering is part of the ICT faculty, so these students might not consider software industry as their field, and thus might have answered the questions differently. 13 students out of 80 ICT students answered that set of questions, 10 male and 3 female. Those students were majoring in electrical engineering (4 students), communication engineering (4 students) and computer science and engineering (5 students).

Table 1 First year students' responses by faculty and by gender

Faculty	Man	Woman	Other/No answer	Total
Human Sciences	7	35	3	45
Education	0	28	0	28
Business School	6	8	0	14
Natural Sciences	12	20	2	34
Medicine	10	38	0	48
Engineering	20	22	3	45
ICT	50	15	2	67
Total	104	167	10	281

Thus, 281 first year students answered the survey, which is 13% of all 2230 students who enrolled in 2021. The ICT field was represented by 67 students, who account for 24.8% of all 270 students that enrolled to the ICT faculty in 2021. The responses by faculty are shown in Table 1.

The survey also checked which majors the students applied to, in order to see if the students were interested in studying IS/SE even if they had enrolled to some other field. However, there were only 14 students who were not IS/SE students, but had applied to it, and those students were quite evenly split between the faculties, so that data was not analyzed further.

4.2 Differences Between Faculties and Genders

There was not much variation between genders across all faculties in their views of software industry. All mean differences (md) between the answers were less than 0.45. The biggest differences were that men saw the field as more human centered ($md = 0.48$) and creative ($md = 0.44$). When focusing on ICT students, the differences between genders disappeared almost completely. The only difference was that women viewed software industry as more difficult ($md = 0.34, p = 0.037$) than men. When examining ICT students' reasons for applying to their major, the differences between genders was again minimal. The only one was that women agreed more with the statements that they applied to their major because it was challenging ($md = 0.85$), prestigious ($md = 0.57$) and they can work with people ($md = 0.61$).

The analysis show that the ICT students viewed software industry as more people oriented than the students from other faculties (mean difference between 0.5–1.3 and always $p < 0.05$). The same difference in the view of the software industry as a solitary profession was not found, as the ICT students had similar perception to other faculties, except for medicine ($md = 0.81$ when compared to ICT) and business school ($md = 0.93$ when compared to ICT) students, who viewed software industry as more solitary than anyone else. Interestingly, even though the ICT students viewed their field as more people oriented than other students, students from other faculties viewed their profession as more people oriented than the ICT students viewed software industry, with an exception among the responses from the students in natural sciences.

Even though the ICT students viewed the field as more people oriented than others, the students did not value the social aspects as much during their major selection, especially compared to education ($md = 1.77$ & $p < 0.001$), business school ($md = 1.14$ & $p < 0.001$) and medicine ($md = 1.46$ & $p < 0.001$) students. Even more drastic was the perception of software industry by the ICT students against engineering students, where ICT students viewed it as more people oriented ($md = 0.80$ & $p < 0.001$) and agreed more with the statement "I selected this field because I can work alone" ($md = 0.96$ & $p < 0.001$) (Table 2).

Another important distinction between the ICT students and students from other faculties is that the ICT students viewed their major as creative, and somewhat applied to ICT because of it. Most of the statistically significant differences were from faculties, that disagreed with the statement that the creativity was the reason they applied to their major. And only education and engineering appreciated creativity more than ICT, and even then only as a reason for applying. (see Table 3).

The most common reason for the ICT students for selecting their major was their interest in technology, computers and mathematics. These were all separate questions in the survey, all of them were clearly shared by the ICT students. While those interests are often cited as stereotypes that hinder girls from applying to the field [6], they also are clearly the most common reason students apply to the ICT field. When compared with the results on ICT students valuing creativity, this seems to indicate that ICT students wanted to work in a creative field, and they understood that there is creativity involved in the work in the ICT field.

Table 2 Mean values of responses from each faculty to the questions "In software industry the work includes working with people", "In my current field the work includes working with people" and "I applied to my major because I wanted to work with people"

Faculty	Software industry is people oriented	Their chosen field is people oriented	Working with people as a reason for applying
Human Sciences	−0.07**	1.31**	0.14
Education	−0.11**	1.79**	1.55**
Business School	−0.36**	1.36**	0.93**
Natural Sciences	0.09**	0.62*	−0.09
Medicine	−0.33**	1.76**	1.24**
Engineering	0.11**	1.25*	0.29*
ICT	0.91	0.91	−0.22

** marks $p < 0.01$ and * $p < 0.05$ when compared to ICT using Mann–Whitney U test

Table 3 Mean values of responses from each faculty to the questions "The software industry is a creative field", "My field is a creative field" and "I chose this field because I want to do creative work"

Faculty	Software industry is creative	Their chosen field is creative	Creativity as a reason for applying
Human Sciences	0.69**	0.24**	0.41
Education	0.68**	1.10	0.72
Business School	0.43**	0.36**	−0.21**
Natural Sciences	0.76**	−0.01**	−0.21**
Medicine	0.77**	0.00**	−0.39**
Engineering	0.71**	0.82*	0.78
ICT	1.2	1.2	0.66

** marks $p < 0.01$ and * $p < 0.05$ when compared to ICT using Mann–Whitney U test

The ICT students were also an interesting outlier in that they represented the only faculty where the students did not choose their major because of the information provided in secondary education. In every other faculty the results for the question "I chose this as my field, because the perception I got from it in secondary education was good" followed even distribution, with slight emphasis on the positive results, but a quarter of the ICT students strongly disagreed with the statement. The differences were big with all faculties, with mean differences going up to 1.18 ($p < 0.001$) for medicine and 1.03 ($p < 0.001$) for engineering. The other faculties were not far behind with mean difference of human sciences at 0.88 ($p = 0.001$) and natural sciences at 1.00 ($p = 0.001$). Education ($md = 0.59$, $p = 0.78$) and business school ($md = 0.53$, $p = 0.24$) did not have significant differences, but their results were still more positive than for the ICT faculty. In addition, when comparing all non-ICT students with the ICT students the mean difference stays at 0.94 ($p < 0.001$).

There were no big differences in the views of software industry between ICT students and others. The views on whether software industry has higher salary or long workdays or if the field is prestigious did not change between faculties to be statistically significant. All answers were also quite equally distributed and mean values among all students close to 0.5, with high salary ($mean = 0.80$) and prestige ($mean = 0.73$) a bit more on the positive side and statement that "software industry has long workdays" ($mean = 0.33$) a bit more on the negative side. The ICT students did find higher salary as a more important factor when applying compared to other students ($md = 0.61$, $p = 0.001$), but that was highly dependent on the faculty. Education ($md = 1.54$, $p < 0.001$), human sciences ($md = 1.30$, $p < 0.001$) and natural sciences ($md = 1.43$, $p < 0.001$) did not value salary, whereas there was no statistically significant difference between ICT and business school, engineering, or medicine students.

5   Discussion

This study focused on students' major choice and their perceptions of the ICT field, more specifically of software industry. It is a widely known and long-lasting concern that young people have problematic perceptions of the ICT field, including IS. Hence, it is important to understand what kind of perceptions young people of today have of the ICT field as well as to understand factors they value in the field they choose to study. This study provides important insights in this respect. We generated two alternative propositions in the introduction regarding students' major choice: that students who apply to IS/ICT find the stereotypical image of the fields as something they want, or that they have an alternative view of the field. We found empirical support for both propositions.

General view of the field. Previous research guides towards examining the existing perceptions of the field or of the professionals working in the field [4, 11, 21, 33]. At large, there seemed to be no difference in our data on how the students perceived software industry, i.e., both those majoring in ICT and those majoring in any other field saw software industry similarly. There was no clear difference between genders either. These are somewhat surprising findings, but also positive ones, telling us that at least the general image of the industry is not problematic as such, at least among the respondents in the University of Oulu, and the reasons for career choice are somewhere else than in a negative image.

Social aspects. A clear difference between the students was that the ICT students viewed working in software industry as more people oriented than the other students. However, social aspects were not considered especially valuable by the ICT students in their career choice, i.e., they did not choose their major based on social aspects, and they consider the possibility to work alone as an asset of the work in software industry. These findings follow a pattern found previously [11] that ICT students understand that interaction is inherent and unavoidable in the field, but they do not necessarily seek interaction with customers or people outside of their group. The same logic can also explain why this study found that ICT students apply to their field because they can work alone. It might be worth emphasizing in student marketing both aspects: there is plenty of social interaction in work in the ICT/IT field, while it is also possible to an extent to choose how much social interaction is involved in own work or profession within the field.

Creativity. An interesting new finding compared to previous research is that the ICT students saw working in software industry clearly as more creative work compared to other students and cited that as a reason for applying to the field. This has not been previously identified as a factor related to the IS or ICT career choice. This finding indicates the ICT students may have a better understanding of what kind of creative aspects the work in the ICT field can contain, compared to other students, as indeed, creativity is at the core of the work in the IS field [24, 27] and in the ICT field in general. This finding indicates that the ICT students want a creative pursuit, and thus they select a field that they see as a creative one. If creativity is one of the career choice factors for an applicant, this finding suggests that there should be more focus on making visible the creative aspects of the work in the ICT field in student marketing, as proposed also by Downey et al. [11]. It seems that the ICT students who have applied to the field can see the creativity involved in the work in this field even without anyone informing of that, while there might be many potential students who cannot see the creativity involved in the ICT field yet, but who might get interested in the field if properly informed. Creativity is definitely involved in the innovation, design, and development of digital technology. Creativity is an essential aspect of human and business-oriented work in our field. Informing potential students better about the creative aspects of our field might make a big difference in the number of applicants, which has been low in many ICT degree programs over the years. Overall, we think we should be digging deeper into the young people's views on creativity: what they think it entails, in different fields, including ours. The students, no matter the major, seemed to see their field as a creative one and emphasized that in their major selection. It might be that creativity of the work is something that generally attracts the young people of today. If that is the case, we should be making the creative aspects of the IS field much more visible when marketing the degree program to potential applicants.

Information gained in secondary education. In Finnish secondary education there are student councilors who try to help the students in making their career choice. We know from previous IS research that they have difficulties in understanding the work in the ICT field in general, and in the IS field in particular, which naturally hinders their capability to give the students a good view of the fields (Vainionpää, Iivari, et al., 2020; Vainionpää, Kinnula, et al., 2020b). This might be at least partly behind the interesting finding concerning information provided during secondary education: the ICT students did not choose their major based on the information they had received in secondary education. ICT students seem to lack information of the ICT field, compared to many other fields. This strongly contradicts with the other majors, where the students mostly reported that the perception of their chosen field given in secondary education had been a factor when making their career choice. Of course, there are big differences between educational systems of different countries, but especially in countries in which students make their major choice already when applying to higher education, it is critical to offer upper secondary students more information of the ICT field and particularly of the IS field [29, 31]. Moreover, we think that informing upper secondary students about the IS field would be valuable even in the case of major selection being made later in the studies. Also other IS studies have pointed out the problem of high school students being poorly informed about or not being even aware of the existence of the IS field when making their career choice [1, 11]. All this indicates we should give high school students more information of what the work in the IS field entails in practice [2, 14], explain how the ICT majors differ from each other [8, 17, 31], and educate pupils during their basic education of this exciting field with career opportunities for those interested in computers, technology and mathematics as well as for those interested in design, people, management and business, not mention all those interested in a career entailing creative work.

Stereotypical and non-stereotypical views. The ICT students in our study showed strong interest in technology, computers, and mathematics. This does not come as a surprise, as they are central in the ICT field, and often reported in the literature on IS and ICT career choice [9, 11]. This is also in line with the stereotypical view of the field, especially when combined with the fact that the ICT students did not value social aspects a lot. It can also be linked with ICT self-efficacy and technical abilities [2, 20], particularly programming [20] and other technical capital [9]. However, important is also to remember that previous research has shown that technical capital does not necessarily lead to interest in the IS career [30]. Then again, the ICT students in our study also produced alternative, non-stereotypical views of the field as a people oriented and creative. These people and creativity related views might be the reasons why the students who chose other majors did not consider ICT as a career choice, especially as everyone seemed to apply to a field that they considered people oriented. All in all, the findings on the perceptions among the ICT students of the ICT field being people oriented and creative enables questioning the prevalent stereotypes.

Implications for student recruitment and marketing programs. If student councilors or university marketing are interested in changing the perceptions of the ICT field in the eyes of future applicants, they could look into how students from other faculties view social aspects, people orientation, creativity and their own career choice. Students similar to them could potentially be swayed if the social, people related, and creative aspects involved in the ICT field were made visible for them. However, that probably is not enough, as most students who apply to the ICT field still select their field because of their interest in computers, technology and mathematics. Probably some interest in them is needed from all students who apply to the ICT field. We need more data on how interested the students from other faculties were in technology, computers and mathematics, compared with the ICT students. This survey only asked if the students applied because of those qualities. From these results it is impossible to say, if the students from other faculties were interested in technology, computers, and mathematics, but did not choose ICT as their career because of other factors.

Gender. As for gender aspects intermingled with the ICT field, an interesting finding was that the ICT field appeared more human centered and creative for men than for women. However, no clear differences could be identified among the ICT students. Overall, as the differences were small, we can say that the perception of software industry is shared by both genders, even if that perception consists of masculine characteristics and even if small difference could be observed in women viewing the field as more difficult than men. This finding is unfortunate but generally in line with the prior research [25–27]. Overall, however, the women who applied to the ICT field did not seem to favor any particular set of views that the men did not. The women who enrolled to ICT enrolled there because they viewed the field as creative, and they liked working with technology. This means that the perception of technology as 'a boys' club' needs to be changed, if we want to make ICT more gender diverse. This all comes to marketing and visibility of the field in the previous stages of education. Given that the ICT students did not see any value from student counseling or student outreach programs from the secondary education, the main reason for their application comes from elsewhere. This survey did not ask about hobbies, which is regrettable, but if the major is not marketed to them within the education system, the main factors likely come from family, peers, hobbies, media and everyday experiences [28–30]. Unfortunately, the existing literature indicates that the society, including media as well as the people close to these young people, still tend to produce very gendered understanding of the ICT field [28–30]. If we want to develop an alternative image of the field to attract more women, the silver bullet is yet to be found.

6 Conclusions

Our findings were refreshing compared to previous research as it seems that at least some elements of the old stereotype of the ICT field (and IS as part of that) as boring, solitary work have vanished or at least somewhat abated. The findings highlight the fact that choosing the ICT career is very much based on interest in the field. In our study, the ICT students considered ICT career as creative and involving working with people. However, their knowledge of and enthusiasm with the field did not originate from information received during their secondary education. It is almost vice versa: we can provocatively say that they seem to have chosen an ICT career despite the information they received during the secondary education, as based on previous research [30, 31] we can assume that they have mostly received information related to other career options and very little related to the ICT careers. In line with Downey et al. [11], we propose IS educators to disembark from the higher education institutes and enter the secondary education schools to inform both the students and their student councillors about the IS field as an interesting, creative, and social career choice with great career opportunities and good salary.

As for the limitations of this work, the study was conducted within one university only, and future studies with a larger sample and across different countries would be needed. There is also room to dig deeper into how and why the qualities like creativity and social needs differ between students who applied to different faculties.

References

1. Acilar, A., & Sæbø, Ø. (2022, June). Exploring the differences between students in IS and other disciplines in the perceptions of factors influencing study program choice: A survey study in Norway. In *35th Bled EConference Digital Restructuring and Human (Re) Action* (pp. 393–402). https://doi.org/10.18690/um.fov.4.2022.24.
2. Alexander, P. M., Holmner, M., Lotriet, H. H., Matthee, M. C., Pieterse, H. V., Naidoo, S., Twinomurinzi, H., & Jordaan, D. (2011). Factors affecting career choice: Comparison between students from computer and other disciplines. *Journal of Science Education and Technology, 20*(3), 300–315. https://doi.org/10.1007/s10956-010-9254-3

3. Alexander, Patricia M., & Pieterse, V. (2010). Indications of personality trait difference between ICT and other students. In *18th European Conference on Information Systems, ECIS 2010*.
4. Andersson, A. (2017). Victim, mother, or untapped resource? Discourse analysis of the construction of women in ICT policies. *Information Technologies & International Development, 13*(2017), 72–86.
5. Berger, K. S., & Thompson, R. A. (2017). The developing person through the life span (Chap. xxvi). In *The Developing Person through the Life Span* (4th ed., 697pp.). https://www.proquest.com/books/developing-person-through-life-span/docview/619171040/se-2?accoun tid=50308%0Ahttps://5531515.odslr.com/resolver/full?atitle=&aulast=Berger&date=1998& issn=&isbn=1-57259-106-4&volume=&issue=&spage=&title=&title=The+developing+.
6. Cheryan, S., Master, A., & Meltzoff, A. N. (2015). Cultural stereotypes as gatekeepers: Increasing girls' interest in computer science and engineering by diversifying stereotypes. *Frontiers in Psychology, 6*, 1–8. https://doi.org/10.3389/fpsyg.2015.00049
7. Clayton, K. L., Hellens, L. A. V., & Nielsen, S. H. (2009). Gender stereotypes prevail in ICT; a research review. In *Proceedings of the Special Interest Group on Management Information System's 47th Annual Conference on Computer Personnel Research* (pp. 153–158). https://doi.org/10.1145/1542130.1542160.
8. Courte, J., & Bishop-Clark, C. (2009). Do students differentiate between computing disciplines? *SIGCSE Bulletin Inroads, 41*(1), 29–33. https://doi.org/10.1145/1539024.1508877
9. Deng, X., Zaza, S., & Armstrong, D. (2020). Factors influencing IT career choice behaviors of first-generation college students. In *26th Americas Conference on Information Systems, AMCIS 2020*.
10. Downey, J. (2011). An empirical examination of the composition of vocational interest in Business Colleges: MIS vs other majors. *Journal of Information Systems Education, 22*(2), 147–158. http://search.ebscohost.com/login.aspx?direct=true&db=ehh&AN=663 39177&site=ehost-live&scope=site.
11. Downey, J. P., McGaughey, R., & Roach, D. (2009). MIS versus computer science: An empirical comparison of the influences on the students' choice of major. *Journal of Information Systems Education, 20*(3), 357–368. http://search.ebscohost.com/login.aspx?direct=true&db= ehh&AN=44447205&site=ehost-live&scope=site.
12. European Commission. (2021). *Communication from the Commission to the European Parliament, the Council, the European Economic and Social Committee and the Committee of the Regions* (pp. 1–21).
13. Eurostat. (2019, October). ICT specialists in employment. In *Eurostat Statistics Explained*. http://ec.europa.eu/eurostat/statistics-explained/index.php/ICT_specialists_in_employment.
14. Ferratt, T. W., Hall, S. R., & Kanet, J. J. (2016). Out of the fog: A program design for understanding alternative career choices: Examples in management information systems and operations management. *Communications of the Association for Information Systems, 38*(1), 106–121. https://doi.org/10.17705/1cais.03804.
15. Giannakos, M. N., Pappas, I. O., Jaccheri, L., & Sampson, D. G. (2017). Understanding student retention in computer science education: The role of environment, gains, barriers and usefulness. *Education and Information Technologies, 22*(5), 2365–2382. https://doi.org/10.1007/s10 639-016-9538-1
16. Granger, M. J., Dick, G., Jacobson, C. M., & Van Slyke, C. (2007). Information systems enrollments: Challenges and strategies. *Journal of Information Systems Education, 18*(3), 303–311.
17. Gupta, U. G., & Houtz, L. E. (2000). High school students' perceptions of information technology skills and careers. *Journal of Industrial Technology, 16*(4).
18. International Labour Organization. (2019). *Skills shortages and labour migration in the field of information and communication technology in India, Indonesia and Thailand*. https://www.ilo.org/sector/Resources/publications/WCMS_710031/lang--en/index.htm.
19. International Labour Organization. (2020). *"The future of the work in ICT" project "The future of work in ICT" project contents*. www.ilo.org/publns.

20. Joshi, K. D., & Kuhn, K. (2011). What determines interest in an is career? An application of the theory of reasoned action. *Communications of the Association for Information Systems, 29*(1), 133–158. https://doi.org/10.17705/1cais.02908.

21. Joshi, K. D., & Schmidt, N. L. (2006). Is the information systems profession gendered? *ACM SIGMIS Database: The DATABASE for Advances in Information Systems, 37*(4), 26–41. https://doi.org/10.1145/1185335.1185343

22. Keller, L., & John, I. (2020). Motivating female students for computer science by means of robot workshops. *International Journal of Engineering Pedagogy, 10*(1), 94–108. https://doi.org/10.3991/ijep.v10i1.11661

23. Kitchen, J. A., Sonnert, G., & Sadler, P. (2020). Campus visits: Impact of a college outreach strategy on student STEM aspirations. *Journal of Student Affairs Research and Practice, 57*(3), 266–281. https://doi.org/10.1080/19496591.2019.1653312

24. Müller, S. D., & Ulrich, F. (2013). Creativity and information systems in a hypercompetitive environment: A literature review. *Communications of the Association for Information Systems, 32*(1), 175–200. https://doi.org/10.17705/1cais.03207.

25. OECD. (2021). Education database: Enrolment by field. *OECD Education Statistics (Database).* https://doi.org/10.1787/33c390e6-en

26. Owuor, J. A. (2009). Examining female students' motivation and preferences for course choices in an undergraduate ICT program in a Californian University. *Canadian Journal for New Scholars in Education, 1*(2). http://downloads.esri.com/archydro/archydro/Doc/Overview ofArcHydroterrainpreprocessingworkflows.pdf, https://doi.org/10.1016/j.jhydrol.2017.11.003, http://sites.tufts.edu/gis/files/2013/11/Watershed-and-Drainage-Delineation-by-Pour-Point.pdf.

27. Seidel, S., Müller-Wienbergen, F., & Becker, J. (2010). The concept of creativity in the information systems discipline: Past, present, and prospects. *Communications of the Association for Information Systems, 27*(1), 217–242. https://doi.org/10.17705/1cais.02714.

28. Vainionpää, F., Kinnula, M., Iivari, N., & Molin-Juustila, T. (2019). Girls' choice - why won't they pick it? In *ECIS 2019.* https://aisel.aisnet.org/ecis2019_rp/31.

29. Vainionpää, F., Iivari, N., Kinnula, M., & Zeng, X. (2020). IT is not for me - women ' s discourses on IT and IT careers. In *Twenty-Eighth European Conference on Information Systems (ECIS2020).*

30. Vainionpää, F., Kinnula, M., Iivari, N., & Molin-Juustila, T. (2020). Career choice and gendered perceptions of it—A nexus analytic inquiry. *Lecture Notes in Information Systems and Organisation, 39 LNISO,* 37–56. https://doi.org/10.1007/978-3-030-49644-9_3.

31. Vainionpää, F., Kinnula, M., Iivari, N., & Molin-Juustila, T. (2020). Girls in IT: Intentionally self-excluded or products of high school as a site of exclusion? *Internet Research.* https://doi.org/10.1108/INTR-09-2019-0395

32. Wang, X. (2013). Why students choose STEM majors: Motivation, high school learning, and postsecondary context of support. *American Educational Research Journal, 50*(5), 1081–1121. https://doi.org/10.3102/0002831213488622

33. Zhang, L. (2007). Do personality traits make a difference in teaching styles among Chinese high school teachers? *Personality and Individual Differences, 43*(4), 669–679. https://doi.org/10.1016/j.paid.2007.01.009

Printed in the United States
by Baker & Taylor Publisher Services